Substance Abuse

Fourth Edition

By
Marilynn Bobst, RN, BS Ed, MA
and
Patricia Habraken, RN, MS

WESTERN®
SCHOOLS
PRESS

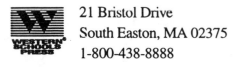

21 Bristol Drive
South Easton, MA 02375
1-800-438-8888

ABOUT THE AUTHORS

Marilynn Bobst RN, BS Ed, MA, is a substance abuse counselor for the County of Riverside Mental Health Dual Diagnosis Program and continues to be in private practice as a substance abuse counselor for Community Behavioral Health Group, Inc. in Riverside, CA. She was perinatal program manager at Inland Behavioral Services in San Bernardino, CA, and an inpatient substance abuse counselor at Riverside Community Hospital, Knollwood Center.

Patricia Habraken, RN, MS, is a certified chemical dependency nurse and is program director of Chemical Dependency Services at Indian River Memorial Hospital, Vero Beach, Florida. Her master's degree is in Counseling Psychology. She is a board member of the National Consortium of Chemical Dependency Nurses (NCCDN) and serves as secretary on that board. She is president of the Florida Network of NCCDN and a member of the Substance Abuse Council of Indian River County. She facilitates several nurse support groups and works with the Intervention Project for Nurses. Ms. Habraken has spoken nationally on a variety of topics related to substance abuse, family roles, and co-dependency.

ABOUT THE SUBJECT MATTER EXPERT FOR NURSING INTERVENTION

Theresa Raphael-Grimm, MSN, RN, is a clinical specialist in Psychiatric-Mental Health Nursing and the psychiatric liaison nurse at Grossmont Hospital, La Mesa, CA. She is a Ph.D. candidate at the University of Pennsylvania. She was clinical nurse specialist for the substance abuse dual diagnosis unit at Thomas Jefferson University Hospital in Philadelphia, PA.

Books from Western schools Press are designed to provide current information which will assist you in providing comprehensive nursing care to clients in a variety of clinical settings. All our books are designed for quality and excellence and are reviewed by experts to meet your professional development needs.

This book is based on *Substance Abuse 2nd Ed.,* 1991 by Robert J. Janke, RN, MFCC and Mary Stein, Western Schools, Inc.

Copy Editor: Barbara Halliburton, PhD

Indexer: Sylvia Coates

Typesetter: Kathy Johnson

Western Schools' courses are designed to provide nursing professionals with the educational information they need to enhance their career development. The information provided within these course materials is the result of research and consultation with prominent nursing and medical authorities and is, to the best of our knowledge, current and accurate. However, the courses and course materials are provided with the understanding that Western Schools is not engaged in offering legal, nursing, medical, or other professional advice.

Western Schools' courses and course materials are not meant to act as a substitute for seeking out professional advice or conducting individual research. When the information provided in the courses and course materials is applied to individual circumstances, all recommendations must be considered in light of the uniqueness pertaining to each situation.

Western Schools' course materials are intended solely for *your* use and *not* for the benefit of providing advice or recommendations to third parties. Western Schools devoids itself of any responsibility for adverse consequences resulting from the failure to seek nursing, medical, or other professional advice. Western Schools further devoids itself of any responsibility for updating or revising any programs or publications presented, published, distributed, or sponsored by Western Schools unless otherwise agreed to as part of an individual purchase contract.

ISBN: 1-57801-005-5

IMPORTANT: Read these instructions *BEFORE* proceeding!

Enclosed with your course book you will find the FasTrax™ answer sheet. Use this form to answer all the final exam questions that appear in this course book. If you are completing more than one course, be sure to write your answers on the appropriate answer sheet. Full instructions and complete grading details are printed on the FasTrax instruction sheet, also enclosed with your order. Please review them before starting. *If you are mailing your answer sheet(s) to Western Schools, we recommend you make a copy as a backup.*

ABOUT THIS COURSE

A "Pretest" is provided with each course to test your current knowledge base regarding the subject matter contained within this course. Your "Final Exam" is a multiple choice examination. **You will find the exam questions at the end of each chapter.** Some smaller hour courses include the exam at the end of the book.

In the event the course has less than 100 questions, mark your answers to the questions in the course book and leave the remaining answer boxes on the FasTrax answer sheet blank. **Use a <u>black pen</u> to fill in your answer sheet.**

A PASSING SCORE

You must score 70% or better in order to pass this course and receive your Certificate of Completion. Should you fail to achieve the required score, we will send you an additional FasTrax answer sheet so that you may make a second attempt to pass the course. Western Schools will allow you three chances to pass the same course…*at no extra charge!* After three failed attempts to pass the same course, your file will be closed.

RECORDING YOUR HOURS

Please monitor the time it takes to complete this course using the handy log sheet on the other side of this page. See below for transferring study hours to the course evaluation.

COURSE EVALUATIONS

In this course book you will find a short evaluation about the course you are soon to complete. This information is vital to providing the school with feedback on this course. The course evaluation answer section is in the lower right hand corner of the FasTrax answer sheet marked "Evaluation" with answers marked 1–25. Your answers are important to us, please take five minutes to complete the evaluation.

On the back of the FasTrax instruction sheet there is additional space to make any comments about the course, the school, and suggested new curriculum. Please mail the FasTrax instruction sheet, with your comments, back to Western Schools in the envelope provided with your course order.

TRANSFERRING STUDY TIME

Upon completion of the course, transfer the total study time from your log sheet to question #25 in the Course Evaluation. The answers will be in ranges, please choose the proper hour range that best represents your study time. You MUST log your study time under question #25 on the course evaluation.

EXTENSIONS

You have 2 years from the date of enrollment to complete this course. A six (6) month extension may be purchased. If after 30 months from the original enrollment date you do not complete the course, *your file will be closed and no certificate can be issued.*

CHANGE OF ADDRESS?

In the event you have moved during the completion of this course please call our student services department at 1-800-618-1670 and we will update your file.

A GUARANTEE YOU'LL GIVE HIGH HONORS TO

If any continuing education course fails to meet your expectations or if you are not satisfied in any manner, for any reason, you may return it for an exchange or a refund (less shipping and handling) within 30 days. Software, video and audio courses must be returned unopened.

Thank you for enrolling at Western Schools!

WESTERN SCHOOLS
P.O. Box 1930
Brockton, MA 02303
(800) 618-1670

Substance Abuse

WESTERN
SCHOOLS®
PRESS

21 Bristol Drive
South Easton, MA 02375

Please use this log to total the number of hours you spend reading the text and taking the final examination (use 50-min hours).

Date	Hours Spent
7-13-01	.5
7-14-01	

TOTAL [   ]

Please log your study hours with submission of your final exam. To log your study time, fill in the appropriate circle under question 25 of the FasTrax® answer sheet under the "Evaluation" section.

Please choose the answer that represents the total study hours it took you to complete this 30 hour course.

A. less than 25 hours   C. 29–32 hours

B. 25–28 hours   D. greater than 32 hours

Substance Abuse

WESTERN SCHOOLS
CONTINUING EDUCATION EVALUATION

Instructions: Mark your answers to the following questions with a black pen on the "Evaluation" section of your FasTrax® answer sheet provided with this course. You should not return this sheet. Please use the scale below to rate the following statements:

A	**Agree Strongly**	**C**	**Disagree Somewhat**
B	**Agree Somewhat**	**D**	**Disagree Strongly**

The course content met the following education objectives:

1. Defined substance abuse and explained the stages of progression.

2. Explained the history of substance abuse treatment, as well a current assessment techniques and treatment modalities.

3. Described the disease process of alcoholism and provided information to access and provide appropriate interventions.

4. Described the progression of sedative-hypnotic dependence, and the current treatment for this dependence.

5. Explained physiological and psychological problems associated with stimulant abuse and withdrawal, as well as therapeutic interventions.

6. Described the effects of opioids, their potential for addiction, and effective treatment.

7. Indicated how the hallucinogens affect users and the best way to treat patients in crisis with these drugs.

8. indicated the short-term and long-term effects of cannabis use.

9. Identified solvents, glues, and aerosols that are abused, and their physiological and psychological effects.

10. Explained how over-the-counter (OTC) drugs are abused and the population that is most likely to abuse them.

11. Identified the scope, signs and resolutions to substance abuse among health-care professionals.

12. The content of this course was relevant to the objectives.

13. This offering met my professional education needs.

14. The objectives met the overall purpose/goal of the course.

15. The course was generally well written and the subject matter explained thoroughly. (If no please explain on the back of the FasTrax instruction sheet.)

16. The content of this course was appropriate for home study.

17. The final examination was well written and at an appropriate level for the content of the course.

Please complete the following research questions in order to help us better meet your educational needs. Pick the ONE answer which is most appropriate. Proceed directly to question #25 to log in your course study time if you do not want to answer the following questions.

18. For your LAST renewal did you take more Continuing Education contact hours than required by your state, if so, how many?

   A. 1–15 hours

   B. 16–30 hours

   C. 31 or more hours

   D. No, I only take the state required minimum

19. Do you usually exceed the contact hours required for your state license renewal, if so, why?

   A. Yes, I have more than one state license

   B. Yes, to meet additional special association Continuing Education requirements

   C. Yes, for professional self-interest/cross-training

   D. No, I only take the state required minimum

20. What nursing shift do you most commonly work?

   A. Morning Shift (Any shift starting after 3:00am or before 11:00am)

   B. Day/Afternoon Shift (Any shift starting after 11:00am or before 7:00pm)

   C. Night Shift (Any shift starting after 7:00pm or before 3:00am)

   D. I work rotating shifts

21. What was the SINGLE most important reason you chose this course?

   A. Low Price

   B. New or Newly revised course

   C. High interest/Required course topic

   D. Number of Contact Hours Needed

22. Where do you work? (If your place of employment is not listed below, please leave this question blank.)

   A. Hospital

   B. Medical Clinic/Group Practice/ HMO/Office setting

   C. Long Term Care/Rehabilitation Facility/Nursing Home

   D. Home Health Care Agency

23. Which field do you specialize in?

   A. Medical/Surgical

   B. Geriatrics

   C. Pediatrics/Neonatal

   D. Other

24. For your last renewal, how many months BEFORE your license expiration date did you order your course materials?

   A. 1–3 months

   B. 4–6 months

   C. 7–12 months

   D. Greater than 12 months

25. **PLEASE LOG YOUR STUDY HOURS WITH SUBMISSION OF YOUR FINAL EXAM.** Please choose which best represents the total study hours it took to complete this 30 hour course.

   A. less than 25 hours

   B. 25–28 hours

   C. 29–32 hours

   D. greater than 32 hours

CONTENTS

PRETEST

Begin by taking the pretest. Compare your answers on the pretest to the answer key (located in the back of the book). Circle those test items that you missed. The pretest answer key indicates the course chapters where the content of that question is discussed.

Next, read each chapter. Focus special attention on the chapters where you made incorrect answer choices. Exam questions are provided at the end of each chapter so that you can assess your progress and understanding of the material.

1. Substance abuse is currently viewed by most professionals as which of the following?

    a. A curable disease

    b. A progressive disease

    c. A disease characterized by abstinence

    d. A disease caused by controlled drinking

2. The early stage of substance abuse involves which of the following?

    a. Difficulty in controlling drug use

    b. Moderate impairment of the user's ability to function

    c. Development of medical problems such as malnourishment

    d. Increased tolerance for the abused substance

3. What is one major factor that determines the intensity of a drug's effect?

    a. Blood pressure

    b. Amount of serotonin released at the synapse

    c. Location of the target cells

    d. Concentration of the drug at the site of action

4. Which of the following is a diagnostic test used to determine substance abuse?

    a. Dexterity test

    b. CAGE

    c. HALT

    d. Intelligence test

5. Steps to prevent relapse in substance abuse include which of the following?

    a. Increasing the dependent's coping skills

    b. Constant supervision by the user's significant others

    c. Recognition by the dependent that he is a failure

    d. Use of methadone

6. Which of the following resulted from the passage of the Controlled Substances Act of 1970?

   a. Establishment of six schedules of controlled drugs

   b. Limitations of refills to two times

   c. Requirement for triplicate prescriptions for controlled substances

   d. Required registration of all prescribing physicians and dispensing pharmacies with the Drug Enforcement Administration

7. Which of the following statements about the metabolism of ethyl alcohol is correct?

   a. It is absorbed primarily from the stomach and small intestine.

   b. It is eliminated primarily through the lungs, kidneys, and sweat glands.

   c. It is metabolized in the stomach to acetaldehyde and finally to acetic acid and carbon dioxide.

   d. It combines initially with neurotransmitters to form rapidly metabolized alkaloids.

8. Alcohol-related medical problems include which of the following?

   a. Increased testosterone levels

   b. Viral hepatitis

   c. Congestive heart failure and hypotension

   d. Osteoporosis and decreased resistance to infection

9. Which of the following statements about the signs and symptoms of alcohol withdrawal is correct?

   a. They are the least serious of any drug withdrawal.

   b. They may include grand mal seizures beginning 12–48 hr after the last drink.

   c. They usually begin 2 weeks after the last drink.

   d. They are no longer experienced after 6 months of sobriety.

10. Which of the following statements about benzodiazepines is correct?

    a. They rarely cause signs and symptoms of withdrawal when their use is suddenly discontinued.

    b. They have generally replaced barbiturates except as anticonvulsants and anesthetics.

    c. They are not considered as safe as barbiturates.

    d. They commonly cause insomnia.

11. Which of the following statements about the elimination half-life of drugs is correct?

    a. It depends on the potency of the drug.

    b. It is correlated with the duration of the withdrawal syndrome.

    c. It is the same as the duration of the drug's action in the body.

    d. It is the time it takes the body to eliminate the entire drug dosage.

12. Which of the following statements about CNS stimulants is correct?

    a. They usually decrease existing circulatory problems.

    b. They decrease the respiratory rate.

    c. They stimulate the appetite.

    d. They alter the function of norepinephrine, dopamine, and serotonin.

13. CNS stimulant withdrawal is characterized by which of the following?

    a. A stable mood

    b. Numbness of the hands

    c. Cessation of cravings within 2 months of the last use of stimulants

    d. An initial "crash" followed in 1-4 hr by intense cravings

14. Which of the following drugs would be the most effective analgesic?

    a. Any parenterally administered analgesic

    b. Cocaine administered by inhalation

    c. Orally administered meperidine

    d. Parenterally administered morphine

15. Which of the following signs is commonly associated with opioid overdose?

    a. Contaminated needles

    b. Runny nose

    c. Fever and chills

    d. Decreased respirations

16. Which of the following statements about hallucinogens is correct?

    a. They are currently the drug of choice in the treatment of asthma.

    b. They have only recently been discovered.

    c. They produce alterations in thought, mood, and perception.

    d. They do not alter neurotransmitters.

17. Timothy Leary is especially known for which of the following?

    a. Promoting medical uses of cocaine

    b. Experimenting with LSD

    c. Accidentally ingesting mescaline

    d. Discovering the anesthetic properties of PCP

18. Which of the following is characteristic of PCP users?

    a. They experience severe withdrawal when they stop using the drug.

    b. They typically do not return to drug use after treatment.

     They have signs and symptoms that are readily differentiated from those of schizophrenia.

    d. They may have persistent speech problems.

19. Which of the following statements about the metabolism of tetrahydrocannabinol (THC) is correct?

    a. Measurable amounts remain in the body for up to 6 months.

    b. It accumulates in areas of low fat.

    c. It has a half-life of 7 days.

    d. Oral doses are metabolized primarily by the lungs.

20. Which of the following statements about marijuana (THC) is correct?

    a. It is used most often by older adults.

    b. It is used predominately by those in lower income levels.

    c. It is usually injected.

    d. It is the most popular illicit drug in America.

21. Which of the following statements about the metabolism of solvents is correct?

    a. They are metabolized solely in the liver.

    b. Their water-soluble metabolites are less harmful than the fat-soluble ones.

    c. They concentrate in tissues that are high in fat.

    d. They are eliminated primarily through the urine.

22. Which of the following statements about OTC drugs in the United States is correct?

    a. Most of them are classified as schedule II drugs.

    b. Their use is limited to the treatment of colds and allergies.

    c. More than 500,000 different preparations are available.

    d. They are most often used by white, middle-class men and the elderly.

23. Which of the following statements about caffeine is correct?

    a. It is rarely the major ingredient in OTC stimulants.

    b. It usually does not produce even mild tolerance unless the dose exceeds 600 mg/day.

    c. It has a half-life of 8–10 hours.

    d. It can exacerbate schizophrenia-type disorders.

24. During the time of Florence Nightingale, which group of people usually provided nursing care?

    a. Volunteers

    b. Trained nurses and doctors

    c. Convicts, prostitutes, and alcoholics

    d. Religious groups

25. Which of the following is an indication of possible drug diversion in a health care setting?

    a. Occasionally incorrect narcotic counts

    b. A decrease in the number of patients' reports of ineffective pain medication

    c. Minor errors in the charting of narcotics

    d. Unusual variation in the quantity of drugs needed on the unit

INTRODUCTION

Few issues in American society are as complicated as substance abuse. In recent years, problems related to substance abuse have emerged as major social and health concerns that affect everyone either directly or indirectly. According to estimates, drug abuse costs the United States $60 billion per year for prevention and treatment programs, for costs incurred by the criminal justice system in dealing with drug-related crimes, and for welfare support paid out to drug abusers and their dependents. The cost in human potential measured as reduced productivity, drug-related health problems, and damages caused by drug-related crime is enormous (Hubbard et al., 1989).

More than 400,000 babies are born each year after intrauterine exposure to illicit drugs, especially crack cocaine (Kandall & Gaines, 1991). Possible adverse effects include prematurity, low birth weight, withdrawal, smaller head circumference, malformations, failure to thrive, developmental delay, stroke, the sudden infant death syndrome, and hyperactivity (McKay & Scavnicky-Mylant, 1991). About 1 child in 600–700 children is born with the fetal alcohol syndrome and may be mentally retarded, malformed, or developmentally delayed or have neurological abnormalities (Streissguth, 1992).

Nearly 2% of children less than 13 years old are infected with HIV (Davis, 1991), and 80% of the infants born with HIV infection have mothers who used intravenous drugs or whose sexual partners did (Kreek, 1992; Streissguth, 1992). Ninety

percent of adolescents drink, and 40% use cocaine, amphetamines, and look-alike drugs (Lewis, Piercy, Sprenkle, & Trepper, 1990). Diet pills, diuretics, amphetamines, and steroids have gained popularity among teenagers as a way to improve physical appearance. Little thought is given to the dangers of sexually transmitted diseases (STDs) and HIV infection so clearly associated with drug use. In 1989, 1% of AIDS cases were in adolescents (Reulbach, 1991).

Drug-related academic, career, and social problems are found in every strata of society, and drug-related accidents and suicides are the leading cause of death among people who use drugs (Nowinski, 1990; Runeson, 1990). About 12 million adults abuse alcohol. This group also has the highest prevalence of illicit drug use; 40% use cocaine and many continue to use marijuana into late adult years. Heroin use has increased slightly and over-the-counter (OTC) pills are popular in this group. Overall, a pattern of multiple drug use has developed in adults (Lee & Bennett, 1991). The result is an increase in family violence, job loss, legal issues, divorce, and health problems (Vannicelli, 1992). With the advent of crack, crime has increased enormously (Lee & Bennett, 1991).

Among the elderly, 10% are thought to have alcohol-related problems. Twenty percent of nursing facility residents and 60% of elderly men admitted to hospital medical wards are problem drinkers. Their drug-related illnesses include dementia, the organic brain syndrome, malnutrition, injuries from accidents, insomnia, incontinence, self-neglect, and depression (Boyd, 1991). Overall, according to estimates, 15–18% of the population of the United States will experience a dependence problem with alcohol, drugs, or both at some point in their lives. This dependence will adversely affect the users, their significant others, and society as a whole (Vannicelli, 1992).

The subject of substance abuse is too vast and complex to discuss every substance that is abused. Therefore, this book does not include information on nicotine, a powerfully habituating substance. The purpose of the book is help the reader recognize substance abuse, assess patients who abuse various substances, and provide appropriate intervention and treatment for these patients.

CHAPTER 1

SUBSTANCE ABUSE: DEFINITION AND PROGRESSION

CHAPTER OBJECTIVE

After studying this chapter, the reader will understand of the definition of substance abuse and recognize the stages of progression.

LEARNING OBJECTIVES

After studying this chapter, the reader will be able to

1. Recognize the disease concept definition of substance abuse.

2. Specify signs and symptoms relative to each stage of substance abuse.

3. Indicate attitudes and behavioral characteristics of a person who is in denial.

4. Indicate physiological factors that influence the effects of a drug.

5. Specify characteristics of withdrawal from abused substances.

6. Recognize risk factors associated with substance abuse.

INTRODUCTION

In this book, the phrase *substance abuse* is used as a synonym for the terms *drug dependence, dependence,* and *addiction.* For simplicity, a person who is dependent on drugs, including alcohol, is referred to as male but should be thought of as male or female.

This chapter reviews how substance abuse came to be viewed as a disease and discusses its progression and underlying characteristics. A list of risk factors thought to increase a person's susceptibility to drug dependence is included.

THE DISEASE MODEL OF ADDICTION

Substance use and abuse have occurred throughout history, often in connection with ceremonies, rituals, religion, use of medication, socialization, and recreation. Before the 19th century, substance abuse (dependence or addiction) was considered a moral failure or a way human beings chose to adapt to their own inadequacies and their environment. In the 1800s, alcoholism came to be viewed as an addiction and a disease characterized by intense cravings, a lack of control, and immoral and criminal behavior, with abstinence as the only remedy (Alexander, 1988). Late in the 1800s, opioid abuse and other addictions were also categorized as diseases (Lewin et al., 1990). However, from 1910 to 1920, the disease model of addiction and its medical approaches to treatment were set aside, and because of underground drug-related crime, addiction was again treated as a moral or criminal problem.

In the 1940s, the disease model was repopularized by Alcoholics Anonymous (AA) (Nace & Isbell, 1991). In 1939, this self-help group published its basic text, *Alcoholics Anonymous,* which states: "We are convinced to a man that alcoholics of our type are in the grip of a progressive illness" (Alcoholics Anonymous, 1976). In 1951, the American Public Health Association presented the Lasker Group Award to AA in recognition of AA's emphasis that alcoholism is an illness (Alcoholics Anonymous, 1976). In 1952, the World Health Organization (WHO) defined alcoholism as follows: "Alcoholism may be characterized as a chronic behavioral disorder manifested by repeated drinking of alcohol beverages in excess of dietary and social uses of the community and to the extent that it interferes with the drinker's health or his social and economic functioning" (Nace & Isbell, 1991). In 1956, the American Medical Association (AMA) recognized alcoholism as a disease and recommended treatment in general hospitals (Beasley, 1990). According to the AMA (1986), "Alcoholism is an illness characterized by preoccupation with alcohol and loss of control over its consumption, such as to lead usually to intoxication if drinking; by chronicity; by progression and by a tendency toward relapse. It is typically associated with physical disability and impaired emotional, occupational and/or social adjustments as a direct consequence of persistent excess use."

By 1960, Jellinek's classification system for diagnosing alcoholism became the basis for treatment of patients who are alcoholic. This system is now applied to addictions in general. It views addiction as a progressive disease characterized by loss of control, cravings, withdrawal, biochemical changes, and genetic etiologic factors. Jellinek recommends abstinence as the only remedy (Selekman & Todd, 1991). Since the late 1960s, professional medical and nursing organizations have been working to promote state legislation and disciplinary sanctions for impaired health care

workers that acknowledge addiction as a health problem rather than as an intentional legal infraction of the state nurse practice acts (Naegle, 1989).

In 1972, the National Council on Alcoholism published its criteria for the diagnosis of alcoholism, focusing on the recognition of early and late signs and symptoms of the disease (Nace & Isbell, 1991). And in 1979, the National Nurses' Society on Addictions recognized alcoholism, or addiction to any mind-altering drug, as a disease (Sullivan, Bissell, & Williams, 1988).

In 1982, the American Nurses Association recognized addiction as a disease and passed a resolution that addicted nurses should be offered treatment before they lose their jobs or their licenses (Sullivan et al., 1988). In 1987, the National Consortium of Chemical Dependency Nurses also recognized addiction as a disease. This national association of professional nurses declared a nursing specialty that requires a specific body of knowledge and competencies to provide appropriate care to patients who alcoholic or addicted. The American Psychiatric Association (1994) defines substance abuse as a continuing pattern of use of a psychoactive substance even though the user knows that it causes or exacerbates persistent or recurrent social, occupational, psychological, or physical problems or that it is being used in physically hazardous situations.

In summary, substance abuse (dependence, addiction) is currently treated by most professionals as a progressive, chronic, incurable, but treatable disease, the remedy of which is abstinence (Selekman & Todd, 1991).

PROGRESSION OF DEPENDENCE

America is a psychoactive (mood-altering), drug-oriented society. We use psychoactive drugs to satisfy curiosity, reduce pain, influence mood, change activity levels, reduce tension and anxiety, decrease fatigue and boredom, improve social interactions, temporarily escape reality, and heighten sensation (Nowinski, 1990).

Psychoactive drugs, including alcohol, may make the user "feel good." Social use of drugs brings people together, because it helps create an atmosphere of openness in which people feel relaxed and able to share more of themselves than they would under ordinary circumstances (Westermeyer, 1991). Unfortunately, every psychoactive substance, including caffeine, nicotine, and some prescription and OTC medications as well as licit and illicit drugs, has the potential for abuse, because the main effect is to produce a pleasant "feeling" (Nowinski, 1990).Many people are able to use drugs without becoming dependent. They do not progress to the point where they experience problems as a result of their drug use, and they do not have psychological cravings, tolerance to the drug, or signs and symptoms of withdrawal when they do not use it. People who become dependent experience progressively severe physical, emotional, familial, social, and occupational problems. Yet, they cannot reduce or stop their drug use and usually deny that it is causing problems.

The progression of dependence has three stages: early, middle, and late. Each stage has specific characteristics.

Early Stage

In the beginning or experimental stage, the ability of the dependent to function is only mildly impaired as a result of his drug use (American Psychiatric Association, 1994).

Drug use. As the amount and frequency of use increase, the dependent periodically decreases or stops using the drug or drugs to prove to himself that he still has control. He may occasionally use drugs as a way to cope with insomnia, lack of confidence, or socialization, but mostly he just uses drugs to feel good. His

family and others may comment on his drug-related behavior and sometimes worry that perhaps he is too involved with drugs. However, when the subject of drugs comes up, the dependent usually either makes light of it or becomes hostile and tries to hide his drug use from them.

Physical effects. The dependent becomes able to use large amounts of drugs without becoming incapacitated (increased tolerance). He may experience insomnia, headaches, cramps, anxiety, epigastric discomfort, heart palpitations and tachycardia, accidental injuries, and increased sexuality.

Emotional effects. The dependent experiences mood swings; decreased self-esteem; negative feelings such as shame, guilt, remorse, resentment, fear, and irritability and tends to focus on drugs.

Family relationships. The dependent may avoid and neglect his family and significant others and argue with them about his drug use and drug-related behavior.

Social effects. The dependent prefers to limit his socialization to activities in which drugs are used and to friends who use moderately to heavily. He may have legal problems or be arrested for driving while intoxicated, for being drunk in public, for disorderly conduct, or for assault.

Occupational effects. The dependent may be late to work or absent from work after a weekend of drug use. His attitude may cause problems at work. He may have financial difficulties related to spending significant amounts of money on drugs. If he is a student, he may be truant and have other drug-related attitudes and behaviors, including decreases in grades and loss of motivation.

Prognosis. Some persons in the early state of dependence improve without treatment. Others continue to progress to later stages (Arif &

Westermeyer, 1988; Ketcham & Gustafson, 1989).

Middle Stage

In the middle stage of dependence, the dependent's ability to function is moderately impaired (American Psychiatric Association, 1994).

Drug use. The dependent has difficulty controlling his drug use. Efforts to stop or reduce use are followed by heavier use, and his drug-related behavior and attitudes continue even when he is not using drugs. He no longer experiences the good feelings that drugs once gave him; now he uses just to feel "normal." He has become sophisticated at finding, buying, and using drugs, and a pattern of using has developed in regard to time, place, and situation.

Physical effects. When he is abstinent, the dependent experiences signs and symptoms of withdrawal that are the opposite of the effects of the drug he has been using. By using the drug again, he can stop the effects of withdrawal. For example, someone who is alcoholic may drink in the morning to relieve tremors. Physical problems increase and may include anorexia, weight change, nausea, diarrhea, malnutrition, gastritis, sexual problems, promiscuity and associated venereal diseases or HIV infection, accidental injuries, suicide attempts, overdoses, blackouts, infections, visual problems, headaches, and memory loss.

Emotional effects. The dependent has extreme mood swings. He feels depressed, ashamed, guilty, remorseful, resentful, fearful, and irritable and is full of self-pity and blame for others. He denies to himself and others that drugs are causing his problems, and he copes with his situation by using more drugs. His thoughts and conversation revolve around drugs.

Family relationships. The dependent embarrasses and alienates his family and others by his drug-related behavior, that is, arguing, fighting, lying, stealing, and self-indulgence. Incest, molestation, physical abuse, and neglect of children may surface. Family members' efforts to keep the family intact and survive involve unhealthy adaptive patterns called codependency, and separation and divorce may occur anyway.

Social effects. The dependent tends to isolate himself or limit his socialization to drug-using friends. He may continue to attend church. He may continue to have legal problems because of driving while intoxicated, being in possession of a controlled substance, disorderly conduct, being drunk in public, assault, warrants for unpaid tickets, and so forth. He may experience drug-related financial problems. If he is a student, he may have escalating problems at school or may drop out.

Occupational effects. The dependent may lose his job because of absences, tardiness, or uncooperative attitudes or because of using drugs on the job or before going to work. Or his employer may ask him to seek treatment.

Prognosis. The dependent may remain in the middle stage for a short time or for many years, or he may bypass it and progress into the late stage. Only a few who have reached the middle stage improve on their own, and if they are multiple-drug users, their progression is even faster (Arif & Westermeyer, 1988; Ketcham & Gustafson, 1989).

Late Stage

In the late stage of dependence, the dependent's ability to function is severely impaired in all areas (American Psychiatric Association, 1994).

Drug use. When the dependent experiences incapacitating effects but cannot control the use of a particular drug, he may replace that drug with another drug that he thinks he has more control over. For example, an amphetamine user who is experiencing paranoia may stop using amphetamines and switch to another drug such as alcohol or marijuana. Drug use is nearly continuous. The dependent uses in an attempt to avoid emotional and physical pain, and he cannot achieve the level of feeling normal.Physical effects. Medical problems may develop, such as malnourishment, impotence, liver disease, pancreatitis, pulmonary edema, toxic psychosis, stroke, kidney failure, overdose, gastritis, and blackouts after even moderate use. If the dependent is an intravenous drug user, he may be exposed to HIV, or septicemia, abscesses, or endocarditis may develop. He may be suicidal or homicidal.

Emotional effects. The dependent loses self-esteem, neglects his personal appearance, and no longer cares about the opinions of his family or society. His judgment and problem-solving skills are poor, and he turns to drugs and crime to survive. He is manipulative; is in denial as to his problems; and externalizes his feelings of guilt, shame, remorse, self-pity, hostility, and resentment.

Family relationships. The dependent is generally alienated from his family and may be institutionalized or homeless.Social effects. The dependent's only associates are drug dealers and the people he uses with.

Occupational effects. The dependent is typically unemployed, on social welfare, and in need of rehabilitation or special education.

Prognosis. Most people in the late stage of dependence do not improve without treatment (Arif & Westermeyer, 1988; Ketcham & Gustafson, 1989).

DENIAL

Denial is a hallmark of the addictive process. It is used by both the dependent and his family to avoid negative feelings, and it is a primary obstacle in their recovery. The dependent person seems unable to recognize the progression of his disease. He minimizes his problems or blames them on others and refuses to seek, help because he feels that he is in control. Typical statements of denial include the following:

* People are over-reacting.

* I'm not as bad as other people.

* I just drink beer.

* I've never been arrested for driving while intoxicated.

Typical behavioral patterns of denial include moving to a new location, looking for a relationship, seeking marriage counseling instead of dealing with the dependency, substituting another drug, decreasing use to get control, and focusing on nutrition and exercise while continuing to use drugs.

Substance abuse is considered a family disease, and treatment is most successful from this perspective. Family members' denial can be seen in the roles they play. These include the hero (the strong family member); the clown (the person who eases tension by eliciting laughter); the lost child (the quiet one); the scapegoat (the one who is blamed for the family's problems); and the chief codependent in charge of seeing that the dependent is protected, the family survives, and the family secrets are kept. The codependent may cope with the situation by taking medications, using drugs, overeating, and so on. Health problems requiring medical attention often occur. Codependents who attend Al-Anon generally develop more appropriate coping skills.The dependent and his family usually have some awareness that their problems are related to their dependencies and that their denial stems from fear of trying to survive without the dependencies (Ketcham & Gustafson, 1989).

PSYCHOLOGICAL DEPENDENCE

All drugs of abuse cause psychological dependence, that is, a need for the drug in order to function and feel good (Schuckit, 1989; Wise & Bozrath, 1985). The degree of psychological dependence ranges from a weak, intermittent desire for the effects of the drug to an overwhelming obsession with the drug. In its extreme, the psychological dependence dominates the life of the dependent through obsessive thoughts and compulsive behavior directed at getting and using the drug. In the middle and late stages of dependence, the dependent usually does not experience pleasure as a result of using the drug, but he continues to use because he fears the emotional and physical pain of withdrawal (Goodwin, 1988). Unfortunately, the search for a good feeling and the instant pleasure gained from using drugs often starts the progression of dependence and ends in a search to avoid both emotional and physical pain.

PHYSIOLOGICAL INFLUENCES ON DRUG INTENSITY

The intensity of a drug's effect is controlled by two major factors: (1) the concentration of drug at the site of action in the body and (2) the tolerance to the drug, or the sensitivity of the target cells to a given concentration of a drug.

Concentration of Drug at the Site of Action

The dose and the way in which the drug is absorbed, distributed, metabolized, and excreted all influence the way a drug becomes concentrated. Drugs that are fat soluble are best able to diffuse across membranes made of a double layer of phospholipids. Thus, drugs that are absorbed across intestinal mucosa; the mucous membranes of the nose, throat, or rectum; or the small air cells of the lung must be fat soluble to be absorbed.

Route of Administration

The four major routes by which drugs are administered are oral, across mucous membranes, inhalation, and parenteral. Each route has its own advantages and drawbacks. Most persons choose a route because of convenience, speed, and duration of action.

Oral route. The most common way to take drugs is to swallow them. Drugs taken orally as capsules, tablets, liquids, or powders are usually absorbed primarily in the small intestine rather than in the stomach. However, if food is present in the stomach, drug absorption may be delayed. Food can delay stomach emptying, or it can dilute the concentration of a drug, delaying absorption and reducing maximum serum levels of the drug. Food can also encapsulate a drug and allow the medication to pass through the body with the feces, without being fully absorbed. Certain drugs are destroyed or their effects are weakened when they are taken orally. For example, heroin is degraded into morphine in the stomach. Once absorbed into the bloodstream, it moves through the liver before it reaches the brain. On the first pass through the liver, so much morphine is destroyed that only a fraction of it ever reaches the brain.

Absorption across mucous membranes. The mucous membranes that line the throat, vagina, and rectum have a larger blood supply than most tissues, and drugs are rapidly absorbed across these membranes. Nitroglycerin, taken for angina, is usually given sublingually because of its speedy absorption when taken by this route. For a number of reasons, most persons do not take drugs sublingually; taste may be one reason.

Sniffing drugs allows the chemicals to be rapidly absorbed across the mucous membranes of the nose and sinus cavities. Drugs commonly taken by this route include cocaine and amyl nitrate. "Sniffing glue" is an incorrect term, because glue and solvent vapors are actually inhaled and absorbed through the lining of the lungs rather than through the lining of the nose and sinus cavities (Cox, Jacobs, LeBlanc, & Marshman, 1983). Sniffing drugs such as cocaine can perforate or destroy the nasal septa.The rectal route is rarely used even though it is an effective alternative route for drugs that cause nausea and vomiting when taken orally.

Inhalation. When a drug is inhaled, it crosses the alveolar membrane and is absorbed into the bloodstream. Inhalation can be an effective route for some drugs, because the surface area of the lungs is large and the diffusion distance is short. However, a drug must be in a gaseous form (as with solvents) or in fine particles or in smoke (marijuana or hashish) to cross the alveolar membrane. The major drawback to this route is that only relatively small amounts of a drug can be absorbed at a time.

Parenteral routes. A drug can be introduced into the bloodstream by subcutaneous, intramuscular, or intravenous injection. Subcutaneous injection, also called "skin popping," involves injecting the drug immediately under the skin. Because this route requires the least skill, it is often used by persons who are just beginning to inject drugs. The effects of a drug occur more rapidly with this route than with the oral route but more slowly than with the intravenous route.

Drawbacks to the subcutaneous route include local or generalized infections that can occur when the needle and drug are not sterile. In addition, insoluble materials tend to remain at the site of injection rather than enter the bloodstream. Thus, the skin may be tattooed or scarred at injection sites; infections may occur there also.

Intramuscular injection sends the drug much more deeply into the body. The drug is injected into the muscle mass, where it is slowly absorbed into the bloodstream. Just as with subcutaneous injection, the risks of infection, scarring, and tissue damage are high, but some drug abusers prefer this route because the drug can be quickly injected right through clothing. Pain at the site of injection is the major drawback. With intravenous injection, that is "mainlining" or injecting a drug directly into a vein, relatively large amounts of a drug can be instantly placed directly into the bloodstream. Usually, the forearms and the area around the elbow are used, although other sites may be used, such as the ankles, scrotum, and the underside of the tongue. Relatively large particles may lead to clot formation, which can block blood vessels and lead to tissue damage or even death. Over time, repeated intravenous injections irritate veins and cause the vessels to collapse. Intravenous drug users are among those at highest risk for AIDS (Arif & Westermeyer, 1988; Nahas 1992; Weiss & Millman 1991).

BIOCHEMISTRY

The biochemical aspects of drug dependence include distribution and excretion of the drug and the development of tolerance.

Drug Distribution

Most drugs are distributed unevenly throughout the body. For example, some drugs bind strongly to blood elements, others dissolve more quickly in body fat, and some have an affinity for bone. To enter the brain, drugs must be highly fat soluble.

Fat-soluble drugs can cross the placenta, affect the fetus, and be present in the milk of lactating women.

Alcohol is a special case. It crosses all barriers, is distributed evenly in the body, and does not bind selectively to any particular tissue (Cox et al., 1983). Some gaseous anesthetics and solvents behave in the same way.

Excretion

Most drugs are excreted via the urine. Blood is filtered as it passes through the kidneys. This filtrate is made up of a considerable amount of the blood's water content, along with all the substances, including drugs, dissolved in this fluid. As the primary water passes farther through the kidney's tubules, the kidney reabsorbs most of the water and some of the dissolved substances. Those substances that are fat soluble tend to diffuse back into the bloodstream and across the membrane of the kidney's tubules (Nahas, 1992; Woolf, 1991a). Urine tests provide only a rough estimate of the serum concentration of a drug because of the reabsorption and active excretion in the renal tubules (Scott, 1990).

Drugs are also excreted in the intestines. For example, some drugs have characteristics that cause them to be actively secreted into the bile as they pass through the liver cells. The drug-filled bile then empties into the intestines (Arif & Westermeyer, 1988).

The breath provides another route of excretion. Volatile drugs such as solvents and general anesthetics are excreted through the breath. Although the breath is a relatively minor excretion route for alcohol, the Breathalyzer test can provide a rough measurement of the blood alcohol level (Arif & Westermeyer, 1988).

Tolerance

Increased tolerance occurs when the body adapts to the long-term use of a drug.

Consequently, larger amounts of the drug must be taken to produce effects. Decreased tolerance occurs when the dependent becomes incapacitated after using even small amounts of the drug.

Cross-tolerance may occur. A person who becomes tolerant to one drug may also become tolerant to all the drugs of that class. For example, alcohol is a central nervous system (CNS) depressant; a person who is alcoholic will be tolerant to all CNS depressants (Woolf 1991a). With multiple drug use, tolerance to two distinct classes of drugs has become common. For example, amphetamine abusers may also abuse alcohol and barbiturates.

Cross-tolerance is used in treatment programs to gradually withdraw a drug. For example, in methadone treatment programs, heroin addicts receive methadone as a substitute for heroin, and the daily dose is gradually reduced and eventually stopped. According to the same principle, alcoholics are detoxified by using chlordiazepoxide (Librium) or other benzodiazepines.

Tolerance will develop to nearly any psychoactive drug that is used repeatedly (Arif & Westermeyer, 1988) Adaption to the long-term use of a drug takes place in the liver (metabolic tolerance) and in the brain (cellular tolerance).

Metabolic tolerance. When large amounts of a drug are repeatedly ingested, the liver adapts by increasing the hepatic enzyme activity needed for detoxification. This adaptation initially results in an increased metabolism of the drug, and the dependent can use large amounts of the drug without becoming incapacitated. If the process continues and the liver cells become damaged and cannot keep up the detoxification, metabolism of the drug decreases and the dependent becomes incapacitated after using even small amounts of the drug (Woolf, 1991a).

Cellular tolerance. In the brain, the cells adapt to large amounts of a drug, so that the dependent must use larger amounts to feel the same effect (Ketcham & Gustafson, 1989). The methods by which drugs affect the CNS are complex. The following discussion is limited to explaining the basic structure and function of the CNS and exploring some of the major effects of drugs on it.

The nervous system can be roughly divided into the CNS (brain and spinal cord) and the peripheral nervous system (all other structures in the nervous system). The psychoactive effects of drugs are due to the actions of the drugs on the CNS.

The CNS consists of billions of neurons (nerve cells) of various shapes, sizes, and functions. The neuron is the base of all activities of the CNS and carries messages in the form of electrical impulses over long distances. Each neuron is made up of a cell body, one or more dendrites that carry electrical impulses (messages) toward the cell body, and an axon that carries electrical impulses (messages) away from the cell body.

The neurons can send messages from one site to another through the transmission of electrical impulses and can synthesize, store, and release highly specific chemicals called neurotransmitters. At the site where the endings of two neurons meet is a gap called the synapse. For an electrical impulse (message) to cross the gap, a neurotransmitter is needed. Thus, when an electrical impulse comes along, vesicles in the ending of one neuron release a neurotransmitter into the gap, and the neurotransmitter migrates to a receptor site on the endings of the adjacent neuron or tissue. This intricate process takes only a few thousandths of a second. After it activates the receptor, the neurotransmitter is released back into the gap and either goes back into the neuron ending from which it originated or is deactivated by the chemical monoamine oxidase in the synapse (Holbrook, 1991a).

Nearly all psychoactive drugs alter the function of neurotransmitters by either stimulating or inhibiting the synthesis, release, reuptake, or breakdown of neurotransmitters and neuropeptides (enkephalin and endorphin). Opioids alter the release of the neurotransmitters acetylcholine, norepinephrine, substance P, and dopamine, causing a decreased response to pain. Opioids bind to the natural receptor sites in the CNS for the neuropeptides, which are thought to influence a number of functions, including mood, alcoholism and hormonal activity, and pain regulation (Woolf, 1991c).

Stimulants alter the release of norepinephrine and dopamine and block their reuptake. Cocaine blocks the reuptake of norepinephrine, dopamine, and serotonin. Both amphetamines and cocaine decrease the electrical stimulus needed to activate feelings of pleasure.

Alcohol metabolizes to acetaldehyde, which has an affinity for endogenous opioid adrenergic receptors and may contribute to withdrawal (Beasley, 1990). Marijuana alters the function of the neurotransmitters serotonin, acetylcholine, dopamine, γ-aminobutyric acid, and tetrahydrocannabinol receptors (Nahas, 1992).

WITHDRAWAL

When a person with a drug dependence suddenly reduces or stops using a drug that he has been habitually (daily) using, painful and distressing physical and psychological signs and symptoms develop. The syndrome is called withdrawal. The signs and symptoms of withdrawal are the opposite of the effects experienced by the dependent while he is using the drug, and they vary in severity and duration.

Opioids have analgesic and calming qualities. Withdrawal from opioids results in extreme excitability and extremely painful, flulike signs and symptoms, which are not generally life threatening. Use of alcohol, barbiturates, and the benzodiazepines can calm, induce sleep, and decrease pain. In contrast, withdrawal from these substances results in tremors, agitation, nausea, diarrhea, insomnia, headache, gastrointestinal distress, psychological pain, and other life-threatening signs and symptoms.

Marijuana produces relaxation and a feeling of well-being, dry mouth, and increased hunger. Withdrawal from marijuana results in irritability, sleep disturbances, headaches, panic attacks, and sweating and is rarely life threatening. Acute signs and symptoms of withdrawal may last anywhere from a few hours after cessation of drug use to several days, depending on the drug, dosage, route of administration, and the user. Protracted withdrawal can last days, weeks, or months. The pain and distress of withdrawal are one of the motivations for a dependent to continue using a drug (Arif & Westermeyer, 1988; Beasley, 1990; Ketcham & Gustafson, 1989; Miller, 1991; Nahas, 1992).

CHRONICITY AND RELAPSE

Basic to the disease concept of addiction is the inability of the addict to return to controlled use of addictive drugs. Because of the chronic nature of the disease, he cannot control the amount of drugs used, the effects, or the cravings associated with use. If he attempts to use drugs after a period of sobriety (nonuse), he quickly becomes as incapacitated as before and is said to have relapsed.

Relapse may occur after any length of sobriety (even years) and is not a random, precipitant event. Relapse is most likely to occur when the dependent experiences negative emotions related to a lack of socialization, peer pressure to use, or conflict with

a person important to him (McKay & Scavnicky-Mylant, 1991).

Even when things are going well the dependent may relapse, perhaps because of a "trigger" (stimulus) that he commonly associates with drug use. A trigger can be an object or an activity, such as a football game, fishing, sex, a place, a holiday, or a particular food. It can be a physical condition such as hunger, fatigue, or pain or an emotion such as anger.

Relapse is much more common for multiple-drug dependents (Ketcham & Gustafson, 1989), and the prognosis of substance abuse is clearly influenced by the intensity of the drug's effects and its route of administration (Arif & Westermeyer, 1988).

RISK FACTORS

A number of risk factors thought to increase a person's susceptibility to drug dependence have been proposed. Some have been supported by research, and others are still hypotheses (Bennett, 1991a).

- **Fetal exposure:** Drugs used during pregnancy may increase the unborn child's susceptibility to drug dependence (Svikis & Pickens, 1988).

- **Heredity:** A family history of alcoholism increases a person's risk for drug dependence (McKay & Scavnicky-Mylant, 1991). Such persons get addicted more quickly, sometimes with the first drink, and their addiction is severe (Goodwin, 1988).

- **Inadequate role models:** Parents and older siblings who use or are apathetic about drug use are modeled. Parental absence (death, divorce) increases the risk of drug dependence in adolescents (Arif & Westermeyer, 1988).

- **Antisocial behavior:** Lack of empathy, lying, the need for immediate gratification, and a lack of responsiveness to punishment are some of the characteristics associated with an increased risk for drug dependence in adulthood (Cahalan, 1991).

- **Peers who use drugs:** An adolescent whose close friends use drugs is at high risk for drug dependence. When drugs are used, it is usually with peers. Peers initiate each other into drug use, talk and experiment together, and model drug-using attitudes and behaviors for each other. Even if a peer uses a drug alone, he will usually also use the drug with others (Oetting & Beauvais, 1988).

- **Low self-esteem:** Insecure adolescents with low self-esteem may try to compensate by using drugs and are at risk for drug dependence (Nowinski, 1990).

- **Daily drinking at a young age:** Adolescents who have a pattern of daily drinking in high school are more likely to progress to multiple-drug use (Schuckit, 1989).

- **Depression:** Adolescents who are chronically angry, anxious, or depressed have a greater risk of drug dependence than adolescents without these characteristics (Oetting & Beauvais, 1988).

- **Poor performance at school:** Academic inadequacies, rebelliousness, alienation, and antisocial behavior increase adolescents' risk for drug dependence (Cahalan, 1991).

- **High activity level in childhood:** Children who are highly active are at greater risk than less active children for alcoholism in adulthood (Tarter & Edwards, 1988).

- **Ethnic group:** Members of various ethnic groups, including the French, Irish, Russian, North American Native Americans, and northern European groups, have an increased risk for alcoholism (Goodwin, 1988) Excretion of alcohol is slower in Native Americans and Eskimos than in other groups (Kolata, 1988).

- **Sex:** Depressed women are at higher risk for alcoholism than depressed men are (Nace & Isbell, 1991).

- **Women who experience trauma and life crisis:** Physical or sexual abuse, a family history of drug abuse, the loss of a parent, role confusion, an abusive spouse or significant other, or divorce are associated with an increased risk for drug dependence (Sumners, 1991).

- **Socioeconomic level:** Research conducted specifically among disadvantaged youth of a very low socioeconomic level showed higher rates of drug use than among youth of higher levels (Oetting & Beauvais, 1988).

- **Occupation:** The armed services have higher rates of alcoholism than the general population does (Schuckit, 1989). A larger than average number of doctors and nurses are treated for drug dependence (Sullivan et al., 1988). Alcoholism is higher among bartenders and journalists than among people in other occupations (Goodwin & Warnock, 1991).

- **Elderly:** The elderly experience social, psychological, physiological, and spiritual stresses that increase the risk of substance abuse (Boyd, 1991).

A High School Study

Newcomb and his coworkers in the UCLA/NIDA Center for Drug Research surveyed 2,926 7th, 9th, and 11th grade students in five school districts in Ventura County, California, in an attempt to isolate risk factors for drug use and abuse. The sample was fairly evenly divided by sex, and five distinct ethnic groups were represented (70% of those responding were white).

The researchers identified 12 risk factors that appeared to lead to drug use (Newcomb, Maddahian, Skager, & Bentler, 1987):

1. **Early alcohol intoxication:** Of the students who responded, 23% had been intoxicated by the time they were 12 years old or younger.

2. **Perceived adult drug use:** The authors used a questionnaire in which students were asked to list the number of adults the students knew who drank beer, wine, or hard liquor or used diet pills at least once a week. The degree of abuse was not graded, so no differentiation was made between use of wine, marijuana, or diet pills, for example. About 30% of students knew at least two adults who engaged in one of these behaviors.

3. **Peer approval of drug use:** The researchers asked students, "What would your 4 or 5 best friends think about another student who usually gets loaded on drugs or alcohol at social events and often at school?" Four responses were offered: (1) Would avoid them, (2) Would see them as okay, (3) Would see them as okay and would sometimes would join in, and (4) My friends are pretty much like that. Thirty percent of the sample picked answer 3 or answer 7

4. **Parental approval of drug use:** The researchers asked two questions to try to determine if parents approved of drug use by teenagers or adults. One question asked about attitudes toward alcohol, and one asked about other drugs. Twenty-five percent of the students were estimated to be at increased risk for drug use because of parental approval of drug use by adults and adolescents.

5. **Absence from school:** One part of the survey looked at the times the student was absent from school for reasons other than illness (including "ditching" school). Sixteen percent of students at risk were in this category.

6. **Low academic achievement:** About 7% of students at risk reported a D or F grade average. These students were at increased risk for drug use, according to the researchers.

7. **Distrust of their teachers' knowledge of drugs:** The survey included the following statement: "In my experience at this school, what my teachers have to say about drugs can be trusted because they are well-informed about the subject." About 12% of the students surveyed thought that their teachers were not well-informed about drugs.

8. **Distrust of their parents' knowledge of drugs:** About 11% of students thought that their parents did not have enough knowledge about drugs or that what their parents said about drugs could not be trusted.

9. **Low educational aspirations:** Students were asked how much schooling they were planning to complete, with choices ranging from dropping out of high school to getting a doctoral degree. Twenty-eight percent of the students at risk were judged to have low educational aspirations.

10. **Little religious commitment:** Twenty-three percent of students rated themselves as not religious at all, on a three-point scale that ranged from not religious at all to very religious.

11. **Emotional distress:** Student were asked to indicate how much they were bothered by seven main problems during the past 30 days. These problems included feeling blue, feeling others were to blame for most of the problems, thoughts of ending their life, and so forth. The results indicated that 29% of the students surveyed had emotional distress.

12. **General dissatisfaction with life:** Students were asked to indicate their level of satisfaction in eight life areas, including the ability to handle feelings and emotions, overall satisfaction with school, general enjoyment of life, relationships with their family and friends, concern about the future, and the ability to be close to someone they cared for. Twenty-six percent of the students were dissatisfied with life.

Overall the researchers found (1) there was no significant difference in risk by gender, (2) the number of risk factors increased significantly with grade level, (3) Native Americans were exposed to many more risk factors than other ethnic groups, and (4) students in continuation school (those removed from regular classes because of adjustment problems) had a much higher risk of substance abuse than those attending regular school sessions.

Twelve percent of the students had abused cigarettes, 3% abused alcohol, 7% abused marijuana, 2% abused cocaine, and 3% abused other types of hard drugs. Abuse was defined as daily use of cigarettes, alcohol, or marijuana or at least weekly use of hard drugs and cocaine during the previous 6 months.

For all types of abused substances, increase in abuse was associated with increased numbers of risk factors. At least 71% of the students with seven or more risk factors abused at least one substance. Also, the researchers showed that the likelihood of drug abuse is directly related to the number of risk factors and not to a single cause. A number of personal, social, and environmental factors have long been implicated in the first and continuing abuse of drugs by teenagers: peer and family models, poor academic achievement, early use of alcohol, and stressful life events. Thus, as this study by Newcomb et al. shows, multiple factors interact to increase a person's susceptibility to substance abuse.

EXAM QUESTIONS

CHAPTER 1
Questions 1–15

1. Which of the following is a risk factor thought to increase a person's susceptibility to drug dependence?

   a. Fetal exposure

   b. Low activity level in childhood

   c. High self-esteem as an adolescent

   d. High socioeconomic level

2. Substance abuse is currently viewed by most professionals as which of the following?

   a. A curable disease

   b. A progressive disease

   c. A disease characterized by abstinence

   d. A disease caused by controlled drinking

3. The early stage of substance abuse involves which of the following?

   a. Difficulty in controlling drug use

   b. Moderate impairment of the user's ability to function

   c. Increased tolerance for the abused substance

   d. Development of medical problems such as malnourishment

4. Which of the following statements about a person in the late stage of drug dependence is correct?

   a. He uses drugs nearly continuously.

   b. He usually receives strong family support.

   c. He typically continues to be employed.

   d. He is rarely institutionalized or homeless.

5. Which of the following statements about denial in drug dependence is correct?

   a. It occurs more often in males than in females.

   b. It is a temporary psychosis.

   c. It seldom occurs before the middle stage of dependence.

   d. It is present when a user seems unable to recognize the progression of his disease.

6. Which of the following statements about the middle stage of drug dependence is correct?

   a. The user increases his social circle.

   b. The user no longer experiences mood swings.

   c. Abuse of drugs is sporadic and not patterned.

   d. Efforts to stop or reduce drug use are followed by heavier use.

7. What is one major factor that determines the intensity of a drug's effect?

    a. Concentration of the drug at the site of action

    b. Blood pressure

    c. Amount of serotonin released at the synapse

    d. Location of the target cells

8. The concentration of a drug at the site of action in the body is determined by which of the following?

    a. Overall body hydration

    b. Degree of psychological dependence

    c. Solubility of the drug in bile

    d. How the drug is absorbed and distributed

9. Which of the following statements about sniffing drugs is correct?

    a. Sniffing of cocaine and amyl nitrite is rare.

    b. Sniffing drugs is the same as inhaling drugs.

    c. Sniffing drugs allows the chemicals to be absorbed slowly.

    d. Sniffing drugs can cause perforation of the nasal septum.

10. Which of the following statements about alcohol is correct?

    a. Excretion is mostly through the lungs.

    b. It does not bind selectively to any particular tissue.

    c. The Breathalyzer gives a precise measurement of blood levels.

    d. It is not evenly distributed through the body.

11. Detoxification of alcoholics may involve the use of which of the following medications?

    a. Chlordiazepoxide (Librium)

    b. Methadone

    c. Disulfiram (Antabuse)

    d. Monoamine oxidase

12. Cocaine blocks reuptake of which of the following biochemicals?

    a. γ-Aminobutyric acid

    b. Acetaldehyde

    c. Dopamine

    d. Tetrahydrocannabinol

13. Which of the following statements about withdrawal from alcohol, barbiturates, or benzodiazepines is correct?

    a. It can cause life-threatening signs and symptoms.

    b. It usually causes an increase in sleep.

    c. It decreases sensitivity to pain.

    d. It is unlikely to occur if the dose is only reduced.

14. How long can protracted withdrawal from alcohol or drugs last?

    a. No more than a few hours

    b. No more than a few weeks

    c. No less than 6 months

    d. Days, weeks, or months

15. Which of the following risk factors appears to lead to drug use among teenagers?

    a.   Peer disapproval of drug use

    b.   Parental approval of drug use

    c.   High educational aspirations

    d.   Strong religious commitment

CHAPTER 2

ASSESSMENT, TREATMENT, AND PREVENTION

CHAPTER OBJECTIVE

After studying this chapter, the reader will be familiar with the history of substance abuse treatment, current assessment techniques, and current treatments.

LEARNING OBJECTIVES

After studying this chapter, the reader will be able to

1. Indicate the historical development of treatment of substance abuse.

2. Specify current techniques for the assessment of substance abusers.

3. Indicate various treatment programs for substance abusers.

4. Specify various tools used in the diagnosis of substance abuse.

5. Choose the definition of relapse in substance abusers.

6. Choose techniques to prevent relapse.

7. Specify current aspects of patients' rights of confidentiality.

INTRODUCTION

This chapter reviews the evolution of treatment in the field of substance abuse. It covers current tools used to assess patients and patients' families and industry-approved treatments, including medical model inpatient treatment, outpatient treatment, self-help groups, community residential treatment, drug therapies, and individual psychotherapy. The chapter concludes with brief discussions on relapses and legal issues covering confidentiality of the patient.

TREATMENT EVOLUTION

Two central methods of treatment of substance abuse were established in the 1700s on the basis of then existing psychiatric treatment methods. The asylum method provided an environment that helped patients abstain from substance use and friends associated with use. The moral treatment method provided both civil and respectful consideration for the recovering abuser.

Both methods are still used, yet neither has been validated by research, and it is generally thought that neither is inevitably successful. Also, these remedies were not always available to the general public because of cost or locality. Consequently, other methods were used.

In the 1700s and 1800s, one treatment was to substitute another drug for the "drug of choice." For example, laudanum (a combination of alcohol and opioids) was prescribed for the treatment of alcoholism, and morphine was recommended for the treatment of opioid addiction. This method is still used today as shown by the prescribing of methadone for long-term heroin addicts.

During the mid-1900s, public detoxification facilities were developed in Eastern Europe and soon became an established form of treatment throughout the world. This course of therapy offered, and continues to offer, many substance abusers an opportunity for recovery.

Also in the mid-1900s, the Minnesota model of treatment was developed. It evolved from the combined program ideas and philosophies of the Wilmar State Hospital treatment program, Hazelden (a private treatment facility in Minnesota), and the Minneapolis Veterans Administration Hospital treatment program.

The following are basic philosophies of the Minnesota model:

1. Inpatient or residential care for a few weeks or months.

2. A focus on use of psychoactive substances with little or no attention to associated psychiatric conditions.

3. Reliance on the concepts, resources, and precepts of AA, including 12 steps central to recovery.

4. Referral to self-help groups such as AA on discharge from residential or inpatient care, with limited or no ongoing professional treatment.

5. Limited family therapy, although the family may be oriented to AA principles and Al-Anon.

6. Nonacceptance of psychotherapy and pharmacotherapy for either substance abuse or psychiatric disorder.

During the 1950s and 1960s, this model helped bridge the gaps between hospital programs and self-help groups. Currently, many treatment facilities use only some aspects of the model and augment it with a wide range of holistic approaches for recovery of the mind, body, and spirit of recovering patients and their families.

From the 1960s to the present, the workplace became a center of early prevention, education, referral for treatment, and rehabilitation through company-sponsored employee assistance programs (Westermeyer, 1991).

CURRENT METHODS

Currently, new diagnostic and treatment methods to improve clinical outcomes are being tested. For example, some programs concurrently treat dual-diagnosis disorders, ranging from associated anxieties, affective disorders, and eating disorders to major psychiatric disorders such as schizophrenia, major depression, and organic brain disorders (Westermeyer, 1991). New treatment philosophies include using inpatient hospital stays for emergency situations until the patient is satisfactorily out of the medical crisis. The patient and his family then become immediately involved in an intensive, structured, outpatient program that addresses the full range of lifestyle issues (including personal, family, social, legal, occupational, financial, and recovery) and focuses on the development of a support system through scheduled attendance at self-help groups.

Treatment of substance abuse in America continues to evolve and change as new knowledge of the disease is gained. A concept of recent years is that, although it is ultimately the dependent person's responsibility to manage his recovery, a combination of involvement of the patient, the patient's family, and society (industry, government, and medical professionals) is more successful and beneficial for all concerned. Involvement begins with recognizing the dependent person and assisting in his recovery (Westermeyer, 1991).

ASSESSMENT

The key to successful recovery is recognition of the addicted person and complete, collaborative assessment and treatment by health professionals, including physicians, nurses, social workers, and trained counselors. The assessment can be a major preventive tool as well as a good indicator of the appropriate level of treatment. No one phase of assessment can be omitted in determining a clinically sound diagnosis and referral (Arif & Westermeyer, 1988).

In general, results obtained through clinical questioning underrate the presence, severity, and duration of substance abuse and its effects. This outcome is due to the reluctance, fear, and denial of the addicted person. Although the assessment may be overpositive about the disease, the time spent with the patient in reviewing his body systems and discussing his addiction is a powerful tool in early intervention and referral.

Assessment includes an initial interview, a physical examination, a psychosocial history, and diagnostic tests (laboratory tests). Confirming and augmenting the assessment through input from the patient's family members and significant others may be helpful. Also helpful are the CAGE questionnaire *(Table 2-1)*, the Brief Michigan Alcoholism Screening Test (MAST; *Table 2-2)*, and the *Diagnostic and Statistical Manual of Mental Disorders: DSM-IV* (American Psychiatric Association, 1994). Nurses should also know the protocol established by the organization in which they are employed.

Initial Interview

Patients are initially screened by a staff counselor or nurse. The purpose of this interview is to gather information that will enable the treatment team to provide appropriate medical care, detoxification, and rehabilitation. Information needed includes a thorough history of health problems,

---

TABLE 2-1
The Cage Questions

1. Have you ever felt you should **C**ut down on your drinking?

2. Have people **A**nnoyed you by criticizing your drinking?

3. Have you ever felt bad or **G**uilty about your drinking?

4. Have you ever had a drink first thing in the morning to steady your nerves or to get rid of a hangover (**E**ye-opener)?

Two or more affirmatives indicates probable diagnosis of alcoholism.

From Mayfield D, McLeod G, Hall P.: More detailed interview screening. *Am J Psychiatry* 1974;131:1121. Reprinted with permission from Essential Medical Information Systems, Inc.

---

medications, drug use, previous detoxifications, seizures, psychiatric diagnosis, and suicidal ideations and attempts. The information gained in this interview is helpful in determining the level of care needed by the patient *(Table 2-3)*. After determining that the patient meets the admission criteria, the nurse (or counselor) consults a medical director of the organization for admission orders.

Physical Examination

The physical examination is performed by a medical doctor and includes assessment of vital signs, autonomic nervous system, mental status, and neurological status.

Vital Signs

Temperature. Fever related to infections resulting from intravenous and other drug use or to withdrawal from sedatives or alcohol.

Pulse. Irregularities related to heavy use of caffeine, tobacco, alcohol, or amphetamines. Bradycardia related to opioid overdose.

TABLE 2-2
The Brief Michigan Alcoholism Screening Test

Question	Circle Correct Answer		Points
1. Do you feel you are a normal drinker?	YES	NO	N2
2. Do friends or relatives think you are a normal drinker?	YES	NO	N2
3. Have you ever attended a meeting of Alcoholics Anonymous?	YES	NO	Y5
4. Have you ever lost friends or girlfriends/boyfriends because of drinking?	YES	NO	Y2
5. Have you ever gotten into trouble at work because of drinking?	YES	NO	Y2
6. Have you ever neglected your obligations, your family, or your work for 2 or more days in a row because you were drinking?	YES	NO	Y2
7. Have you ever had delirium tremens (DTs) or severe shaking, or heard voices or seen things that weren't there after heavy drinking?	YES	NO	Y2
8. Have you ever gone to anyone for help about your drinking?	YES	NO	Y5
9. Have you ever been in a hospital because of drinking?	YES	NO	Y5
10. Have you ever been arrested for drunk driving or driving after drinking?	YES	NO	Y2

Score 6 indicates probable diagnosis of alcoholism.

Source: *A Manual on Drug Dependence,* 1992, by G. Nahas. Essential Medical Information Systems, Inc. Reprinted with permission.

Blood pressure. Hypertension related to long-term alcohol intoxication or withdrawal. Hypotension related to overdose of various drugs, but characteristic of opioid or PCP intoxication.

Mental Status

General behavior. Poor personal hygiene related to long-term drug abuse. Relationship with examiner evasive, suspicious, manipulative, seductive, directing, seeking nontherapeutic ends.

Mood. Sad, euphoric, irritable, anxious, rapid mood swings.

Thinking processes. Logical, connected, appropriate, delusional, hallucinatory.

Orientation. Time (year, month, date, day, season, hour), place, person (name of self and the examiner), current situation, and purpose for being in the current location.

Memory. Distant (childhood, birthplace), recent (events of day or weeks prior), immediate (recall what was said in the current interview).

Organs and Systems

Head. New or old trauma, pediculosis.

Eye. Pupils constricted related to opioid intoxication or dilated with opioid withdrawal. Dilated and nonreactive related to alcohol or sedative overdose. Conjunctiva congested as with use of cannabis and alcohol, pale with anemia. Lacrimation related to opioid withdrawal. Sclerae yellow with liver disease. Oculomotor indication of ophthalmoplegia with thiamine deficiency. Both horizontal and vertical nystagmus related to PCP use. Toxic amblyopia related to use of tobacco, alcohol, and methanol.

Nose. Rhinorrhea, septal ulcers, and perforations related to sniffing drugs. Rhinophyma and acne rosacea related to heavy use of alcohol.

TABLE 2-3
Admission Criteria for Substance Abusers

I.   Criteria for Acute Hospital Care

1.   Failure to make progress in less intense levels of care

2.   High-risk chemical withdrawal (seizures, delirium tremens)

3.   High tolerance to one or multiple substances

4.   Acute exacerbation of medical or psychiatric problems related to chemical dependence (cardiomy-opathy, hepatitis, depression)

5.   Concomitant medical or psychiatric problem that could complicate treatment (diabetes, bipolar disor-der, hypertension)

6.   Severely impaired social, familial, or occupational functioning

II.   Criteria for Nonhospital Residential Care

1.   Failure to make progress in less intensive levels of care

2.   Ability to undergo chemical withdrawal without close medical supervision

3.   Stable medical or psychiatric problems that require monitoring

4.   Impairment of social, familial, or occupational functioning requiring separation from environment

5.   Sufficiently developed interpersonal and daily living skills to permit a satisfactory level of functioning

III. Criteria for Partial Hospital Care

1.   No need for 24-hour medically supervised chemical withdrawal

2.   Stable psychiatric or medical problems

3.   Sufficiently developed interpersonal and daily living skills to permit a satisfactory level of functioning in this setting

4.   No need for intensive psychiatric care

5.   Freedom from drugs that alter the state of consciousness, other than prescribed medication approved by the program

6.   Need for daily support rather than weekly or biweekly sessions

7.   Social system—that is, family, friends, or employment—capable of providing support

IV. Criteria for Outpatient Care

1.   Ability to function autonomously in present social environment

2.   Stable psychiatric or medical problems

3.   Sufficient capacity to function in individual, group, or family therapy sessions

4.   No need for 24-hour medically supervised chemical withdrawal

5.   Willingness to work toward goal of abstinence from harmful drug use

Ears. Gouty tophi related to alcohol use and increased serum levels of uric acid.

Breath. Odor of alcohol, poor care of mouth, odor of tobacco or cannabis. Lips showing malignant or premalignant lesions due to use of alcohol and tobacco. Possible cyanosis in heavy smokers. Perioral rash related to solvent use.

Teeth. Dental caries and periodontal infection related to use of any drug, particularly drugs that are chewed.

Tongue. Tremors related to withdrawal from depressants.

Uvula. Edema related to heavy use of hashish.

Pharynx. Inflammation or tumor related to use of alcohol, tobacco, or betel.

Neck. Nodding related to opioid intoxication. Muscle rigidity and spasm related to PCP intoxication.

Chest. Findings on inspection and palpation: spider angiomata related to liver damage, gynecomastia in males related to liver damage and decreased testosterone, rib fracture related to trauma incurred while intoxicated.

Lungs. Findings on percussion and auscultation: bronchitis or emphysema related to heavy smoking of opium, tobacco, marijuana, or hashish. Lung abscess related to aspiration during intoxication. Acute pulmonary edema related to use of opioids. Asthma related to use of LSD, cannabis, opium, and other drugs. Cor pulmonale related to long-term smoking.

Heart. Cardiomegaly; alcoholic cardiomyopathy; acute cardiac dilation related to inhalant intoxication. Cardiac murmurs related to bacteremia from intravenous drug use causing valvulitis and endocarditis. Dysrhythmias related to use of alcohol, solvents, tobacco, caffeine, or stimulants.

Abdomen. Distension due to ascites related to long-term use of alcohol or inhalants. Dilated superficial veins due to obstruction of the portal vein related to alcoholism; surgical scars from peptic ulcer, liver biopsy, paracentesis. Hematemesis from esophageal varices due to hepatic cirrhosis related to alcoholism. Findings on palpation: hepatomegaly with or without tenderness. Tenderness of right upper quadrant due to hepatitis; periumbilical or epigastric alcoholic pancreatitis. Ascites: fluid wave. Findings on auscultation: decreased peristaltic sounds related to use of opioids or stimulants; increased peristaltic sounds related to alcoholic malabsorption syndrome or to opioid withdrawal. Findings on percussion: shifting dullness due to ascitic fluid; hepatomegaly.

Genitourinary system. Females: Chancre, herpes infection, STDs, urethral and vaginal discharge, cervicitis related to multiple sexual partners, amenorrhea related to effect of alcohol or opioids on ovaries. Males: penile lesions of chancre, herpes progenitalis; urethral discharge (gonorrheal, trichomonal); testicular atrophy, decrease in pubic hair related to alcoholism or opioid dependence; pediculosis. Some of these conditions may be due to lifestyle rather than to drug use.

Musculoskeletal system. Muscle wasting; muscle spasm and rigidity related to PCP use. Fractures due to trauma, accidents. Osteomyelitis and septic arthritis from intravenous drug use. Muscle tenderness especially in the calves due to kidney disease related to intravenous drug use.

Nervous system. Tremors; liver flap with hepatic encephalopathy; withdrawal from alcohol or sedatives. Abnormal gait resulting from alcoholic cerebellar degeneration.

Skin. Stained fingers from holding cigarettes, marijuana. Intravenous tracks occurring as pigmented linear marks along the course of superficial veins. Thrombophlebitis, abscesses. Pruritus, chronic papular seborrheic dermatitis, cheilosis due to vitamin deficiency; stress. Perspiration associated with withdrawal from opioids, alcohol, or sedatives. Piloerection associated with opioid withdrawal. Pyoderma due to poor hygiene or to white blood cell suppression because of alcoholism.

Lymphatic system. Enlarged lymph nodes due to AIDS as related to intravenous drug use (Arif & Westermeyer, 1988).

Psychosocial History

A thorough history is generally obtained by a substance abuse counselor who is also responsible for developing the part of the treatment plan that addresses substance abuse. The history includes the following:

- Identifying data.

- Medical history, including past and current prescribed or OTC medications, hospitalizations, past and current medical problems, nutrition.

- Substance abuse history, including current and past drug use, patterns of use, problems experienced because of drug use, previous treatment and detoxification, periods of sobriety and relapse.

- Psychiatric history, level of self-esteem, diagnosis, treatment, suicidal ideations and/or attempts.

- Social history, including the patient's relationships with family members and peers both as a child and currently; education; work history; hobbies; leisure time use; past and current legal problems; financial problems; marital status; children; relationship with spouse or significant other; history of abuse, incest, or molestation.

- Motivation for seeking treatment and goals while in treatment.

- Recommendations, including further diagnostic testing.

Psychiatric signs and symptoms may not become completely evident until the user has been abstinent for a substantial period—generally 3 months to 1 year (Crist & Milby, 1990; Huggins, 1990).

Diagnostic Tests

Psychological Tests

The Minnesota Multiphasic Personality Inventory (MMPI) is used to determine preexisting psychopathological conditions. The major advantage of the MMPI over other psychological tests is that it differentiates addiction from psychiatric disorders with an 85% accuracy (Crist & Milby, 1990).

Laboratory Tests

Laboratory tests are used to help the clinician develop an overall diagnosis. Testing is done to evaluate current or recent use of drugs or alcohol, level of tolerance, use of multiple drugs, and possible physical complications that may need to be addressed.

It is important to know the half-life of drugs screened for and detected. Many drugs are detectable within 12–48 hr after use, and some may be detected up to weeks later (e.g., cannabis).

Generally, two methods are used to test blood and urine: immunoassay and chromatography. Urine screening is used primarily for identification; opioids, sedative-hypnotics, stimulants, hallucinogens, and alcohol can be detected. Blood screening is used for quantitative analysis.

When a urine drug screen is ordered, the substance abuser should be monitored during collection of the urine sample, because his level of denial may influence him to attempt to alter or manipulate the screen in an attempt to avoid detection of his drug use.

Self-Rating Scales

Self-rating scales consist of direct questions about drug use and its effects. Two examples of self-rating scales are the CAGE inventory and the MAST. The CAGE inventory consists of four questions about feelings and behavior associated with addiction. The MAST, developed by Selzer, provides questions along the same line as the CAGE inventory but covers specific areas such as family history, work history, psychiatric history, and physical effects. As in the CAGE inventory, an increased number of positive responses indicates a higher probability of chemical dependency (Crist & Milby, 1990).

Family Assessments

Family assessments are excellent tools for determining the progression of dependence in a substance abuser. Families often provide information about length of use and validate drug-related behavior. When made comfortable, families may begin to discuss the dysfunction and the individual coping methods each family member uses, preliminary to seeking treatment for themselves (Arif & Westermeyer, 1988; Sparks, 1993).

CORRELATING AND RELATING THE DIAGNOSIS

After the assessment is completed, and all information and facts are on hand, the findings and a course of therapy can be proposed to both the patient and his family. Several methods are used to accomplish this goal. One method is to directly discuss the findings with the user, depending on his denial, interest, and cooperation. Another method involves intervention. This process is a coordinated effort between the clinician and the user's significant others to confront the user with the problems caused by his drug-related

behavior. Intervention requires understanding, empathy, and compassion toward the disease and the user, with care taken to attack the denial, but not the person. The process also provides the user and his family a suggested course of therapy and may convince him to seek treatment (Arif & Westermeyer, 1988).

TREATMENT

As described previously, the history of treatment of substance abuse is relatively short. However, within the past 50 years, excellent advancements in assessment, diagnosis, and treatment have produced a spectrum of therapeutic models that, in many cases, can work synergistically to provide a broad range of therapy to both the user and his family members.

Detoxification

Treatment begins with admission to a detoxification service. Usually inpatient facilities admit all patients, regardless of the level of the patient's intoxication or reported drug abuse, to detoxification for a minimum of 24 hr; the average time is 3 days. This protocol is followed because the level of denial is usually high at the time of admission, and the history of the substance abuse may be minimized. Therefore, it is thought safer to observe behavior and monitor vital signs for at least 24 hr before the patient is discharged to rehabilitation services (Merlin, 1990).

Detoxification services have standing orders that may include diagnostic tests to screen for frequently seen complications of substance abuse (Magarian, Lucas, & Kumnar, 1992). The standing orders are modified to meet the needs of each patient.

Vital signs are monitored regularly every few hours for the first day and then at least every 8 hr while the patient is in detoxification. Medications commonly required by any patient in detoxification

---

TABLE 2-4
Maternal Drug and Neonatal Consequences

DRUG	DURATION OF SIGNS	SIGNS/ONSET
Alcohol	18 months	Hyperactivity, crying, irritability, tremors, poor sucking reflex, convulsions, disturbed sleep, hyperphagia, diaphoresis; ONSET: at birth
Amitriptyline	9 months	Tremors, disturbed sleep, abdominal pain, feeding difficulties
Barbiturates	4–6 months	Irritability, hyperacusis, severe tremors, diarrhea, excessive crying, vasomotor instability, restlessness, hypertonicity, hyperphagia, vomiting, disturbed sleep; ONSET: first 24 hr 10–14 days
Bromide	2½ months	Lethargy, dilated pupils, hypotonia, hypertonus, high-pitched cry, feeding difficulties, decreased reflexes
Chlordiazepoxide	9 months	Irritability, tremors; ONSET: 21 days
Chlorpromazine	9 months	Extrapyramidal dysfunction, intention tremor, opisthotonos, masklike faces; ONSET: 24–36 hr
Diazepam	8 months	Hypotonia, poor sucking reflex, hypothermia, apnea, hyperreflexia, tremors, vomiting, hyperactivity
Lithium	10 days	Respiratory distress, lethargy, cyanosis, poor sucking reflex, hypotonia
Phencyclidine	8–15 days	Jitteriness, hypertonia, vomiting, lethargy, vertical nystagmus

Source: Diagnosing and Managing Chemical Dependency, 1990, by J. Beasley. Comprehensive Medical Care, Amityville, NY.

---

are ordered but may be omitted by order of the physician (Merlin, 1990).

Pregnant women are treated with extreme care because of the severe risks that can accompany drug use, especially use of alcohol, cocaine, and opioids. Drug use of any kind, including use of nicotine and caffeine, should be stopped or decreased during pregnancy, because any drug that enters the bloodstream and has CNS activity can cross the placenta and affect the fetus. Fetal activity is monitored throughout detoxification. Signs and symptoms of acute withdrawal are curtailed, because they can cause spontaneous abortion.

Detoxification of neonates consists of supportive care until the drug is excreted. If signs of withdrawal are severe, the baby may be treated with phenobarbital, with blood levels monitored throughout treatment to prevent intoxication. *Table 2-4* gives the effects on the neonate of maternal use of drugs (Beasley, 1990).

During detoxification, counselors may work with the patient to evaluate, motivate, and advise him about the next step, which is rehabilitation services.

The written treatment plan, begun in detoxification and continued in rehabilitation, is based on the data from the history and physical examination, results of diagnostic tests, consultation reports, nursing admission evaluation, and staff members' observation of the patient. The treatment plan is developed as data are received. When a problem is noted by a nurse or counselor, it is included on the treatment plan so that reasonable, measurable objectives can be formulated and plans created to reach the objectives. Daily charting is done by nurses while the patient is in detoxification and by both nurses and counselors after the patient is transferred to the rehabilitation service (Epstein, 1990).

Rehabilitation

A patient detoxified in a hospital setting may complete rehabilitation as an inpatient or may be referred to an outpatient program, residential program, self-help group, individual therapy, or a combination of these. In many cases, both detoxification and rehabilitation can be accomplished outside the hospital setting.

Inpatient Programs

After successful detoxification and complete assessment of the patient's family and social setting and his current capabilities, further therapeutic sessions within the hospital may be recommended. Therapy may include group therapy, education about the disease, communication workshops, education on use of leisure time, development of support systems, 12-step study, and individual and family therapy. These sessions are generally conducted by licensed or certified specialists, and programs are 3–4 weeks long. When the patient is discharged from rehabilitation, a plan is made to address his need for a sponsor, 12-step therapy, an ongoing support system, leisure time development, or volunteer work. The plan is individualized to address particular problems.

Inpatient programs also provide a few weeks of once-a-week continuing group therapy (Kaufman, 1985). Inpatient programs for adolescents and other specialized programs (Rawson, Obert, McCann, Castro, & Ling, 1991) use essentially the same structure. Dual-diagnosis programs for patients who have psychiatric disorders in addition to drug or alcohol addiction may be inpatient or may be located in board-and-care facilities and run

more like day-care programs. Structure and curricula are similar to those of programs restricted to treatment of addiction except that the dual programs have shorter, more concrete lectures, include groups that address the mental illness, and provide necessary medications (Hendrickson & Schmal, 1993; Miller & Gold, 1991a; Roberts, Shaner, Eckman, Tucker, & Vaccaro, 1992).

Outpatient Programs

Structured outpatient programs usually have a medical director and use treatment philosophies developed by inpatient hospitalization and self-help groups. This level of therapy may provide ambulatory detoxification for patients with minor or no acute medical complications. Thus, the patient can reside at home, continue to be employed, or need only minor time off from work.

This method often generates immediate recovery work within the patient's community and provides immediate family involvement. Because of the time commitment (8–12 weeks with three to four meetings each week and 1 year of structured continuing care), outpatient therapy may allow the recovering user and his family more opportunities to address deeper, underlying issues. Self-help groups such as AA and Al-Anon are involved for long-term support. Discharge plans may include weekly group therapy, 12-step study, or involvement in outside support groups such as AA (Stainback & Walker, 1990).

Day-Treatment Programs

Day-treatment programs have a structure similar to that of inpatient and outpatient programs and may specialize in the treatment of certain populations. For example, perinatal programs offer similar curricula with special emphasis on parenting and life-management skills. Mothers are observed as they interact with children in the nursery, and children in the nursery are observed and assisted developmentally as well as medically. The goals are to help the mother be abstinent, address underlying issues that contribute to substance abuse, assist the mother with parenting skills, and promote the optimum development of the child. Prenatal programs are similar and include educational aspects of pregnancy (Sparks, 1993).

Individual Psychotherapy

Individual psychotherapy is generally considered an excellent augmentation to ongoing participation in a support group for the recovering patient and his family members. However, because of the high degree of denial, manipulation, and selective discussion, this form of treatment is thought to be ineffective as the single primary source of recovery.

Some patients may require individual psychotherapy because they need more therapy than is offered in self-help groups. Others may have achieved sobriety but have psychiatric disorders for which they are seeking help. Individual psychotherapy benefits both the patient and his family by providing the patient an avenue to address sensitive issues that he feels uncomfortable discussing in group settings. Psychotherapy provides immediate feedback with possible rectification or alternatives (Dodes & Khantzian, 1991).

Social Detoxification and Residential Treatment

Social detoxification and residential treatment involves the patient in detoxification without direct medical supervision yet may provide close physical monitoring by trained nurses and assistance by skilled counselors and recovering peers. If a medical emergency develops, the patient may be returned to medical care. After detoxification, the patient may complete his therapeutic goals while residing in place that is drug- and alcohol-free (Lewis, Dana, & Blevins, 1988).

The length of stay may be 1–6 months or more, depending on criteria set by the treating facility. Some residential treatment centers use the services of trained recovering patients and offer group support meetings, 12-step study, and individual counseling. These facilities are generally operated on a sliding-scale or ability-to-pay basis and are usually federally, state, or locally funded. This model of treatment and recovery is best suited for patients who have no history of detoxification and medical problems and are in no imminent medical danger.

Self-Help Groups

Self-help groups, a centuries-old tradition, are often associated with religious and social temperance groups. The effectiveness and continual evolution of such groups led the way to the development of AA in the 1940s and 1950s with its 12 steps and 12 traditions (Kaufman, 1985).

The 12 steps were developed as a method of suggestion rather than as a mandate for sobriety. The only requirement for membership in AA and many other self-help groups is the desire to be sober. After the evolution of AA, other groups targeting specific drugs developed (e.g., Cocaine Anonymous, Narcotics Anonymous, Marijuana Anonymous). The availability of these groups differs from group to group and from community to community. Listings of local meetings can be obtained at meetings or by telephone.

Many different types of self-help meetings are available to promote participation: speaker, 12-step study, closed, open (meaning anyone including nonaddicted people may come) gay, stag (all male or all female). Meetings are held throughout the day, including the lunch hour. Confidentiality is expected among the group members.

The following statement by a member of an AA group describes the benefits of attending a self-help group:

> In my groups, I find people who have the same disease that I do. They understand me. They empathize with me. They laugh with me, and I know that they are not laughing at me. They love me without judging me for what I am thinking, saying, or doing. My friends help me by giving me their experiences, both the good in their

lives and the not so good. The people with the good experiences are telling me things I can try. The people with the not so good experiences are telling me the things I can avoid. All I have to do is be willing one day at a time. Today, I wouldn't have it any other way. —*Doug B.*

Participants are encouraged to read further the Big Book of AA and the 12 steps and 12 traditions published by AA and available at local meetings.

Treating Family Members and Significant Others

Chemical dependency is not a disease that affects the individual user alone. It also affects the user's significant others, including family, friends, and employers, and the community and society as a whole. Clinicians have a responsibility during diagnosis and referral to make means available so that both the user and his significant others can begin recovery.

To date, many of the legitimate therapy programs incorporate family treatment in their regimens. These provide opportunities to educate the user's family and significant others about the disease and the recovery process. Family members are encouraged to determine their coping skills, their abnormal reactions and responses, and a means to develop their own recovery. Long-term support groups are also available for family members and significant others. The most prominent groups are Al-Anon, Families Anonymous, and Alateen. These groups use essentially the same 12 steps as AA but insert, where appropriate, words related to control and sanity (Beattie, 1987; Stainback & Walker, 1990).

RELAPSE AND RELAPSE PREVENTION

Relapse is defined as a return to drinking or using behavior that may culminate in the uncontrolled return to drug or alcohol use.

A relapse may be short or may last a long time. In either instance, intervention may be necessary.

The primary goal of relapse prevention is to minimize the risk that the person will return to substance use. Prevention includes helping the former user increase his adaptive coping and problem-solving skills and thus his confidence and self-efficacy.

The first step is to educate the user and his significant others about the warning signs of a possible relapse. Support groups and treatment centers use the easy-to-remember acronym HALT, which means don't get too hungry, angry, lonely, or tired.

Determinants that increase the possibility of relapse include high-risk situations that cause the former user to lose a sense of control (e.g., walking into a room where people he used to drink with are drinking). Other factors are negative emotions such as anger, depression, and anxiety and interpersonal conflicts and social pressure. Less obvious stressors are lifestyle imbalances (e.g., being a workaholic) that lead the person to rationalize that he deserves to indulge in drugs or alcohol.

Intervention strategies include self-monitoring, whereby the former user keeps a complete record of his drug use (i.e., where, when, and so forth) or, if abstinent, keeps a record of cravings, thus increasing self-awareness. Another strategy is using the Situational Confidence Questionnaire. The person imagines himself in each of 100 situations and reports his level of confidence in resisting drinking or using. One of the most effective tools is labeling and detaching, actions that are accomplished by verbalizing cravings and the reason for the cravings. Behavioral contracting is a tool designed to limit a relapse. Some formers users carry a "reminder card" with suggestions on how to handle a slip from abstinence.

Of all the techniques and strategies, coping skills and stress management are the most important. These include adherence to AA slogans such as "one day at a time," "easy does it," "live and let live," and "keep it simple, stupid." Other stress management techniques are flexibility, getting help, exercise, spending time alone, humor, and good nutrition.

If a relapse does occur, the user will be more likely to recover if he reminds himself that the relapse does not mean that he is a failure or a bad person, and he uses the occasion as a learning tool to avoid future relapses (Lewis et al., 1988).

CONFIDENTIALITY

Health clinicians must be aware of their state's requirements and laws covering patient treatment confidentiality. In the state of California, the individual's rights are protected under the California Mental Health Services Act of 1981, with subsequent revisions under federal law. Patients and families are covered under the Federal Privacy Act (42-CFR-2) 1975 and subsequent revisions. Both of the cited acts spell out the rights of the individual and the treating professional.

By law, disclosure of information to anyone about a patient's admission, diagnosis, therapeutic process, or medical or psychological findings requires that (1) all concerned explain to the patient the patient's rights of confidentiality and (2) the patient sign a consent authorizing release of the requested information. The information to be released must be stated specifically and must be requested by persons who have a "need-to-know right." A confidentiality request covers not only written or documented material but also verbal (face to face or by telephone) requests. The duration of authorization must be stated by either date or event and can be revoked by the patient at any time (Barr, 1990).

The confidentiality of patients' records of persons being treated for substance abuse is protected

by federal law *(Figure 2-1)*. This law also applies to drug-abusing patients who have AIDS. Because AIDS-related legal issues are a developing area of law, health professionals should read the protocol for the organization by which they are employed and keep abreast of any changes that may occur (Barr, 1990; Schleifer, Delaney, Tross, & Keller, 1991).

DEVELOPMENT OF DRUG LAWS

The recognition of abuse and the need to prevent addiction spearheaded legislation by Congress to protect members of the public who are uneducated about the effects of chemicals or alcohol. The Pure Food and Drugs Act of 1906 was the first federal attempt to control the accuracy of labeling and to force manufacturers to substantiate their claims. In accordance with this act, all OTC products involved in interstate commerce had to be clearly labeled. The content and percentage of certain agents, including opioids, cannabis, cocaine, and chloral hydrate, had to be indicated on the label. This measure limited the amount of drugs in popular products and also hurt sales. However, no similar measure was enacted to control the actions of physicians, and they readily prescribed opiates and cocaine to anyone who asked for these drugs. Most persons could also order the same products from mail-order companies. President Theodore Roosevelt convened the Shanghai Opium Commission in 1909 in an effort to help the Chinese stamp out opium addiction. The Smoking Opium Exclusion Act outlawed imported opium prepared for smoking.

The Harrison Act, sponsored by New York congressman Francis Burton Harrison in 1914, imposed standards for quality, packaging, and labeling of narcotics but did not outlaw the use of these substances. This act required all those who imported, manufactured, produced, compounded,

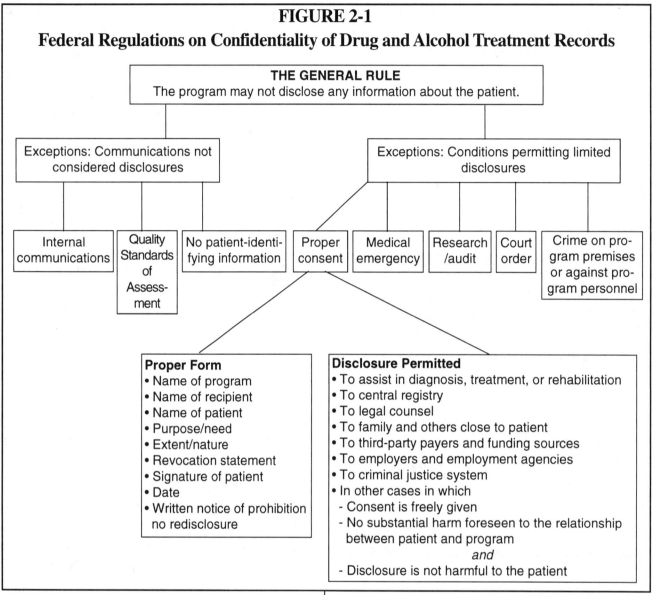

FIGURE 2-1
Federal Regulations on Confidentiality of Drug and Alcohol Treatment Records

sold, dispersed, or distributed cocaine and opioids to register with the Treasury Department. These persons were also required to pay a special tax and to keep records of all transactions. The purpose of the act was to exercise some control over, rather than penalize, the estimated 200,000 users of narcotics in the United States at that time.

Some parts of the act allowed physicians to prescribe, dispense, or administer narcotics "for legitimate medicinal purposes" and only "in the course of professional practice." Most physicians at the time claimed addiction was a disease for which drugs could be prescribed. In contrast, the Treasury Department interpreted the Harrison Act to mean that a physician's prescription of an opioid was illegal.

This debate led to a ruling in 1919 that a physician could not prescribe narcotic drugs to an addict for the purpose of maintaining the addict's use or comfort. Three years later, the ruling was extended in *U.S. v. Behrman,* which held that a "narcotics" prescription written for an addict was illegal, even when the drugs were prescribed as part of a program to cure the addiction. This ruling made it almost impossible for addicts to obtain drugs legally.

In 1925, the U.S. Supreme Court reversed itself in *Lindner v. U.S.,* which disavowed the Behrman opinion and held that addicts were entitled to medical care the same as everyone else. This ruling had almost no effect, because many physicians were unwilling to treat addicts under any circumstances. As a result, a well-developed illegal drug marketplace emerged to cater to the needs of addicts.

In 1922, the Narcotic Drug Import and Export Act strengthened the prohibition against drugs such as morphine, coca leaves, and derivatives of coca leaves. The Commissioner of Narcotics had control over the amount of narcotics that could be legally imported and was necessary for medical and scientific uses only. In addition, drugs manufactured in the United States were strictly controlled so that those exported were needed for medical purposes only.

The Porter Act of 1929 was sponsored by Captain Richard Pearson Hobson Porter, hero of the Spanish-American War who later became a congressman. He undertook a nationwide educational campaign against narcotics abuse. Captain Porter was an energetic and overzealous speaker and campaigner, particularly against heroin. For example, he often warned women to check their face powder for traces of heroin, and he claimed that one dose of heroin could lead to addiction. He also stated that a single ounce of heroin could cause the addiction of up to 2,000 persons.

One of his efforts was to develop two "narcotic farms" where narcotic addicts could be treated and researchers might find a cure for addiction. As a result of his efforts, and the fact that existing federal prisons were overflowing with persons convicted under the Harrison Act, two federal treatment centers were established, one in Fort Worth, Texas, and another in Lexington, Kentucky. In addition, the Public Health Narcotics Division was founded, which eventually became the National Institute of Mental Health and the National Institute on Drug Abuse. Captain Porter

also carried an act through congress that established the Federal Bureau of Narcotics in 1930.

The Marijuana Tax Act of 1937 was passed in response to reports in the southwestern United States of a plant-based narcotic grown and used by Mexican laborers. Marijuana use was blamed for stimulating violence; its enemies claimed that it was secretly being sold to school children. The Federal Bureau of Narcotics described it as a fearful substance but maintained that it was under control.

The Federal Food, Drug, and Cosmetic Act of 1938 gave the federal government far-reaching authority over the manufacture, distribution, and labeling of drugs. Amendments in 1962 and 1965 established new record-keeping procedures and inspection requirements. They also established standards for handling certain types of drugs by persons who register to do so.

In 1942, the Opium Poppy Control Act prohibited the growth of opium poppies in the United States except by license from the Secretary of the Treasury. Thus, anyone growing opium poppies (and thus supposedly illegally marketing opium) would go on public record. Not surprisingly, no such license has ever been issued (Wilford, 1982).

The Boggs Amendment in 1951 established minimum mandatory sentences for narcotic and marijuana sales. Later, in 1956, the death penalty was allowed at a jury's discretion in some sales of heroin.

The mid-1950s could be viewed as the peak of punitive action against drug addiction. During this time, numerous efforts were made to stop substance abuse through increasingly stringent laws. In the years that followed, a much greater effort was made to examine the psychosocial effects of substance abuse and to treat, rather than punish, persons who abused drugs.

The Narcotic Manufacturing Act was established in 1960 for licensing manufacturers to produce narcotics. It also set manufacturing quotas for the basic classes of these drugs.

In 1970, the Comprehensive Drug Abuse Prevention and Control Act consolidated more than 50 federal drug-related laws into one far-reaching act. This measure was designed to help control the underground drug industry and to curtail imported distribution of illegal drugs. The act established five schedules of controlled drugs, giving various degrees of control for each group of drugs.

Each controlled drug is assigned to a schedule according to the following criteria:

1. Current scientific knowledge of the drug's pharmacological effects.

2. The state of current scientific knowledge about the substance.

3. The history of the drug and the current pattern of abuse.

4. The scope, significance, and duration of abuse.

5. The risk, if any, that the drug poses to public health.

6. The drug's psychic or physiologic dependence liability.

7. Whether or not the drug is an immediate precursor of a substance that is already controlled.

Because of strong political and social pressure, the Bureau of Drug Abuse Control (established in 1965) of the Food and Drug Administration was placed under the Department of Justice. In 1970, the Controlled Substances Act added many drugs not previously classified as controlled substances to the list and established stricter requirements for obtaining and using these drugs. The Drug Enforcement Administration (DEA) is the leading federal agency responsible for enforcing the act (Ray & Ksir, 1993).

CONTROLLED SUBSTANCES

All prescribing physicians and dispensing pharmacies must be registered with the DEA. Separate records must be kept of all purchases and dispensations of controlled substances, and a physical inventory of all controlled substances must be made every 2 years. Prescriptions for controlled substances must be made in ink and must include the date issued; the full name and address of the patient; and the full name, address, and DEA registration number of the physician. Prescriptions for controlled substances may not be dispensed or refilled more than 6 months after the prescription was issued, and they cannot be refilled more than five times.

For schedule II drugs, a written prescription order signed by the physician is required. In an emergency, a verbal prescription may be filled; however, the physician must then provide a signed prescription within 72 hr. Prescriptions for schedule II drugs cannot be refilled.

The schedules of controlled substances are as follows (Nahas, 1992):

Schedule I

Drugs on schedule I have no accepted medical use in the United States and have high potential for abuse. They are heroin, marijuana, LSD, peyote, mescaline, psilocybin, the tetrahydrocannabinols, levomoramide, dihydromorphine, morphine methysulfonate, nicocodeine, nicomorphine, acetylmethadol, fenethyline, tilidine, and methaqualone.

Schedule II

Schedule II drugs have high potential for abuse but approved medical usage. They are opium, morphine, codeine, hydromorphone, methadone, pantopon, meperidine, cocaine, oxycodone, oxymorphone, amphetamines, methamphetamines, phenmetrazine, methylphenidate, amobarbital, pentobarbital, secobarbital, etorphine, phenylacetone, and phencyclidine.

Schedule III

The abuse potential of schedule III drugs is less than that of drugs in schedules I and II. Schedule III drugs include compounds containing limited quantities of certain narcotic drugs and nonnarcotic drugs, such as derivatives of barbituric acid, glutethimide, methyprylon, chlorhexadol, sulfonmethane, nalorphine, chlorphentermine, clortermine, mazindol, phendimetrazine, and paregoric. Any suppository dosage form containing amobarbital, secobarbital, or pentobarbital is in this schedule.

Schedule IV

The abuse potential of schedule IV drugs is less than that of drugs in schedule III. Schedule IV drugs include barbital, phenobarbital, methylphenobarbital, chloral betaine, chloral hydrate, ethchlorvynol, ethinamate, meprobamate, paraldehyde, methohexital, fenfluramine, diethylpropion, phentermine, dextropropoxyphene, pentazocine, mebutamate, chlordiazepoxide, diazepam, oxazepam, clorazepate, flurazepam, clonazepam, prazepam, alprazolam, halazepam, femazepam, triazolam, and lorazepam.

Schedule V

Schedules V drugs have less potential for abuse than schedule IV drugs do. Schedule V includes preparations containing limited quantities of certain narcotic drugs for antitussive and antidiarrheal purposes that may be distributed without a prescription.

EXAM QUESTIONS

CHAPTER 2
Questions 16–24

16. Since the early 1960s, who or what has been a center of early prevention, education, and referral for treatment and rehabilitation of substance abuse?

    a. The workplace

    b. Hospitals

    c. The legal system

    d. Individual therapists

17. Assessment tools for determining dependence include which of the following?

    a. Bone density tests

    b. History and physical examination

    c. Lie-detector tests

    d. Mandatory HIV testing

18. Which of the following is a diagnostic test used to determine substance abuse?

    a. CAGE

    b. Dexterity test

    c. HALT

    d. Intelligence test

19. Which of the following is a common feature of inpatient, outpatient, and day-treatment programs for substance abusers?

    a. Education in social drinking

    b. Group and individual therapy

    c. Social detoxification

    d. Immediate recovery work in the community

20. Which type of treatment of substance abuse is ineffective when used as the sole primary source of recovery?

    a. Individual psychotherapy

    b. Dual-diagnosis programs

    c. Perinatal programs

    d. Structured outpatient therapy

21. Steps to prevent relapse in substance abuse include which of the following?

    a. Increasing the dependent's coping skills

    b. Constant supervision by the user's significant others

    c. Recognition by the dependent that he is a failure

    d. Use of methadone

22. Disclosure of information about a patient's admission, diagnosis, therapeutic process, or medical or psychological findings requires which of the following?

    a. Written consent from the patient before the release of any information either written or verbal

    b. Verbal consent from the patient before the release of any information either written or verbal

    c. The consent allows all patients information to be released.

    d. Confirmation by the patient that once given, authorization cannot be revoked

23. Which of the following resulted from the passage of the Controlled Substances Act of 1970?

    a. Establishment of six schedules of controlled drugs

    b. Limitations of refills to two times

    c. Requirement for triplicate prescriptions for controlled substances

    d. Required registration of all prescribing physicians and dispensing pharmacies with the DEA

24. Relapse occurs when a recovering drug dependent does which of the following?

    a. Drinks or uses drugs in a controlled fashion

    b. Stops attending therapy or support groups

    c. Returns to drinking or using drugs for fewer than 7 days

    d. Returns to drinking or using behavior that may culminate in the uncontrolled return to use of drugs or alcohol

CHAPTER 3

CNS DEPRESSANTS: ALCOHOL

CHAPTER OBJECTIVE

After studying this chapter, the reader will understand the disease process of alcoholism and be able to access and provide appropriate interventions.

LEARNING OBJECTIVES

After studying this chapter, the reader will be able to

1. Recognize the social effects of alcohol.

2. Specify historical characteristics of alcohol use.

3. Specify how alcohol is absorbed, distributed, metabolized, and excreted from the body.

4. Indicate alcohol-related medical problems.

5. Recognize signs and symptoms of alcohol withdrawal.

6. Choose a treatment plan for a patient in withdrawal.

INTRODUCTION

Alcoholism is a disease that affects the dependent, his family, and society as a whole. The devastating impact of the disease can be seen in alcohol-related health problems, child and spouse abuse, divorce, job loss, accidents, crime, homelessness, and other losses.

HISTORY

Alcohol has always been used to enhance life, socialize, celebrate traditions and religious rituals, and medicate (Arif & Westermeyer, 1988). Ethyl alcohol, the oldest of the sedative-hypnotic drugs, dates back to 8000 B.C.E., when mead was first brewed. Around 800 B.C.E., distillation was discovered, making it possible, with repeated distillation, to bring a liquid to nearly 100% alcohol. The alcohol content of most beverages is 3–50% (Nahas, 1992).

In the early 1800s, Dr. Benjamin Rush popularized the view that alcoholism is an addiction and a disease rather than a moral failure. Since then disagreement has existed as to the cause of alcoholism. Some think that it is an inherited disease, whereas others think it is merely a habit gone out of control. Currently, the concept that alcoholism is a disease and an addiction is widely accepted by professionals in the field (Nace & Isbell, 1991).

CURRENT IMPACT

In our society, the average person drinks alcohol but is not an alcoholic. More than two thirds of American men drink; the peak drinking years are between the ages of 16 and 25 (Schuckit, 1989). However, of about 12 million persons recognized as alcoholics in the United

States, 20–50% are women (Boyd, 1991; Sumners, 1991).

When does alcohol begin to be a problem? The key appears to be "loss of control." Clinically, a person is considered an alcoholic if he continues to drink even though alcohol is causing physical, emotional, family, social, and occupational problems (Borders, 1986).

Alcoholism is a health problem surpassed only by heart disease and cancer. About one third of adult patients in hospitals have problems related to alcohol, and about 240,000 deaths a year are directly linked to alcohol abuse, an average of 1 in 10 deaths in the United States (West, Maxwell, & Noble, 1984).

In this country, 67% of the incidents of domestic violence, 50% of all traffic fatalities, 33% of the cases of child abuse, 50% of deaths by fire, 67% of homicides and aggravated assaults, 40% of forceful rapes, and 35% of suicides can be traced directly to alcohol abuse (West et al., 1984). About 5% of American alcoholics end up homeless (Ropers & Boyer, 1987).

Alcoholism is found in all socioeconomic classes and cultures (Diamond, 1992). Although the ritualistic use of alcohol is thought to inhibit the development of alcoholism, American Italians and Jews, Native American tribal groups, and people in France and Italy have alcohol-related health problems, and all have incidence of alcoholism. Asian-Americans have lower rates, possibly because of their metabolism (Nace & Isbell, 1991).

The family of an alcoholic may be completely disrupted and emotionally exhausted by the interpersonal stress imposed on them by alcoholism. The risk is high that children of alcoholic families will become alcoholic themselves (Rogers & McMillin, 1989).

SCHEDULE OF CONTROLLED SUBSTANCES

Ethyl alcohol (also called ethanol) is not a controlled substance for adults, except for restrictions on operating a vehicle while under the influence of alcohol. Most state legislatures have deemed that a blood alcohol level (BAL) of 0.10% is incompatible with safe driving. Recently, some states lowered the acceptable BAL to 0.08%.

Therapeutic Uses

Ethanol is used as a base in more than 700 medicinal preparations in the United States. The concentration ranges from 0.3% to 68.0% (Nahas, 1992).

Nontherapeutic Uses

Ethyl alcohol is used worldwide, except in Islamic countries, for recreational purposes (Nahas, 1992).

Routes of Administration

Ethyl alcohol is used orally almost exclusively. Therapeutically, it may be used intravenously or topically (Woolf, 1991a).

BIOCHEMISTRY

Ethyl alcohol is a CNS depressant. It is a clear, colorless, hydrophilic molecule. It is absorbed primarily from the stomach and intestine and is distributed into the total body water and from there to virtually every cell in the body (Nace & Isbell, 1991).

Although ethanol is a CNS depressant, at lower doses it has a stimulating effect. This effect is due to a lessening of inhibitions rather than to true physical stimulation. As the dose is increased, progressive depression of cerebral function occurs. The dose needed to produce the depressant effect depends on variables such as the drinker's age, weight, sex, and physical condition; coingestion of food; and level of tolerance (Nahas, 1992).

At a BAL of 0.05% (measured in milligrams per deciliter, mg/dl), most persons have impaired coordination and euphoria. At BALs of 100–199 mg/dl (0.10–0.19%), ataxia, decreased mentation, poor judgment, and a labile mood set in. When the BAL reaches 200–299 mg/dl (0.20–0.29%), most persons have marked ataxia and slurred speech, poor judgment, nausea and vomiting, and a labile mood. At a BAL of 300–399 mg/dl (0.30–0.39%), the drinker will be in stage I anesthesia with memory lapse and a labile mood. Finally, at BAL levels of 400–700 mg/dl (0.40–0.70%) and higher, respiratory failure, coma, and, ultimately, death occur. However, drinkers who are tolerant to the effects of alcohol have been known to be awake and talking with a BAL of more than 700 mg/dl (Schuckit, 1989).

For several reasons, ethanol can damage or destroy every cell in the body. First, it is found in all the body fluids surrounding the cells, including blood, urine, saliva, spinal fluid, and tears. Second, used repeatedly in certain concentrations, it is toxic to body tissue. Third, it is converted to acetaldehyde, a metabolite that is even more toxic than the parent compound ethanol.

After ingestion, ethanol is absorbed primarily from the stomach and the small intestine. About 5–15% is eliminated through the lungs, kidneys, and sweat glands. The remainder is metabolized in the liver, where it is converted to acetaldehyde by the enzyme alcohol dehydrogenase. Acetaldehyde, more toxic than ethanol, is quickly converted by another liver enzyme, aldehyde dehydrogenase, to acetic acid, which is broken down into carbon dioxide and water and eliminated through the kidneys and lungs (Schuckit, 1989).

This is the normal process that occurs when a person drinks alcohol. The metabolism of someone who is alcoholic is dramatically different in one important way. Although most of the ethanol is broken down by the usual process into carbon dioxide and water and is eliminated through the kidneys and lungs, about 1% is diverted to an alternative fate. Biochemical dependency on ethanol is due to this small part of diverted acetaldehyde (Schlaadt & Shannon, 1986). Acetaldehyde combines with the neurotransmitter dopamine to form an addictive alkaloid that is closely related to the opioids. In addition, it combines with other neurotransmitters in the CNS, forming other addictive alkaloids. Most now think that these substances are not metabolized or eliminated, but remain in the body and act much as heroin does (see chapter 6, "The Opioids"). Because these substances remain in the body, once a person is an alcoholic, he will always be one. The reasons are similar to those for the recurrence of opioid dependency. Thus, even though an alcoholic may abstain from alcohol for 20 years, if he starts drinking again, he will be unable to control his intake (Nace & Isbell, 1991; Miller, 1991).

In addition to alcohol dehydrogenase, the metabolism of ethanol requires the coenzyme nicotinamide adenine dinucleotide, which is also found in the liver. If an insufficient amount of alcohol dehydrogenase is produced in the liver, ethanol cannot be metabolized. Thus, the active ingredients in ethanol remain in the system longer. Aldehyde dehydrogenase, another enzyme involved in the metabolism of ethanol, has at least four clinically significant isoenzymes. Aldehyde dehydrogenase I, the most active isoenzyme, is missing in up to 50% of Asians. The lack of this enzyme is tied to the facial flushing that occurs in many Asians when they drink alcoholic beverages. Native Americans and Eskimos also have high rates of facial flushing and alcoholism (Nace & Isbell, 1991).

Oxidation of alcohol also leads to release of excess hydrogen in the liver, causing an overabundance of the reduced form of nicotinamide adenine dinucleotide. Inadequate feedback regulation of the metabolism of alcohol results in imbalances in the liver, which ultimately lead to alcohol-related liver disease (Woolf, 1991a).

ALCOHOL-RELATED MEDICAL PROBLEMS

Alcohol produces a wide variety of physiological disturbances and tissue damage. It affects all the cell membranes of the body, the activity of neurotransmitters and neuroreceptors in the brain, the production of hormones, and the replication of cells (Arif & Westermeyer, 1988).

Liver Disease

Liver disease occurs because the metabolic machinery of the liver is disturbed by the presence of alcohol. Metabolizing alcohol is a high-priority function. Normal and necessary hepatic functions are not carried out when alcohol is present. Liver disease is commonly associated with alcoholism. Three major forms of liver disease occur: fatty liver (hepatic steatosis), alcohol hepatitis, and alcoholic cirrhosis.

Fatty liver occurs because metabolism of fat by the liver is decreased during the metabolism of ethanol, and deposits of fats build up in normal liver cells. This condition can develop in persons who drink heavily for a brief time. Fatty liver is characterized by nausea, vomiting, hepatomegaly, and pain and tenderness in the right upper quadrant. Acute fatty liver is reversible if alcohol use is stopped. Among heavy drinkers, 90–100% show evidence of some features of fatty liver.

Alcoholic hepatitis is a more serious form of liver disease with a mortality rate of 10–30%. This illness usually follows a prolonged or severe bout of heavy drinking. Liver metabolism is disturbed, and both inflammation and damage to liver cells occur. Jaundice is a sign of hepatitis. Other characteristics include weakness, loss of appetite, easy fatigability, occasional nausea and vomiting, mild weight loss, low-grade fever, dark urine, and light stools. In some persons, hepatitis, like fatty liver, is reversible when alcohol use is stopped. In others, it may be fatal or go on to become a chronic disease. Alcoholic cirrhosis will develop in 20% of those who stop drinking and in 50–80% of those who continue drinking. Alcoholic cirrhosis can occur without previous occurrence of fatty liver or alcoholic hepatitis.

Cirrhosis means scarring. Liver cells are widely destroyed and are replaced by nonfunctioning scar tissue. Once scar tissue has developed, the damage is irreversible; the affected liver cells will not function again. Long-term heavy consumption of alcohol is the cause in approximately 80% of cases of cirrhosis. Alcoholic cirrhosis develops in approximately 10% of long-term heavy drinkers. More than 50% of people who continue to drink after alcoholic cirrhosis is diagnosed are usually dead within 5 years.

Life-threatening complications of cirrhosis include gastric or esophageal varices, ascites, renal failure, and encephalopathy (Woolf, 1991a). Serious hepatotoxic effects can develop in chronic alcoholics who are taking therapeutic doses of acetaminophen. These persons usually seek help after jaundice and liver disease have already developed. Often the blood level of acetaminophen is low or unmeasurable, and the diagnosis is based largely on the level of aspartate aminotransferase, prothrombin time, and a medical history (Rex & Kumar, 1992).

Gastrointestinal Disease

Alcohol can damage the lining of the esophagus, stomach, and small intestine by irritating the mucosa and causing inflammation. Alcohol increases the secretion of gastric acid and combines with other irritants such as aspirin to cause bleeding. Alcoholics may mask nausea and pain associated with gastrointestinal irritation by drinking.

However, in cases of severe alcoholism, more serious gastric erosion can develop.

As heavy drinking continues, the entire digestive system is irritated, starting with the mucous membranes of the mouth and esophagus. Increased secretion of gastric acid and vomiting occur and may cause esophagitis because of the inflammatory effects of alcohol.

Ethanol stimulates the production and release of gastric acid even while it delays emptying of the stomach. Because of disturbances in the gastric mucosal barrier and the presence of excess acid, most heavy drinkers have gastritis. Erosive gastritis is the most common stomach disorder associated with alcoholism and is often the first complaint that will send an alcoholic to a doctor. The signs and symptoms include nausea, vomiting, and epigastric pain, and some patients may have bleeding because of the erosion of blood vessels. Long-term alcoholics also often have gastric ulcers. Hemorrhage in the upper part of the gastrointestinal tract is also common. This abnormality is due to the ingestion of alcohol alone or alcohol plus aspirin.

A serious cycle is now in place. The gastritis caused by heavy drinking decreases the patient's appetite, leading to malnutrition. Even alcoholics who are eating a fairly good diet may be affected by worsening gastritis and eventually become malnourished. Vitamin and mineral deficiencies may develop because of alcohol-related defects in absorption and storage of vitamins. These deficiencies lead to impairment of the liver, the primary organ involved in vitamin storage and the conversion of vitamins to their active metabolites. With breakdown of the liver accompanied by vitamin deficiency and poor nutritional status, long-term heavy drinkers become extremely susceptible to infections and other types of disease (Nace & Isbell, 1991). This pattern of systemic malnutrition and toxic effects is a hallmark of alcoholism (Nahas, 1992).

Pancreatic Disease

Gallstones and heavy alcohol consumption are two of the leading causes of acute pancreatitis. Research shows that more than 75% of patients who have pancreatitis are long-term, heavy drinkers. Alcohol modifies the pancreatic enzymes, releasing proteolytic enzymes that damage the pancreas. The signs and symptoms of acute pancreatitis are severe abdominal pain, nausea, vomiting, fever, and tachycardia. In advanced stages, when little pancreatic tissue is left, diabetes mellitus and malabsorption can occur (Arif & Westermeyer, 1988). The mortality rate for severe pancreatitis with complications can exceed 30%. Stopping the use of alcohol may decrease the pancreatic pain, but it does not stop the progression of pancreatic dysfunction (Woolf, 1991a).

Cardiovascular Effects

Long-term heavy use of alcohol is associated with hypertension, vascular abnormalities, cardiomegaly, and cardiac arrhythmias (Arif & Westermeyer, 1991). The atrial fibrillation that is so commonly observed after a large intake of alcohol is called holiday heart syndrome (Woolf, 1991a).

Alcohol abuse can cause myocardial damage, affecting the heart muscle itself, and can produce cardiac dysrhythmias. Long-term use of alcohol may play a role in ischemic heart disease and in cerebrovascular disorders, including stroke. According to estimates, cardiac or cardiovascular diseases develop in 25% of alcoholics (Schuckit, 1989). In severe withdrawal reactions, myocardial infarction or congestive heart failure can occur.

Endocrine Disorders

Hyponatremia, hypokalemia, hypoglycemia, signs and symptoms of diabetes, and abnormal results on thyroid tests can be caused by long-term heavy use of alcohol (Arif & Westermeyer, 1988). Alcohol affects virtually every endocrine organ. Alcohol-induced hormonal changes alter metabolism and predispose to organ damage. Endocrine effects include alterations in thyroid hormones, growth hormones, and vasopressin. Alcohol may have a toxic effect on the thyroid gland independent of the degree of liver damage.

Immune System Effects

Alcohol depresses the movement of white blood cells into areas of inflammation, thereby decreasing resistance to infection. Alcoholics are less resistant than the general population to tuberculosis (Solari-Twadell, 1991) and to infections and abscesses caused by organisms such as *Staphylococcus, Pneumococcus, Streptococcus, Hemophilus influenzae, Klebsiella pneumoniae,* and *Legionella pneumophila* (Arif & Westermeyer, 1988). Burns are more likely to be associated with complications, and the hospital stay may be longer (Kelley & Lynch, 1992). Respiratory herpesvirus infections may occur in long-term alcoholics who have liver disease (Pol et al., 1992).

So far no evidence indicates a direct association between use of alcohol and the development of AIDS. However, by reducing inhibitions, drinking alcohol may lead to an increase in risk-taking behavior. Alcohol could increase the risk of primary infection during initial exposure to HIV. For those already infected with HIV, alcohol could result in progression from asymptomatic to clinical infection by depressing the immune mechanisms that work to limit the adverse effects of HIV infection.

Musculoskeletal Disorders

Alcoholics have an increased risk for metabolic bone diseases, including osteonecrosis. Toxic effects of alcohol on skeletal muscles increase the risk for acute or chronic alcoholic myopathy (rhabdomyolysis), which causes pain and swelling in the large muscle groups. Patients who also have alcoholic polyneuropathy may experience a painless, progressive muscle wasting (Nace & Isbell, 1991). The most commonly affected areas are the proximal muscles of the extremities and the thoracic cage.

Excessive use of alcohol also causes osteoporosis and an increased risk of fractures, probably because of the effects of alcohol on calcium and phosphorus metabolism. Persons who are intoxicated are also at an increased risk of trauma. Heavy use of alcohol is also associated with different types of arthritis (Kinney & Leaton, 1987). Gouty arthritis is caused by increased levels of uric acid. Degenerative arthritis (osteoarthritis) is due to the increased frequency of falls, injuries, and fractures. Septic arthritis (infection in joint spaces) occurs because the body's defense against infections are diminished in alcoholics. Aseptic necrosis or bone death due to diminished blood supply is another condition that often occurs in alcoholic men. Approximately 50% of patients with this condition have a history of heavy use of alcohol.

Kidney Disorders

Alcohol is a diuretic, so when the BAL is high, the secretion of the antidiuretic hormone is suppressed. Because this diuretic effect does not occur when the BAL is constant or decreasing, a person who is alcoholic may retain water (Woolf, 1991a).

Cutaneous Effects

Long-term use of alcohol affects the skin in many ways. The most pronounced is dilation of the vessels of the skin. The following cutaneous changes all reflect significant liver dysfunction: itching, jaundice, chronic flushed appearance, changes in hair distribution, thinning of the skin, a grayish cast to the skin, changes in the fingernails, and the presence of spider angiomas. Bruising, paleness, and skin infections may be the result of abnormalities in the hematological system.

Heavy or long-term intake of alcohol aggravates or precipitates rosacea in predisposed persons. The signs and symptoms include flushing and inflammation of the nose and the middle part of the face. Rhinophyma or "rum nose," the excessive growth of subcutaneous tissue of the nose, is particularly striking in alcoholics.

Hematological Effects

Alcohol decreases the production of all types of blood cells. Macrocytosis (also called macrocythemia, a condition in which the red blood cells are larger than normal) caused by a deficiency in folic acid is often a sign of alcoholism. Decreased production and efficiency of white cells make alcoholics susceptible to more infections, and decreased production of clotting factors and platelets leads to increased bruising and gastrointestinal bleeding. The higher incidence of cancer in alcoholics may be related to the decrease in thymus-derived lymphocytes (Schuckit, 1989).

Cancer

Alcohol consumption is associated with cancers of the mouth, larynx, tongue, esophagus, liver, lung, head, and neck (Kato, Nomura, & Stemmermann, 1992). The risk of cancer is increased about one third in those who drink heavily and may be due to numerous factors. These include nutritional deficiencies, a damaged liver that cannot detoxify carcinogens, and cellular injury resulting in metabolic changes. In addition, alcohol itself causes cancer (Woolf, 1991a).

The risk of cancer due to the excessive use of alcohol is increased by about 33% in the 20% of the population who drink most heavily. Besides the possibility that alcohol itself causes the cancer, alcohol might act as a solvent for the cancer-causing agent (Bennett & Woolf, 1991). Drinkers who consume large amounts of alcohol have a higher incidence of skin, thyroid, and breast cancer than persons who drink less.

Abnormalities of the Nervous System and Brain

Alcohol acts as a depressant on various brain structures (Bennett, 1991b) and damages the CNS

and the peripheral nervous system by modifying neurotransmitter levels and the fluidity and function of cell membranes. A peripheral neuropathy occurs in 5–15% of alcoholics.

Organic brain syndrome can be temporary or permanent and is associated with both the direct effect of alcohol and vitamin deficiencies. Korsakoff's psychosis is an organic mental syndrome in which patients are disoriented, confused, unable to recall events, and extremely susceptible to suggestion. Usually patients also have polyneuropathy and Wernicke's encephalopathy. The latter is characterized by ataxia, nystagmus, and ocular muscle palsies. Neuritic and hemorrhagic lesions develop in the brainstem. The underlying problem is a deficiency in thiamine. Patients with Wernicke's encephalopathy should be immediately admitted to a hospital and given parenteral doses of 50–100 mg of thiamine daily, supplemented by oral B-complex vitamins and ascorbic acid.

Dementia associated with alcoholism is another organic brain syndrome. Patients with dementia have severe loss of intellectual function, interference with social or occupational function, and memory impairment. This pattern is seen in long-term alcoholics. In its most severe form, the patient may have emotional instability, disintegration of personality and social function, and overt signs of dementia. The diagnosis is based on the results of neuropsychological tests. The mild form can be treated in an ambulatory, alcoholic treatment program, but strong efforts must be made to get the patient to stop drinking. If he cannot do so, he should be placed in a residential treatment center.

Alcohol idiosyncratic intoxication is a rare phenomenon that produces a severe change in mental state and behavior after a person drinks only a small amount of alcohol. Patients may become confused and have transitory delusions, visual hallucinations, and transient loss of consciousness. They may also become enraged, aggressive, and destructive or be depressed and suicidal. This state lasts for a few hours to a few days and is best treated with sedation in the hospital. These patients can be dangerous to themselves and others. After a period of sleep, the condition clears, and the person does not recall the episode (American Psychiatric Association, 1994; Nace & Isbell, 1991).

Changes in Sleep Patterns

Alcohol interferes with normal sleep by decreasing the deep sleep stages and causing frequent awakenings. These problems may persist for 3–6 months during abstinence, and gradually a normal sleeping pattern returns (Schuckit, 1989).

Changes in Nutrition

Alcoholics may obtain more than one half their daily calories from alcohol, which has no nutritional value, and neglect eating food. In addition, alcohol suppresses appetite through its effect on the CNS. Diseases of the gastrointestinal tract, liver, and pancreas may further decrease intake and absorption of food and contribute to malnutrition. Alcoholics are lacking in vitamins, particularly the B vitamins. The metabolism of iron is altered by alcohol; alcoholics should be examined for possible idiopathic hemochromatosis only after a complete review of their case. A reversal of overload is possible with B vitamin therapy and abstinence (Woolf, 1991a).

The results of nutritional deficiencies include depressed cellular and hormonal functions, Wernicke's encephalopathy, neuropathy, and anemia. Nutritional deficiencies also may contribute to the fetal alcohol syndrome, pancreatic disease, liver disease, malabsorption, and carcinogenesis. Fasting and a zinc-deficient diet decrease the activity of the important alcohol-metabolizing enzyme alcohol dehydrogenase, which contains zinc. Alcohol interferes with the absorption of many nutrients, including amino acids, glucose, choline, zinc, and vitamins. Abnormal metabolism of proteins, carbo-

hydrates, lipids, vitamins, and minerals occurs with heavy, long-term consumption of alcohol (Editorial Experts, Inc., 1990). Alcohol-dependent persons are also susceptible to acute and chronic muscle injury. Sixty percent may have biopsy-proved atrophy of muscle fibers. The occurrence of this atrophy is more likely in patients with severe liver disease, peripheral neuropathy, or malnutrition. If the patients abstain from alcohol, significant improvement in muscle can be detected within 3 months, and often complete recovery occurs within a year (Editorial Experts, Inc., 1990).

Abnormalities of the Reproductive System

Chronic alcoholism inhibits normal testicular, pituitary, and hypothalamic function. Impotence, decreased libido, and decreased testosterone levels may occur. Hyperestrogenization (feminization) may develop in men who have cirrhosis of the liver (Nace & Isbell, 1991). After 3 months of abstinence from alcohol, sperm count, motility, and volume of ejaculate tend to improve.

Most clinical and reproductive studies of alcohol have been carried out in men. The few studies of alcohol-dependent women showed that the women had a higher prevalence of amenorrhea, anovulation, dysfunction in the postovulation phase of the menstrual cycle, and pathologic ovarian changes than non-alcohol-dependent women (Editorial Experts, Inc., 1990). The findings suggest that repeated or sustained episodes of alcohol intoxication may suppress hormonal activity in women.

Fetal Alcohol Syndrome

Alcohol crosses the placenta and can cause the fetal alcohol syndrome. The syndrome is characterized by physical abnormalities and developmental retardation and is the leading known cause of mental retardation (Ray & Ksir, 1993; Sparks, 1993). The severity of the effects depends on the amount of alcohol ingested during pregnancy. With total abstinence, there is no risk; with two or three drinks daily, the risk and the severity of the effects are moderate. With six or more drinks daily, the risk of severe abnormalities, including mental retardation, poor coordination, irritability, hyperactivity, microcephaly, and low birth weight, is high (Beasley, 1990).

CASE STUDY

The following case study from the *AA Big Book* illustrates the chronic, progressive, incurable but treatable characteristics of alcoholism (Alcoholics Anonymous, 1976).

How was I to know that I was an alcoholic? No one ever told me that I was or even hinted that I had passed the point of no return.

Some years ago my thinking was that alcoholics just did not live in my world. Yes, I had seen them on my infrequent visits to the seamy side of town. I had been panhandled by them in nearly every city in Canada. In my estimation an alcoholic was a down-and-out, a badly dressed bum who much preferred drinking to working. If I would have been asked, I would have said that I did not even know an alcoholic. As for being one, it was the very farthest thing from my mind. I would have bitterly resented any such suggestion. Besides, I thought that any alcoholic was a misfit with a mental quirk of some kind. It was my opinion that they were all introverts and on tests I had twice been classified as an extrovert. (After I)…got out of the army, my drinking dropped away to a drink or two on very special occasions two or three times a year. So it went for the next 10 years, no pattern, no problem.

Toward the end of the twenties, my company went through a merger. I was given a more responsible position, which entailed a great deal of traveling from coast to coast. I found that a few drinks with agreeable companions, in sleeping cars or hotels, helped while away the time.

Frankly, I preferred the company of those who took a drink or two to those who did not. For the next few years I had a lot of fun with alcohol. I liked the effect of it. I conducted myself properly and no harm came of it. Without realizing it, I came to look forward to several drinks before dinner and then to some during the evening. I gradually developed into a heavy drinker, with the result that I didn't feel so well in the mornings…Neither business pressure nor added responsibility had anything to do with my drinking. I had the capacity for handling business without any fear of criticism. I enjoyed the companionship of drinking friends, but I began to notice that there was this difference between us. They were still satisfied with one or two drinks, but alcohol was having a different effect on me. My system seemed to need more alcohol than theirs. In retrospect, my only conclusion is that at the time I was becoming more physically sensitive to and losing my tolerance for alcohol.

But obviously my illness was progressing, because it wasn't long until I started experiencing blackouts. There were times when I would lose my car. At this distance it seems funny, but in those days it was a serious business. With some serious drinking in mind, I would take great care to park my car in some inconspicuous place, some distance from where I intended to do this drinking. After several hours, I would return to find that it wasn't there. At least it wasn't where I thought I had left it. Then I would start walking up blocks one way and down blocks the other way until I would finally locate it, usually in an entirely different direction than where I was sure I had parked it. On these occasions I would always end up with a feeling of remorse not far removed from a loathing of myself and the condition I was in. And, of course, I was always terribly afraid of being seen by someone who knew me.

It wasn't long until traveling even by train became a hazard. I would manage to catch a train, but all too often it was not the train which I intended to catch. Sometimes it would be going in the wrong direction and I would end up in a town or city where I had no intention of being, and therefore had no business to transact.

Having blackouts meant that I couldn't clearly remember all of what had transpired the night before and then it was only a short step to not being able to remember any of it. This became very embarrassing to me. I began to avoid discussing the very happenings of the night before. In fact, I no longer wanted to talk about my drinking. I began drinking alone.

Up to this point, my rise in the business world had been steady. I had become vice-president of the Canadian end of a large company known the world over. Now I found myself delaying making decisions, putting off appointments because my eyes were bloodshot and I didn't feel so well. It was difficult for me to concentrate and even to follow closely a business conversation.

Time and again I went "on the wagon"; I said I was through with drink and at the time actually meant what I said. The end result was always the same. Sooner or later, I started in all over again and binges came closer and closer together.

From time to time friends and relatives spoke to me about my drinking. My wife and family asked me to control it, to pull myself together, to use my willpower, to drink like a gentleman. I made dozens of promises and at the time of making them, I sincerely meant to keep every one. I became two different people, one person when I was sober and an entirely different one when I was drinking.

As alcoholism progresses, the alcoholic reschedules his daily activities so that two goals can be met: First, he must have a supply of alcohol, and second, he needs enough time to drink it. Job, family, marital relationships, and health may be neglected or lost (Ketcham & Gustafson, 1989).

WITHDRAWAL

Although alcohol is a licit drug, socially acceptable and widely used, it is more physically destructive when abused than nearly any other popular drug. Not only is it physically destructive when abused, but withdrawing from its use can be life threatening (Ray & Ksir, 1993).

Physical dependence on alcohol occurs gradually and progresses in severity over time. The severity of the signs and symptoms of withdrawal depends largely on how much the person has been consistently drinking, for how long a time, and his general condition (Merlin, 1990). One study showed that 68% of alcoholics who had abused alcohol for 3–5 years had mild indications of withdrawal, including tremors and autonomic hyperactivity. Alcoholics who had abused alcohol for 6 or more years had more severe signs and symptoms, including seizures. Among those who had severe signs and symptoms of withdrawal that included delirium tremens, 80% had abused alcohol 10 years or more (Woolf, 1991a).

Acute Withdrawal

Acute withdrawal from alcohol is usually complete in 5–7 days if no complications occur. If complications occur, the person will need medical supervision for a longer period. Of note, withdrawal from alcohol can be unpredictable, and signs and symptoms can overlap (Woolf, 1991a).

Withdrawal Syndromes

Four different major withdrawal syndromes have been described. In real life, these different syndromes sometimes blend together. The most common and earliest indication of alcohol withdrawal is a generalized state of hyperarousal. This state includes anxiety, insomnia, loss of appetite, irritability, rapid heart beat (tachycardia), and tremulousness. Wanting to avoid this state often is what motivates actively drinking alcoholics to have the first morning or midday drink. With increasing tolerance, increasing amounts of alcohol are necessary to ward off the signs and symptoms of withdrawal, and only a relatively lowered BAL is necessary to induce withdrawal. With all addicting drugs, including alcohol, progressively increasing amounts are consumed, not for their positive effects but as a means to avoid the signs and symptoms of withdrawal.

The cause of delirium tremens is unknown, but the higher centers in the brain may be overstimulated by alcohol, or the centers in the brain that act as a governor over the activity may become exhausted and can no longer function (Woolf, 1991a). Seizure activity is absent during delirium tremens. Without treatment, the delirium gradually worsens and then disappears in a week to 10 days. Fluid loss and metabolic imbalances can cause cardiovascular failure and death (Merlin, 1990).

When and if the physically dependent person abstains completely, the signs and symptoms of withdrawal increase markedly. The appearance is one of stimulation. Patients in this stage startle easily, feel irritable, and in general are "revved up" in an unpleasant way. The signs include a fast pulse, increased body temperature, elevated blood pressure, sweating, dilated pupils, and a flushed face. Sleeping is usually affected and will be difficult. Usually these effects subside over 2–3 days. The vital signs return to normal, and the shakes go away. Some signs and symptoms can persist for 2–3 weeks or even longer, including feeling awful, being irritable, and having difficulty sleeping. Generally, this acute withdrawal syndrome by itself does not require medical treatment. However, the patient should not be left alone and should be observed for indications of incipient delirium tremens. When the acute stage passes, the possibility of delirium tremens developing is greatly decreased. If the acute signs and symptoms do not resolve or if they worsen, progression to delirium tremens is likely.

Alcoholic hallucinosis is another syndrome of withdrawal from alcohol. This condition occurs in approximately 25% of cases, usually within the first 24 hr of withdrawal. Alcoholic hallucinosis is characterized by true hallucinations, both auditory and visual. Illusions also are common, that is, the misperception or misinterpretation of real environmental stimuli. Persons with this syndrome are oriented, know who they are, where they are, and what time it is.

Bad nightmares often accompany this syndrome. They may be due to REM rebound after the release from long-term suppression of dreaming sleep associated with alcohol abuse. This rebound effect usually clears by the end of the first week of withdrawal.

In a few cases, a chronic and persistent form of alcoholic hallucinosis may develop and continue for weeks to months. It is important to recognize alcoholic hallucinosis as a common withdrawal phenomenon and not be misled into thinking that the hallucinations are necessarily indicative of an underlying, primary psychiatric disorder.

The chronic form is often thought of as a separate syndrome. It is primarily characterized by persistent, frightening auditory hallucinations. Generally, the hallucinations have a distinctly paranoid aspect and are auditory. The patient usually hears familiar voices, often those of relatives or acquaintances. During the early stages, the voices are threatening or demeaning or arouse guilt. The person believes the voices are real, because they are true hallucinations, and he acts on them as if they were real. These actions may lead to the person doing harm to himself or others. When the hallucinations persist, they become less frightening and may be tolerated with greater equanimity by patients.

In most cases, alcoholic hallucinosis does not indicate an underlying psychiatric diagnosis but simply is the response of the CNS to the absence of alcohol. Appropriate treatment includes observing someone in an environment in which he will be safe; use of mild sedation may be needed. Alcoholic hallucinosis, unless extremely severe, should not be treated with antipsychotic medications during the first 2–4 days of withdrawal. The risk for seizures is increased during that period, and such drugs lower the seizure threshold.

Convulsive seizures, often referred to as "rum fits," also occur in association with acute alcohol withdrawal. Convulsive seizures are almost always generalized, grand mal, major motor seizures. The eyes roll back in the head, the body muscles contract and relax and extend rhythmically and violently, and loss of consciousness occurs. These seizures are so typical that the occurrence of any other type of seizure should raise concern about causes other than alcohol withdrawal. The seizure

usually lasts 1–2 min, but the person may be stuporous and groggy for as long as 6–8 hr. Treatment during a seizure is limited to preventing injury and protecting the person's airway. A serious complication of one of these single, isolated seizures is the development of status epilepticus, in which seizures follow one another with virtually no intervening seizure-free periods. Normally, only one or two seizures occur with acute alcohol withdrawal. Status epilepticus is uncommon and, its occurrence suggests causes other than alcohol withdrawal.

Unless a person in alcohol withdrawal has a history of seizures, anticonvulsant drugs are not normally prescribed. However it is critical to rule out any other possible cause of the seizures. Infections, electrolyte disturbances, and falls with associated head trauma or subdural hematoma, to which alcoholics are prone, can be causes. Seizures can occur 12–48 hr after a person stops drinking alcohol, but they can occur up to 1 week after the last drink. Delirium tremens, which can be fatal, develop in one third of all alcoholics who have had seizures.

Delirium tremens are the most serious form of alcohol withdrawal syndrome. In the past, the mortality rate was as high as 15–20%. Now, with modern treatment, the mortality rate is still 1–2%. The word *delirium* refers to the confusion, disorientation, and hallucinations. The word *tremens* refers to the elevated autonomic nervous activity, agitation, marked tremulousness, fast pulse, elevated blood pressure, and fever. When someone is in this emotional and physical state of heightened agitation, infections, fluid loss, respiratory problems, and physical exhaustion create further difficulties. These difficulties or complications contribute to the mortality rate. The acute phase of delirium tremens can last from 1 day to 1 week. In 15% of cases, it is over in 25 hr; in 80% within 3 days. Normally the person will have little memory of what has happened.

Once a person goes into delirium tremens, there is no cure or way to stop the condition. Treatment consists of providing supportive medical care, reducing the agitation, conserving energy, and preventing exhaustion while the condition runs its course. However, delirium tremens can be prevented if adequate medication is given at the first indication of any signs and symptoms withdrawal and is continued throughout the withdrawal period. The dose of the medication is reduced when possible until medication is not needed to keep the person out of danger.

A major concern in delirium tremens is liver function. The liver, usually damaged by alcohol, is the organ that metabolizes virtually all drugs. When it is damaged and cannot metabolize drugs, they will not be removed from the body as speedily as they should, a situation that can lead to further problems. The benzodiazepines (lorazepam, chlordiazepoxide, diazepam, and oxazepam) are usually the drugs of choice for treatment of delirium tremens. They have a wider margin of safety and are less toxic than some of the alternative drugs. In addition, they also have a marked anticonvulsant effect.

Who will or will not go into delirium tremens cannot be predicted, but the most likely candidates fit the following descriptions. Statistically, a person who is a daily drinker who has consumed a fifth or more of alcohol a day for at least a week before abstinence and who has been a heavy drinker for 10 years or more is very susceptible. Persons who have ever had convulsions, extreme agitation, marked confusion, disorientation, or delirium tremens during a previous period of abstinence are more likely to have these signs and symptoms again. Another predictor is recent abuse of other sedatives, especially barbiturates, because these drugs also have serious withdrawal syndromes, much like that seen with alcohol.

Protracted Withdrawal

Some alcoholics experience signs and symptoms of withdrawal that may last up to a year after cessation of drinking. These signs and symptoms include autonomic nervous system irregularities, such as labile blood pressure and pulse, irregular breathing, tolerance to sedatives, a fine tremor of the hands, persistent anxiety and depression, insomnia, fatigue, inability to concentrate, and memory impairment (Schuckit, 1989).

Neonatal Withdrawal

For mild withdrawal in neonates, supportive care is preferred. This includes swaddling to decrease sensory stimulation, frequent small feedings of hypercaloric formula, and caloric intake that provides 150–250 calories per kilogram of body weight every 24 hr. The high-calorie diet is needed to replace calories lost through vomiting, diarrhea, drooling, and increased motor activity. The neonate's sleeping patterns, body temperature, weight, electrolyte levels, and signs and symptoms of illness should be monitored. Fluids and electrolytes should be given intravenously if needed.

Sleeplessness, dehydration, fever, seizures, and serious weight loss indicate severe withdrawal, and medications should be administered with doses adjusted according to the patient's birth weight. Paregoric can be administered at feeding times. The initial dose is 0.2 ml orally every 3–4 hr. This is increased by 0.05 ml per dose until the signs and symptoms are controlled or the dose is up to 0.75 ml or seizures occur. If seizures occur, phenobarbital is added; the dosage is 5 mg/kg per day in three divided doses. This regimenshould be maintained for 5–7 days and then decreased by 0.05 ml/day (Beasley, 1990). A protracted withdrawal may last 6 months, with irritability, tremors, and poor sleeping patterns, but medication should not be continued.

ASSESSMENT

Most people will admit that they drink alcohol, but few will admit their addiction. Therefore, appropriate questions must be asked about problems in physical and emotional health, family relationships, socialization, occupation, legal status, and use of medications and illicit drugs. The inventory of medications and drugs is important for treating the withdrawal syndrome (Merlin, 1990). A psychiatric evaluation is needed if signs and symptoms persist over many weeks into sobriety or immediately if suicide or homicide is a threat.

Patients who abuse alcohol often smell of alcohol and are middle-class. They may have insomnia, nervousness, depression, and interpersonal problems. Medical problems such as ulcers, high blood pressure, and anemia are common, and medical emergencies may include toxic reactions, overdose, and accidents (Schuckit, 1989).

The history and physical examination should always include assessment for concurrent drug abuse, which can complicate withdrawal from alcohol. Drugs concurrently abused by alcoholics, in descending order of frequency, are marijuana, cocaine, PCP, benzodiazepines, barbiturates, and the psychedelics (Miller & Giannini, 1991).

In addition to the history and physical examination, other diagnostic tests may be needed, for example, an electrocardiogram and laboratory tests. Nurses should follow the protocol established by their place of employment. Tools that may be helpful in the assessment process include the CAGE and MAST (see chapter 2) and the section on alcoholism in the *DSM-IV* (American Association of Psychiatry, 1994).

TREATMENT

Treatment of alcoholism incorporates both short- and long-term goals.

Short-Term Goals

Short-term goals include safe detoxification, control of behavior and suppression of signs and symptoms of delirium tremens without endangering the patient, normal vital signs, results of laboratory tests in the normal range, stabilization of mental status, initial education for the patient and his family about the concept of alcoholism as a disease, and referral for appropriate treatment (see chapter 2).

Treatment for toxic reactions and overdoses involves establishing adequate ventilation, circulation, and control of shock; ruling out other medical problems; and establishing supportive measures while the body metabolizes the alcohol. If opioids were also ingested, naloxone (Narcan) may be given intramuscularly or intravenously, depending on the protocol of the detoxification center.

All patients should be given thiamine intramuscularly daily for at least 3 days and multiple vitamins orally after that. Good general nutrition and rest are an important part of recovery (Merlin, 1990).

Treatment begins with administration of fruit juices, oral electrolyte solution, magnesium gluconate, benzodiazepines as needed for sedation, and anticonvulsants. If the patient has chronic obstructive pulmonary disease or emphysema, dosages of antianxiety drugs will need to be titrated gradually and continuously. ß-Blockers are indicated in patients with blood pressure more than 170 mm Hg systolic and 110 mm Hg diastolic, pulse more than 120 beats per minute, and a history of cardiac problems.

If the patient is on the verge of delirium tremens, treatment includes decreasing environmental stimulation, providing reassurance, periodically orienting the patient, continual monitoring during hallucinations, and eliminating other possible causes of the hallucinations. Other causes of seizure should be ruled out, the response to medication reevaluated, and the medical regimen followed as prescribed.

If delirium tremens develop, the initial treatment is 5–10 mg or more of diazepam intravenously every 5–15 min until the patient is calm. Once the patient is calm, diazepam is given every 1–4 hr to control behavior and suppress signs and symptoms. As much as 200 mg of diazepam may be required initially (O'Brien, 1992). If the patient does not respond to initial measures, or his condition deteriorates, the attending physician should be notified to transfer the patient to an intensive care unit. The patient should be examined for bleeding, embolism, infection, trauma, electrolyte imbalance and dehydration, and blood glucose levels and body temperature should be determined (Nahas, 1992).

Long-Term Goals

Long-term goals may include involvement in a drug treatment program and community support groups and lifestyle changes in areas of socialization, leisure-time use, exercise, and nutrition. These goals should also involve the patient's family (Finney & Moos, 1992).

Anxiety, depression, emotional liability, and insomnia are all part of the protractedwithdrawal syndrome. Patients should be educated about coping with these signs and symptoms and advised that these effects will clear spontaneously with time and abstinence, generally without use of medications such as benzodiazepines, antianxiolytics, sedatives, or depressants, which may be abused and only enhance craving for alcohol (Ray & Ksir, 1993).

Some patients find disulfiram (Antabuse) helpful for a time. This drug is metabolized to acetaldehyde and causes uncomfortable signs and symptoms such as flushing, headache, nausea, vomiting, tachycardia, chest pain, dizziness, blurred vision, difficulty breathing, and confusion if an alcoholic drinks while taking it (McNichol, Sowell, Logsdon, Delgado, & McNichol, 1991).

EXAM QUESTIONS

CHAPTER 3
Questions 25–32

25. Alcoholism affects which of the following?

    a. Only the older children in the family

    b. The dependent, his family, and society as a whole

    c. The physical health of the dependent only

    d. Communication patterns of the dependent only

26. When was distillation discovered?

    a. 800 B.C.E.

    b. 200 B.C.E.

    c. The 1500s

    d. The 1800s

27. Which of the following statements about the metabolism of ethyl alcohol is correct?

    a. It is metabolized in the stomach to acetaldehyde and finally to acetic acid and carbon dioxide.

    b. It is eliminated primarily through the lungs, kidneys, and sweat glands.

    c. It is absorbed primarily from the stomach and small intestine.

    d. It combines initially with neurotransmitters to form rapidly metabolized alkaloids.

28. Alcohol-related medical problems include which of the following?

    a. Increased testosterone levels

    b. Osteoporosis and decreased resistance to infection

    c. Congestive heart failure and hypotension

    d. Viral hepatitis

29. Which of the following statements about the fetal alcohol syndrome is correct?

    a. It is reversible over time.

    b. It is not the leading cause of mental retardation.

    c. It is unlikely to occur if alcohol intake is limited to two or three drinks a day during pregnancy.

    d. It is characterized by physical abnormalities and developmental retardation.

30. Which of the following statements about the signs and symptoms of alcohol withdrawal is correct?

    a. They may include grand mal seizures beginning 12–48 hr after the last drink.

    b. They are the least serious of any drug withdrawal.

    c. They usually begin 2 weeks after the last drink.

    d. They are no longer experienced after 6 months of sobriety.

31. When treating a patient with delirium tremens, it is safer to do which of the following?

    a. Undersedate the patient.

    b. Control the patient's behavior and suppress signs and symptoms.

    c. Avoid giving the patient thiamine.

    d. Avoid giving phenytoin if the patient has a history of withdrawal seizures.

32. Which of the following is a sign or symptom that can occur as a result of drinking while taking disulfiram (Antabuse)?

    a. Hyperventilation

    b. Drowsiness

    c. Bradycardia

    d. Blurred vision

CHAPTER 4

CNS DEPRESSANTS: SEDATIVE-HYPNOTIC MEDICATIONS

CHAPTER OBJECTIVE

After studying this chapter, the reader will be able to recognize the progression of sedative-hypnotic dependence and the current treatment for this dependence.

LEARNING OBJECTIVES

After studying this chapter, the reader will be able to

1. Indicate a cause of overdose with CNS depressants.

2. Differentiate by name the benzodiazepines from the barbiturates.

3. Discriminate between the half-life of a drug and the drug's duration of action in the body.

4. Specify characteristics of benzodiazepines.

5. Recognize characteristics of withdrawal from CNS depressants.

6. Choose treatment for a neonate in withdrawal from benzodiazepines.

7. Indicate educational topics for a patient in withdrawal from CNS depressants.

8. Recognize physiological effects of CNS depressants.

INTRODUCTION

Sedative-hypnotic medications include benzodiazepines, antianxiety agents, and barbiturates. This large and varied group of drugs probably contains more prescribed and overprescribed drugs than any other group (DuPont & Saylor, 1991).

The WHO has determined that benzodiazepines are "essential drugs" that should be available for medical needs in all countries ("Abuse of benzodiazepines," 1988). Most of these products are used in a therapeutic way, but persons who use them, especially patients with emotional or physical pain, can become dependent on them.

HISTORY

Until the early 1800s, ethyl alcohol was the only sedative-hypnotic agent available. In the mid-1800s, bromides were introduced, originally to manage epilepsy. Bromides were popular and widely used as sedative-hypnotics until the middle of the 20th century despite the serious side effects their accumulation produced in the body. Bromism, as it was called, produced abnormal behavior and a rash that could affect the entire body. Bromides are no longer used medically because of their slow onset of action and high toxicity (Woolf, 1991b).

In the late 1800s, two other compounds, paraldehyde (1882) and chloral hydrate (1869), were developed. Paraldehyde, a by-product of the oxidation of ethyl alcohol, was thought to be a safe and nonaddictive sedative-hypnotic for many years. However, it decomposes easily when stored, and the decomposed drug produces a difficult-to-manage type of intoxication. Eventually, clinicians discovered that paraldehyde induces tolerance and dependence. Its use declined after the introduction of the barbiturates (Arif & Westermeyer, 1988; Woolf, 1991b).

The barbiturates began a long and successful history with the introduction of barbital in 1903. All barbiturates are derived from the compound barbituric acid and are used clinically as sedatives, hypnotics, anesthetics, and anticonvulsants.

Although once thought to be safe, barbiturates have major liabilities, including depression of the respiratory control centers in the brain, rapid development of tolerance, development of physical and psychological dependence, and the problems inherent in sudden withdrawal. In an effort to reduce side effects, a number of products were developed that did not offer any improvement over the earlier products. Only the benzodiazepine flurazepam (Dalmane) appears to be as powerful as the earlier agents but does not pose the serious drawbacks of the other sedative-hypnotics. Chlordiazepoxide (Librium), a benzodiazepine introduced in 1961, is a safer drug than the barbiturates (Woolf, 1991b).

Diazepam (Valium), another benzodiazepine, was introduced in 1963 and was used as an antianxiety agent, a sedative-hypnotic, an anticonvulsant, and a muscle-relaxant. It soon became the most commonly prescribed medication in the world. The adverse effects of the drug, including addiction and overdose, became apparent by the mid-1970s. In 1979, a U.S. Senate subcommittee on health and scientific research held a hearing to discuss the impact of diazepam on the public health. By 1981, diazepam had dropped to the sixth most frequently prescribed drug (Lee & Bennett, 1991; Ray & Ksir, 1993).

In 1965, Rohrer Pharmaceuticals introduced the nonbarbiturate CNS depressant methaqualone (Quaalude) as a safer alternative to the barbiturates. By the late 1960s, methaqualone had become the most popular drug on many college campuses. Students discovered that it produced sedating effects without the hangover of alcohol and that in combination with alcohol, it produced a sense of well-being and a higher pain threshold. It was also thought to have aphrodisiac properties, because it reduced inhibitions and led to sexual desire. However, a pattern of abuse and a number of deaths from overdoses (88 persons in 1974) emerged. Visits to the emergency department because of use of methaqualone also jumped from 1,161 in 1974 to 5,500 in 1977 (Schlaadt & Shannon, 1986).

Other agents such as glutethimide (Doriden) were introduced as safe, nonaddictive substitutes for barbiturates. Manufacturers developed them to overcome some of the side effects of the barbiturates, such as hangover, drowsiness, and drug-induced sleep disturbances, and to counteract the highly lethal overdose potential of barbiturates.

For purposes of identification, the generic names of all the barbiturates in the United States end with the suffix *-al (Table 4-1)*. Generic names for some nonbarbiturate CNS depressants are ethclorvynol, chloral hydrate, glutethimide, meprobamate, methaqualone, methyprylon, and paraldehyde (Schuckit, 1989).

By the 1970s, the leading method of suicide was barbiturate overdose. This situation led to the development of the benzodiazepines, which are considered to be more effective and safer than the barbiturates and other sedative-hypnotics.

TABLE 4-1
Routes of Abuse and Half-Lives of Barbiturates and Miscellaneous Sedatives and Hypnotics

Generic Name	Trade Name	Slang	Routes of Abuse[a]	Half-Life (in hours)
Barbiturates				
Amobarbital	Amytal	Blue velvet, bluebirds, blue devils, blue heavens, blues	PO, IV, IM	8–42
Secobarbital	Seconal	Reds, redbirds, red devils, seggy	PO, IV, IM	15–40
Pentobarbital	Nembutal	Nembies, yellows, yellow jackets	PO, IV, IM	15–48
Phenobarbital	Luminal and others		PO, IV, IM	80–120
Butabarbital	Butisol		PO	34–42
Secobarbital/ amobarbital	Tuinal	Rainbows, reds and blues, tooies, double trouble	PO, IV, IM	15–40
Others				
Ethchlorvynol	Placidyl		PO, IV	10–25
Chloral hydrate	Noctec and others	Mickey Finn	PO	4–9.5[b]
Glutethimide	Doriden		PO	5–22
Meprobamate	Equanil, Miltown		PO	6–17
Methaqualone	No longer on market	Ludes, Sopors, quads	PO	10–40
Methyprylon	Noludar		PO	3–6
Paraldehyde	Generic		PO	3.4–9.8

[a] PO = oral
 IM = intramuscular
 IV = intravenous
[b] Includes half-life of major metabolite

Note: The data in column 5 are from Harvey, 1985; Olin, 1987.

CURRENT IMPACT

Currently, benzodiazepines *(Table 4-2)* are the most frequently prescribed drugs in the Western world. Approximately 90% of hospitalized patients are given hypnotics, antianxiety medication, or both (Schuckit, 1989).

In the United States, long-time users of the benzodiazepines are older than nonusers, are depressed, and have health problems such as cardiovascular disorders and arthritis (Salzman, 1990). According to estimates, 40% of the elderly use 25% of all prescribed drugs, with sedative-hypnotics, tranquilizers, and analgesics among the most frequently used. Substance abuse among the elderly causes added health problems such as dementia, malnutrition, accidental injuries, insomnia, incontinence, and self-neglect (Boyd, 1991).

Women are twice as likely as men to take benzodiazepines for medical problems (Salzman, 1990). If a woman takes a CNS depressant during pregnancy, her baby will experience signs and symptoms of withdrawal as a neonate (Arif & Westermeyer, 1988).

Persons dependent on other drugs are at risk for abuse of CNS depressants (DuPont & Saylor, 1991). Diazepam is a popular street drug, especially among heroin addicts who are on methadone programs, because it enhances the CNS-depressing effects of methadone while adding its own antianxiety properties. About one third of alcoholics also take benzodiazepines (Salzman, 1990). As benzodiazepines have become more controversial, there is danger that clinicians will return to prescribing the more toxic sedative-hypnotics, particularly those younger physicians to whom these drugs may be new (DuPont & Saylor, 1991).

TABLE 4-2
Routes of Abuse and Half-Lives of Benzodiazepines

Generic Name	Trade Name	Routes of Abuse[a]	Half-Life (in hours)
Chlordiazepoxide	Librium and others	PO, IM, IV	5–15
Diazepam	Valium and others	PO, IM, IV	30–60
Lorazepam	Ativan	PO, IM, IV	10–20
Oxazepam	Serax	PO	5–10
Prazepam	Centrax	PO	24–200[b]
Flurazepam	Dalmane	PO	50–100[b]
Chlorazepate	Tranxene, Azene	PO	50–80[b]
Tenazepam	Restoril	PO	10–17
Clonazepam	Klonopin	PO	18–50
Alprazolam	Xanax	PO	12–15
Halazepam	Paxipam	PO	14
Triazolam	Halcion	PO	1.5–5.4

[a] PO = oral
 IM = intramuscular
 IV = intravenous
[b] Includes half-life of major metabolite

Note: The data in column 4 are from Harvey, 1985; Olin, 1987.

Reproduced by permission. *Substance Abuse* edited by E. Gerald Bennett and Donna Woolf, Delmar Publishers, Inc. Albany, NY, Copyright, 1991.

SCHEDULE OF CONTROLLED SUBSTANCES

All the benzodiazepines are schedule II or schedule III drugs. Of the barbiturates and other sedative-hypnotics, methaqualone is a schedule I drug. Nonsuppository dosages of amobarbital and secobarbital are schedule II; suppository dosages are schedule III. Glutethimide and methyprylon are schedule III drugs, and pentobarbital, phenobarbital, ethchlorvynol, chloral hydrate, meprobamate, and paraldehyde are schedule IV (Nahas, 1992).

Therapeutic Uses

Clinical uses of the benzodiazepines include treatment of neuroses, anxiety, depression, hypertension, epilepsy, insomnia, muscular tension, and the withdrawal syndrome. Barbiturates and other sedative-hypnotics have similar clinical uses but have largely been replaced by the benzodiazepines except as anesthetics and anticonvulsants (Beasley, 1990; Ray & Ksir, 1993).

Nontherapeutic Uses

CNS depressants are used and abused recreationally for their effects of relaxation and decreased inhibition. They are also used with other drugs to enhance intoxication and to decrease the discomfort of withdrawal from the abuse of stimulants (Beasley, 1990; Ray & Ksir, 1993).

Routes of Administration

The CNS depressants are usually taken in pill or liquid form, although some are available as injectables, suppositories, and intravenous drugs. Some of the general anesthetics are inhaled as gases (Beasley, 1990).

BIOCHEMISTRY

Different CNS depressants have markedly different lengths of duration of action in the body. Accordingly, they have been classified as long acting, short-to-intermediate acting, and ultrashort acting. They have also been classified according to elimination half-life *(Tables 4-1 and 4-2)*, which is the length of time it takes for the body to eliminate one-half of the drug dosage (Woolf, 1991b). The half-life of many drugs does not necessarily correspond to their duration of action in the body (long, short-to-intermediate, ultrashort, an observation to keep in mind to avoid confusion). The intensity and duration of the withdrawal syndrome can generally be correlated with the half-life of the abused drug.

The short-to-intermediate–acting barbiturates, including secobarbital and pentobarbital, are the most commonly prescribed and abused of the barbiturates. The intermediate-acting benzodiazepines, such as lorazepam and alprazolam, also have a high rate of abuse. Diazepam, the most rapidly absorbed of the benzodiazepines, produces euphoria quickly and is the most abused of that class.

Each of the CNS depressants varies in potency and action. All are capable of producing sedation, relaxation, stupor, coma, and death, depending on the potency and the dosage of the drug.

Long-term use of CNS depressants leads to tolerance. Dispositional tolerance is due to changes in the body (such as increased liver metabolism) and may occur after only a few doses of the drug. Pharmacodynamic tolerance develops when higher doses of the drug are needed to get the same effects. Because the lethal dose never changes, a person trying to get the same effects may overdose as he continues to increase his dosage.

Overdose can also occur as a result of day-to-day accumulation of drug dosages in the body. The signs of overdose include severe inebriation, coma, depressed respiration, lowered body temperature, hypotension, pulmonary edema, pneumonia, and renal failure. The fatal dose of short-to-intermediate–acting CNS depressants is usually lower than the fatal dose of long-acting CNS depressants (e.g., it takes less pentobarbital than phenobarbital to overdose) (Woolf, 1991b).

The barbiturates are among the most lethal of abused drugs. Death has occurred when three times the recommended dosage was taken. When barbiturates are combined with other CNS depressants, such as alcohol, the probability of fatal reactions is greatly increased. Barbiturates are also often implicated in drug-related suicides. Unlike the situation for narcotic analgesics, no specific antidotes are known for overdose with any barbiturate or sedative-hypnotic.

Long-term use of a CNS depressant, besides resulting in tolerance to the drug, results in cross-tolerance to all other CNS depressants. The cross-tolerance probably occurs because all CNS depressants affect γ-aminobutyric acid, the major inhibitory neurotransmitter. When any of the CNS depressant drugs is combined with any other CNS depressant, the effects are additive or synergistic.

Side effects of CNS depressants include drowsiness, motor incoordination, ataxia, rage, confusion, dry mouth, a metallic taste in the mouth, blurred vision, and headache. High doses of benzodiazepines over a period of a month will result in a withdrawal syndrome comparable to that of the barbiturates or alcohol. Because of the similarities of the signs and symptoms, withdrawal from CNS depressants is termed the general depressant withdrawal syndrome (Schuckit, 1989; Tabakoff & Hoffman, 1991; Woolf, 1991b).

MEDICAL PROBLEMS RELATED TO USE OF CNS DEPRESSANTS

CNS depressants shorten stage-four sleep, so that stopping their use results in rebound dreaming, nightmares, and night terrors (Arif & Westermeyer, 1988; Woolf, 1991b). All CNS depressants can cause excessive respiratory depression in a person who has chronic obstructive pulmonary disease (Woolf, 1991b). These drugs are metabolized in the liver and may accumulate there in a person who has liver impairment such as occurs with alcoholism. The drugs profoundly affect the metabolism of other drugs by stimulating the microsomal enzyme system that metabolizes the other drugs. Patients with acute intermittent porphyria could become paralyzed or die if given CNS depressants (Ray & Ksir, 1993; Woolf, 1991b).

High doses of CNS depressants can depress cardiovascular function. They decrease systolic blood pressure and increase heart rate (Woolf, 1991b). CNS depressants can also cause impairment in short- and long-term memory, abstract thinking, and judgment (Boyd, 1991).

There is no absolute proof that benzodiazepines cause birth defects, but several studies have reported abnormalities resembling the fetal alcohol syndrome in children exposed to benzodiazepines in utero. The time that a drug is taken during gestation is critical; a small dose during the first 8 weeks may have a far greater effect than several large doses taken later in gestation (McKay & Scavnicky-Mylant, 1991).

WITHDRAWAL

Rapid withdrawal from all depressants, including the benzodiazepines, after continuous high doses produces a dramatic withdrawal state similar to alcohol withdrawal. The effect is hyperexcitability, or body reactions nearly opposite to the usual effects of these drugs. The severity of the signs and symptoms of withdrawal depends on the strength of the drug, the doses taken, and the length of time the drug has been taken. Most persons have a confusion-disorientation syndrome upon withdrawal. With a drug such as meprobamate (Miltown), severe withdrawal may occur with doses of 3–6 g/day over 40 days (American Medical Association, 1983; Schuckit, 1989). About 500 mg of a barbiturate or an equivalent dose of other drugs will place the patient at risk for withdrawal seizures. For the benzodiazepines, mild-to-moderate signs and symptoms of withdrawal can occur when persons take two to three times the usual clinical dose for only 16 weeks (Ray & Ksir, 1993; Schuckit, 1989).

Patients who are in withdrawal usually have a strong mixture of physical and psychological signs. Physically, the patient has fine tremors, gastrointestinal effects, muscle aches, and autonomic nervous system problems. With the benzodiazepines, patients often have headache, malaise, and abrupt weight loss. With any of the CNS depressants, grand mal convulsions develop in 5–20% of patients. The most typical psychological symptoms of withdrawal from CNS depressants are a high level of anxiety and a strong drive to obtain more of the drug. An organic brain syndrome with hallucinations and delirium develops in a few patients. With barbiturates, delirium will develop in about half of patients if they are not treated (Schuckit, 1989).

In neonates, withdrawal from barbiturates and benzodiazepines may range from mild to severe *(see Table 2-4)*. The signs and symptoms may last for several months (Beasley, 1990).

ASSESSMENT

Withdrawal from CNS depressants should be evaluated in any patient who has anxiety, tremors, anorexia, weakness, nausea or vomiting, cramps, hypotension, and increased reflexes and requests a prescription for a CNS depressant. The history should include the patient's drinking patterns. An inventory of all medications and drugs is necessary to evaluate for potential additive effects. Diagnostic tests may be required.

For neonates, withdrawal from sedative-hypnotics acquired in utero or through breast-feeding can be evaluated through questioning of the mother and family, laboratory tests, and observation (Merlin, 1990; Sparks, 1993).

TREATMENT

Withdrawal from CNS depressants is more safely accomplished in the hospital setting because of potential hallucinations or convulsions. A flow sheet may be useful. Every 4 hr, all signs and symptoms evaluated and the drug doses given should be entered on the sheet.

Patients can be treated for withdrawal with pentobarbital or phenobarbital. With the pentobarbital method, the patient is given an oral test dose of 200 mg and is evaluated 1–2 hr later. If the patient falls asleep during the test period, he is probably not addicted to depressant drugs, and no active medication will be needed. However, if after 2 hr the patient has severe tremors, orthostatic hypotension, or other signs or symptoms of withdrawal, an alternative schedule of withdrawal is established. Treatment consists of giving titrated doses of phenobarbital until the patient becomes quiet or drowsy or falls asleep. This level of drug is probably the patient's normal tolerance level. The dosage of phenobarbital is gradually decreased by

10% each day until the patient is no longer receiving phenobarbital. The patient is reevaluated at regular intervals. An example of the decreases in doses is as follows:

Day	Dose (mg)	10% Decrease (in mg)	New Dose (mg)
1	500		
2	500	50	450
3	450	45	405
4	405	41	364
5	364	37	328
6	328	33	295
7	295	30	265

and so on.

General supportive care should include good nutrition, rest, and multivitamins. The patient and his family should be taught about the dangers of using a CNS depressant for more than 2–3 weeks and how to taper off the medication appropriately. Patients may require referral for further counseling and assistance in finding alternative ways of coping.

Pregnant women should be advised to avoid these agents, especially during the first trimester. This warning is also pertinent during the neonatal period, because some of these agents, particularly the benzodiazepines, can be passed through the mother's milk to the baby and may lead to increased accumulation of bilirubin (Dupont & Saylor, 1991; Schlaadt & Shannon, 1986).

Infants born to mothers taking benzodiazepines may be at risk for signs of withdrawal. If the signs are severe, the infant should be treated with phenobarbital. The loading dose is 8–10 mg per kilogram of body weight in divided doses over 24 hr. The maintenance dose is 3–5 mg/kg over 24 hr continued no more than 6–8 weeks. Blood levels should be monitored throughout to prevent intoxication (Beasley, 1990).

SUMMARY

The barbiturates, benzodiazepines, and other CNS depressants all have effects in common with each other and with alcohol. At lower doses, they act as a sedative and at higher doses as a hypnotic.

The barbiturates have been replaced mostly by the benzodiazepines over the past 20 years. The benzodiazepines appear less likely than barbiturates to result in overdose and are thought to be less addictive. However, all CNS depressants can produce both psychological and physical dependence.

EXAM QUESTIONS

CHAPTER 4
Questions 33–40

33. Which of the following statements about overdose with CNS depressants is correct?

    a. It usually is not due to tolerance.

    b. It can be due to day-to-day accumulation of drug dosages in the body.

    c. It is less likely to occur with barbiturates than with benzodiazepines.

    d. It is not generally life threatening.

34. Which of the following statements about barbiturates is correct?

    a. Most of them are not generally addictive.

    b. The generic names all end in -al.

    c. They no longer have a medical use.

    d. They are the most frequently prescribed drug in the Western world.

35. Which of the following statements about the elimination half-life of drugs is correct?

    a. It depends on the potency of the drug.

    b. It is the same as the duration of the drug's action in the body.

    c. It is correlated with the duration of the withdrawal syndrome.

    d. It is the time it takes the body to eliminate the entire drug dosage.

36. Which of the following statements about benzodiazepines is correct?

    a. They have generally replaced barbiturates except as anticonvulsants and anesthetics.

    b. They rarely cause signs and symptoms of withdrawal when their use is suddenly discontinued.

    c. They are not considered as safe as barbiturates.

    d. They commonly cause insomnia.

37. Which of the following is characteristic of withdrawal from CNS depressants?

    a. More than 50% of patients have organic brain syndrome or convulsions.

    b. Meprobamate typically is given for detoxification.

    c. Safe detoxification rarely requires hospitalization.

    d. A high level of anxiety and craving for more of the drug are typical.

38. What drug is used to treat infants in withdrawal from benzodiazepines?

    a. Disulfiram

    b. Phenobarbital

    c. Ephedrine

    d. Methadone

39. Patients taking CNS depressants should be educated about which of the following?

    a. Avoiding use of pentobarbital

    b. Doubling the dose if anxiety occurs

    c. Tapering off CNS depressants gradually

    d. The dangers of using a CNS depressant for more than 2–3 days

40. Which of the following statements about CNS depressants is correct?

    a. At higher doses, they act as sedatives.

    b. They are considered safe for persons with liver impairment.

    c. They do not have addictive effects when combined with other CNS depressants.

    d. At higher doses, they act as hypnotics.

CHAPTER 5

CNS STIMULANTS: COCAINE AND AMPHETAMINES

CHAPTER OBJECTIVE

After studying this chapter, the reader will recognize physiological and psychological problems associated with cocaine and amphetamine abuse and withdrawal and be familiar with therapeutic interventions for patients who have these problems.

LEARNING OBJECTIVES

After studying this chapter, the reader will be able to

1. Indicate characteristics of amphetamines.
2. Specify a current medical use of amphetamines.
3. Indicate the history of cocaine.
4. Indicate characteristics of cocaine.
5. Specify the effectiveness of different routes of administration of cocaine.
6. Indicate physiological effects of CNS stimulants.
7. Recognize signs and symptoms of withdrawal from CNS stimulants.

INTRODUCTION

CNS stimulants comprise a large category of a wide variety of substances. The category ranges from caffeine, the most widely and regularly consumed psychoactive substance in the world (Cox et al., 1983), to cocaine and amphetamines.

Cocaine is extracted from the coca plant (*Erythroxylon coca*) by soaking the leaves in kerosene and sulfuric acid and forming the mixture into a crude paste called coca paste, which consists of 70% cocaine in coca alkaloids and oil. Hydrochloric acid is added to the paste to form a 90% pure cocaine salt. This salt (rocks or white flakes) is crushed into powder and sold to an underground market, where it is diluted ("cut") with one or more products such as amphetamine, ephedrine, procaine, xylocaine, lidocaine, or quinine.

Cocaine is a natural stimulant. In contrast, the class of stimulants called amphetamines is a group of compounds synthesized from ephedrine. Amphetamines include racemic amphetamine, dextroamphetamine, and methamphetamine. Other CNS stimulants include synthetic amphetamine-like anorectics, caffeine, and nicotine.

All the stimulants have similar mechanisms of action, effects, and treatment approaches. Therefore, they are discussed as a group (except for nicotine), with special focus on cocaine and the amphetamines (Nahas, 1992; Ray & Ksir, 1993; Schuckit, 1989).

HISTORY

Cocaine has been used for its stimulating effects for centuries. Coca leaves are combined with lime, made into balls *(cocada),* and chewed to appease hunger, increase stamina, and provide a pleasant sensation lasting about 40 min.

In the mid-1800s, the Spanish arrived in South America, recognized the value of coca, and brought the leaves back to Europe. In Europe, the alkaloid cocaine was extracted in 1857 and used as an anesthetic in ophthalmic surgery.

In addition to being recognized as an anesthetic, cocaine became famous as an ingredient in a popular tonic, Vin Mariani, made by a French chemist, Angelo Mariani. The tonic was thought to nourish, fortify, refresh, aid digestion, strengthen the entire body, and be a medical miracle.

Sigmund Freud promoted the use of cocaine in medicines. Teas, lozenges, and the drink Coca-Cola became popular. The use of cocaine grew to epidemic proportions in Europe and the United States in the 1880s, resulting in large numbers of cocaine addicts (Holbrook, 1991c; Schuckit, 1989).

By 1891, recognizing the addictive and corruptive potential of cocaine, physicians spearheaded efforts to regulate its use. In 1906, the U.S. Congress initiated regulation of cocaine by passing the Pure Food and Drug Act, halting interstate shipment of cocaine-containing products, and requiring cocaine to be listed on labels of cocaine-containing products. The Harrison Act of 1914 further restricted the use of cocaine by making it a prescribed medicine. As a result of these measures, cocaine use declined sharply before World War I and remained obscure until a resurgence in the late 1970s (Holbrook, 1991c).

The amphetamines, a group of synthetic stimulant compounds derived from ephedrine, were initially used in the United States in bronchial dilators to relieve nasal congestion and for the treatment of narcolepsy, hyperkinesis, and obesity. Abusers could dismantle the inhaler, extract the paper inside containing 250 mg of amphetamine sulfate, and drink the medication in a beverage or chew it in gum for the stimulating effects (Burton, 1991; Musto, 1992). The abuse continued until 1949 when the amphetamine used in the inhaler was replaced with a mild CNS stimulant (Holbrook, 1991c).

Between 1932 and 1946, amphetamines were used medically to treat narcolepsy, heart block, schizophrenia, morphine and codeine addiction, cerebral palsy, hyperactivity, parkinsonism, obesity, and depression (Lukas, 1985).

Most amphetamine abuse of the 1950s and 1960s was abuse of prescription forms of the drug by patients who obtained prescriptions from one or more doctors. In 1970, the Controlled Substance Act was passed, making it more difficult for manufacturers to market the drug. Afterward, the number of clandestine laboratories manufacturing amphetamine and the number of abusers of the street form of the drug increased.

The purity of amphetamines produced in clandestine laboratories declined in the 1970s. On average, the product contained about 10% amphetamine and 90% an OTC stimulant such as caffeine, ephedrine, or phenylpropanolamine.

In the 1980s, use of an illicit injectable form of amphetamine known on the street as "speed," "crystal," "crank," or "go" became popular. In addition, "crack," a cheap, smokable form of cocaine, and "ice," a freebase form of methamphetamine, were available (Lee & Bennett, 1991).

CURRENT IMPACT

The number of cocaine users decreased from 12 million in 1985 to 8 million in 1988. Yet, the number of cocaine-associated emergencies increased, from 8,831 in 1984 to 46,020 in 1988. A corresponding increase occurred in the number of cocaine-related deaths, from 628 in 1984 to 1,589 in 1988. This increase was probably related to the strength and toxicity of crack (Karan, Haller, & Schnoll, 1991).

Female users prefer crack over other street drugs. Because of this preference, prostitution and spread of STDs, including HIV infection, have increased. An increasing number of "crack babies" are born with health, behavioral, and learning problems of long-term consequence. Significant numbers of infants and young children may be exposed to cocaine through either intentional or accidental ingestion, cocaine-contaminated household dust, breast-feeding, normal hand-to-mouth activity, and passive inhalation of vapors (Dyer, 1991; Kharasch, Glotzer, Vinci, Weitzman, & Sargent, 1991).

Because of its low cost, the intense high it produces, and the presence of well-developed distribution networks in the inner city, crack has become popular in lower socioeconomic groups. In that population, it is associated with an earlier onset of use, decreased maturation, and increased psychiatric morbidity and crime (Lee & Bennett, 1991).

Cocaine continues to have a substantial impact on the rates of violence, especially in the inner city. It was estimated in 1987 that one of every five homicide victims in the United States had evidence of recent use of cocaine (Karan et al., 1991).

The reemergence of methamphetamine use in parts of the United States since the mid-1980s has contributed to violence and crime. Demographics of its use have changed to include more ethnic minorities, adolescents, women, and homosexuals. Currently, the typical methamphetamine abuser in treatment (nationwide) is white, male, of low to middle income, high school educated, and 20–35 years old (Helschober & Miller, 1991). The seizure of amphetamine laboratories throughout the United States has been increasing over the past 10 years, particularly in California, Texas, Oregon, and Washington. More than 80% of these laboratories manufacture methamphetamine (Irvine & Chin, 1991).

The manufacture of methamphetamine does not require knowledge of chemistry, and recipes are easy to obtain. Manufacture of this drug in makeshift laboratories (e.g., private homes, rentals, motel rooms, garages, campgrounds, vans, boats, commercial buildings, and storage facilities) is dangerous. Deserted laboratories legally require decontamination, which typically costs the property owner thousands of dollars; in some cases the property is not salvageable.

Clandestine drug laboratories place the persons who are manufacturing the drug, innocent bystanders, public officers, and the general population at risk for serious health problems due to explosions, fire, and the dumping of hazardous chemicals (Irvine & Chin, 1991).

Stimulant drugs continue to be taken by members of all social strata, from athletes to truck drivers, students at examination time, medical abusers, and street abusers. Enough stimulants are legally manufactured to give each man, woman, and child in the United States 50 doses a year. Half of these doses end up being used illegally (Schuckit, 1989). Because the stimulants have been so widely abused in recent years despite strict federal regulations, they may be removed from the legal drug market in the future (Holbrook, 1991c).

SCHEDULE OF CONTROLLED SUBSTANCES

Cocaine and the amphetamines are schedule II drugs. They have a high abuse potential but are approved for medical use.

Therapeutic Uses

Cocaine is used as a topical, local, and regional anesthetic and vasoconstrictor for some types of surgeries, such as ear, eye, nose, and throat (Beasley, 1990; Nahas, 1992). By producing anesthesia while reducing blood circulation to the areas to which it is applied, cocaine can help provide a clearer operating field and prevent large blood losses during surgery.

Amphetamines are used in the United States for treatment of attention deficit hyperactivity disorder, for the short-term treatment of obesity, for relief of migraine headaches, as an additive in OTC diet and cold medications, and to potentiate the effects of narcotics used in the treatment of severe pain (Beasley, 1990; Nahas, 1992).

Nontherapeutic Uses

Generally, stimulants are used and abused by persons who seek euphoria without sedation; relief from fatigue; and feelings of renewed energy, confidence, and alertness. With larger oral doses, a temporary sense of exhilaration, excess energy, extended wakefulness, and loss of appetite are achieved. Stimulants are sometimes used to enhance the effects of marijuana, depressants, and hallucinogens and vice versa (Beasley, 1990).

Routes of Administration

Stimulants can be taken orally, inhaled (sniffed), smoked (freebased), or injected intravenously (Beasley, 1990).

Oral route. Oral cocaine is less effective than cocaine taken by other routes. When it is taken orally, only about 10% of the drug enters the bloodstream, and the resulting stimulation is of low intensity (DuPont, 1984). Amphetamines are effective when taken orally and act for prolonged periods (Arif & Westermeyer, 1988). They can be dissolved in liquids, such as coffee, sodas, or juice, or used in pill form.

Inhalation. The most common route for cocaine ingestion is inhalation through the nose (sniffing). The powder is measured out with a spoon into a small pile on a piece of glass or mirror and divided with a razor blade or other sharp tool into "lines." The user sniffs the cocaine through a tube such as a glass straw, a drinking straw, or a rolled-up bill.

The initial effects are quickly felt, because the drug passes rapidly into the bloodstream. Further absorption is slowed, because cocaine is also a vasoconstrictor and narrows the small blood vessels lining the nose at the point of administration. This vasoconstriction can cause perforated septum, rhinitis, sinusitis, and damage to the nasal mucosa (Nahas, 1992). Overall, about 60% of the cocaine reaches the bloodstream.

Traces of cocaine can be found in the blood within 10 min after inhalation of the drug. Peak levels occur in 60 min, and euphoria lasts about 20 min (DuPont, 1984).

Like cocaine, amphetamine in powdered form can be prepared in lines and inhaled (sniffed).

Smoking (freebasing). Freebase cocaine is obtained by using an alkali (e.g., buffered ammonia) to extract cocaine hydrochloride, which is then mixed with a solvent (e.g., ether). The solvent is separated and volatilized, leaving small amounts of residual freebase cocaine (Karan et al., 1991).

The cocaine freebase can be smoked by burning the substance and inhaling the fumes, by sprinkling it over the tobacco in a cigarette and smoking the cigarette, or by placing a small amount of the freebase (called a "hit") on a screen in the neck of a glass pipe and heating it over a torch to a high temperature while smoking it. This last method produces a high that lasts 2–5 min and is equal in intensity to that obtained by injection.

Crack is an <u>inexpensive form</u> of cocaine that can be bought illicitly. It is ready to use, although it may not be free of the adulterant (baking soda) used to prepare it. Crack is <u>easily made</u> by mixing baking soda and cocaine paste and can be processed in about 8 min. It is called crack because of the crackling sound that the sodium bicarbonate and other ingredients make as they burn when the substance is smoked in a pipe. A 300-mg dose may be sold in a vial or a foil package for as little as $5–$10 (Karan et al., 1991).

Freebasing delivers high doses of cocaine to the brain and produces an intense, rapid euphoria. The short high is followed by a "crash." During the crash, the user is agitated and irritable and has an intense craving for more of the drug. Crack addiction occurs very rapidly.

Bodily injury from burns can result from freebasing. The highly flammable, caustic chemicals induce pulmonary conditions such as bronchitis, pneumonitis, and hemoptysis (Nahas, 1992).

In the early 1990s, an illicit, inexpensive freebase form of methamphetamine called ice became available (Burton, 1991). Ice is convenient to use, provides an 8-hr high (Cahalan, 1991), and like cocaine freebase is smokable and potent (Ray & Ksir, 1993).

Intravenous route. With intravenous injection, cocaine is taken directly into the bloodstream. The "rush" occurs in about 30 sec but is short-lived because the cocaine is rapidly metabolized by the liver. The intravenous route offers rapid, potent euphoria but exposes the user to HIV infection, hepatitis, and other infections and communicable diseases common among users of injectable drugs (Karan et al., 1991; Nahas, 1992).

According to national data, in the United States, the intravenous route is the most com-

mon route of administration of methamphetamine (Cook, 1991; Helschober & Miller, 1991). Most users who turn to the intravenous route have been taking amphetamines orally for some time. Intravenous use quickly leads to tolerance, and soon the user must inject 100–200 mg to achieve the same effects that 10 mg originally provided (Ray & Ksir, 1993).

BIOCHEMISTRY

All the drugs in the stimulant class *(Table 5-1)* produce their effects by stimulating the central nervous, respiratory, and circulatory systems (Nahas, 1992).

CNS Effects

Stimulants enter the nerve synapses in the CNS; <u>block reuptake of the neurotransmitters norepinephrine, dopamine, and serotonin;</u> and promote release of neurotransmitters from the neurons sending the transmitters (Beasley, 1990). Chemicals that are not taken up, that remain in the synapse, promote a high nerve-firing rate, which produces euphoria and excitement. The body adapts to the overstimulation by making adjustments to establish homeostasis. Cessation of stimulant use produces depression and lethargy, because the neurotransmitters are depleted. Days or weeks are required for the reserves to be built up again. The more intense the cocaine (or amphetamine) high, the more profound is the depression that occurs after drug use (Holbrook, 1991c).

Respiratory Effects

Stimulants affect the medulla and thus increase the respiratory rate. As the dosage is increased, respiration and heart rate increase. Large doses can cause tremors and convulsive movements, medullary depression, and respiratory and cardiac failure (Holbrook, 1991c).

TABLE 5-1
Common Legal Amphetamines in the United States

Generic Name	DEA Schedule	Trade Name	Usual Therapeutic Dose
Amphetamines			
Amphetamine	II	Benzedrine Biphetamine Others	2.5–10 mg one to TID
Dextroamphetamine	II	Dexamyl Dexedrine	2.5–5 mg one to TID
Methamphetamine HCL	II	Desoxyn Fefamine Others	2.5–5 mg one to TID or 5–15 mg of extended release once daily
Amphetamine Analogues			
Phenmetrazine HCL	II	Preludin	25 mg BID or TID; maximum of 25 mg TID or 75 mg of extended release once daily
Methylphenidate	II	Ritalin	Adults: 20–30 mg daily Children: 5 mg BID to start
Benzphetamine HCL	III	Didrex	25–50 mg once daily to a maximum of 50 mg TID
Phendimetrazine tartrate	III	Plegine	35 mg BID or TID; maximum of 70 mg TID
Diethylpropion HCL	IV	Tenuate Tepanil Dospan Ten-Tab	25 mg TID or 75 mg extended release once daily
Fenfluramine HCL	IV	Pondimin	20 mg TID to a maximum of 40 mg TID
Phentermine	IV	Ionamin	15–30 mg of resin complex once daily
Pemoline	IV	Cylert	37.5–112.5 mg daily

Note: DEA = Drug Enforcement Administration, TID = Three times a day, BID = twice a day.

Source: A Manual on Drug Dependence by G. Nahas. Essential Medical Information Systems, Inc. 1992. Reprinted with permission.

Cardiovascular Effects

Cocaine taken in small doses can slow the heart rate because of central vagal stimulation, but larger doses increase both heart rate and blood pressure; these effects seem to be dose related. A large intravenous dosage of cocaine can cause cardiac failure, which would lead to immediate death due to a direct toxic action on the heart muscle. Cocaine can cause hypertension and tachycardia. It also can cause ventricular ectopic beats, accelerated ventricular rhythm, ventricular fibrillation, angina, a subsequent subendocardial myocardial infarction. and death. Interestingly, there is no consistent or definite dose at which any of these toxic effects occur. Some users have taken up to 224 mg of cocaine intravenously over 1 hr and had no evidence of cardiac arrhythmias or other cardiovascular indications of toxic effects. Others have taken as little as 22 mg injected submucosally and have had fatal reactions.

Long-term use of cocaine or amphetamines affects the cardiovascular system by interfering with circulation and producing poorly oxygenated blood. The ability of stimulants to constrict blood vessels aggravates any existing circulatory problems and can lead to angina or heart attacks. Cocaine or amphetamines can have a powerful and unpredictable effect on the heart. Increased heart rate and blood pressure follow their use, and death can occur as a result of fatal arrhythmias or epileptic seizures. For some users, even moderate doses can cause a sudden, extreme increase in heart rate, in which the heart quivers instead of beats. The ineffective pumping reduces cardiac output, and without immediate medical assistance, the user will die quickly (Karan et al., 1991).

Effects on the Fetus

Cocaine use during pregnancy causes constriction of blood vessels in the fetus. This constriction reduces the blood supply to fetal cells during periods of rapid growth. Consequently, babies tend to be undersized and have a smaller head circumference, traits associated with lower IQ scores. If the mother continues drug use throughout the pregnancy, a clot may form in the fetus and cut off the blood supply to a part of the body. At birth, the baby might be missing a kidney or sections of intestine, have a shriveled arm or leg, or have a stroke (Sparks, 1993).

Exposure to cocaine also affects the brain in the fetus by altering the action of the neurotransmitters that control mood and responsiveness. After birth, these effects are noticeable as impulsiveness, moodiness, difficulties in bonding, and easy overstimulation (Parker et al., 1990). By school age, the child often has behavioral problems and difficulty concentrating and remembering (Toufexis, 1991).

Fetal exposure to cocaine also affects the respiratory system by decreasing the response to carbon dioxide. This condition is thought to be related to the increased (15% higher) rate of sudden infant death syndrome among babies who were exposed to crack in utero (McKay & Scavnicky-Mylant, 1991).

The effects of methamphetamine use on the fetus are similar to the effects of cocaine use. These include decreased growth, birth defects, and morbidity (Zimmerman, 1991).

Tolerance

With long-term use of stimulants, tolerance develops to their anorectic, euphoric, hyperthermic, and cardiovascular effects. For example, the therapeutic dosage of dextroamphetamine is 5–10 mg orally two to three times a day, but a person addicted to this drug may use up to 10 g/day intravenously (Senay, 1983). With cocaine, the frequency of use is usually increased rather than the dosage (Beasley, 1990). The lethal dose can vary, but prolonged use of any of the stimulants can cause an imbalance of the neurotransmitters and a buildup of toxins that cause toxic psychosis (Senay, 1983). Most of the stimulant drugs produce cross-tolerance.

Users who are tolerant to the effects of amphetamine can take up to 2,000 mg (2 g) of the drug for the euphoric effects, whereas someone who is not tolerant can overdose on as little as 30 mg. Signs and symptoms of amphetamine overdose include hyperreflexia, restlessness, irritability, tremors, confusion, delirium, psychosis, palpitations, seizures, circulatory collapse, bleeding, and coma. Death may occur (Beasley, 1990).

COCAINE- AND AMPHETAMINE-RELATED MEDICAL PROBLEMS

Use of cocaine, amphetamine, and similarly acting sympathomimetics can cause a variety of medical problems. Some are related to the drug itself. Others are related to adulterants in the drug or to the route of administration.

Problems Due to Adulterants and Route of Administration

Adulterants and route of administration are associated with the following: loss of sense of smell, intestinal ischemia (Yang, Han, & McCarthy, 1991), necrotizing enterocolitis (Czyrko, Del Pin, O'Neill, Peckham, & Ross, 1991), inflammation of nasal mucosa, necrosis, perforation of the nasal septum (Sercarz, Strasnick, Newman, & Dodd, 1991), paralysis of the pharynx and larynx, aspiration pneumonia, optic atrophy, osteolytic sinusitis, pneumomediastinum and emphysema, granulomatous pneumonitis, pulmonary edema, burns, AIDS, skin abscesses, phlebitis, deep venous thrombosis (Lisse, Thurmond-Anderle, & Davis, 1991), cellulitis, septic emboli, pulmonary abscesses, bacterial endocarditis, eye infections, fungal cerebritis, hepatitis, tuberculosis, rhabdomyolysis and its complications, acute renal failure (Horst, Bennett, & Barrett, 1991), headaches (Dhopesh, Maany, & Herring, 1991), and STDs (Shernoff, 1991).

Problems Due to Stimulant Abuse

Problems due to stimulant abuse include sinus tachycardia, ventricular premature contractions, ventricular tachycardia and fibrillation, myocardial infarction or arrhythmia seizures, status epilepticus, cerebral hemorrhage, cerebral vascular accidents, transient ischemic attacks, hyperpyrexia, respiratory paralysis or arrest, migrainelike headaches, rhabdomyolysis, weight loss, dehydration, nutritional deficiencies, endocrine abnormalities(Karan

et al., 1991), and organic mental disorders including intoxication, delirium, delusional disorder, and withdrawal.

Delirium. Delirium associated with abuse of cocaine, amphetamines, and similarly acting sympathomimetic delirium develops within 24 hr after stimulant use. Often the patient is aggressive or violent and may need to be restrained. Delirium usually appears within an hour of substance use and is over in about 6 hr. When the stimulant is taken intravenously, the onset of delirium is immediate. On rare occasions, it follows a period of intoxication. When the other pharmacological effects of the drug have worn off, the delirium disappears completely. The diagnostic criteria for this type of delirium include delirium developing within 24 hr after stimulant use and delirium not due to any other physical or mental disorder (American Psychiatric Association, 1994).

Delusional disorders. Cocaine or amphetamine delusional disorders are characterized by rapidly developing ideas of persecution shortly after cocaine or an amphetamine is used. The patient often has a distorted body image and people's faces may look strange to him. At first, he may be merely suspicious and curious and feel pleasure from the drug, but later this reaction turns to aggression or violence against his "enemies." Hallucinations about bugs, snakes, or vermin crawling under the skin may lead to scratching and extensive scarring of the skin. Such delusions can last for a week or longer but sometimes last for more than a year. The diagnostic criteria for these delusional disorders include an organic delusional syndrome that develops shortly after the drug is used, rapidly developing delusions of persecution as the predominant clinical characteristic, and the absence of any other physical or mental disorder that could produce the delusions. Cocaine, either smoked or taken intranasally, is currently a common cause of mental illness (American Psychiatric Association, 1994; Galanter, Egelko, De Leon, Rohrs, & Franco, 1992).

Intoxication. Intoxication due to use of cocaine, amphetamines, or similarly acting sympathomimetics is characterized by the recent use of the stimulant and behavioral changes that include fighting, grandiosity, psychomotor agitation, impaired judgment, and impaired social or occupational functioning. Physical indications of amphetamine intoxication include at least two of the following within 1 hr of use of the drug: tachycardia, dilated pupils, elevated blood pressure, excess perspiration or chills, and nausea and vomiting. The list is identical for cocaine except that it also includes visual and tactile hallucinations (American Psychiatric Association, 1994). Long-term cocaine, amphetamine, or similarly acting sympathomimetic intoxication produces marked weight loss, hallucinations, paranoid delusions, and compulsive stereotyped behavior such as sorting objects into neat piles (Nahas, 1992).

WITHDRAWAL

Withdrawal from cocaine, amphetamine, or similarly acting sympathomimetics progresses through several stages. It is characterized by irritability, anxiety, depression, possible suicidal ideations, fatigue, cravings, insomnia, hypersomnia, and psychomotor agitation due to stopping frequent doses or reducing the amount used of a stimulant drug.

The initial crash is followed in 1–4 hr by intense cravings, prolonged sleep that may be interrupted to eat large amounts of food, numbness of the throat, diaphoresis, tachycardia, and abdominal cramps. These signs and symptoms, not due to other physical or mental disorders, last more than 24 hr after cessation of stimulant use and usually peak in 2–4 days, although depression and irritabil-

ity may last for months (American Psychiatric Association, 1994).

Cravings can occur after months or even years of abstinence and appear to be "conditioned"; that is, they are triggered by events, either internal or external, that the patient associates with stimulant use. If the patient remains abstinent, the cravings are less after each exposure (O'Malley & Gawin, 1990).

If cocaine is combined with alcohol, the signs and symptoms of withdrawal are more severe that those associated with withdrawal from cocaine alone, and the risk of death from heart attack or stroke increases. Alcohol and cocaine in combination are metabolized by the liver to cocaethylene, which produces a more intense high and consequently more severe withdrawal signs and symptoms (Randall, 1992).

In neonates, cocaine withdrawal is similar to opioid withdrawal except that it is usually mild to moderate (see *Table 2-4;* Beasley, 1990; Sparks, 1993).

CASE STUDY

Lauren had it all—brains, beauty, and success. At 38, she was headed for the vice presidency of a large ad agency, a testimony to years of hard work and successful client campaigns. She had not been exposed to cocaine beyond a few lines now and then, mostly as a social obligation; a number of her clients and coworkers carried cocaine with them nearly all the time. Then, as time went on, she began to use cocaine once or twice a month. The high seemed to get better and better, and Lauren believed she had a million more ideas while on the drug. Within 7 months she was buying $100 of cocaine a week and spending weekends with an ever-growing circle of new friends who were also using cocaine as a recreational drug.

One of her new friends described the terrific rush that injecting cocaine could produce, but Lauren resisted injecting it; after all, that was too much like the horrible heroin addicts she'd read about. She wasn't an addict, after all. However, eventually her curiosity got the best of her, and she tried injecting cocaine. It was fabulous, she said, and she couldn't wait for the next shot. After a short time, her weekly bill for cocaine rose to $500, and she found she could inject the drug herself without help from her friends.

Before long, Lauren began to arrive late for meetings, even though she had always prided herself on being on time and prepared. She lost weight, and her once perfectly tailored suits now hung loosely. She was dreamy and distracted and then hostile and defensive. Finally, her boss gave her a warning: one more mess up (and there had been many) and she was out. In 12 months, she had spent thousands of dollars; had depleted her savings, her health, and almost all her friendships; and now was facing the loss of her job. The confrontation with her boss drove her to a counselor, and eventually to an outpatient cocaine treatment program. After 2 years, she is still cocaine-free.

In many ways, Lauren was a typical cocaine abuser. She was atypical in that she avoided arrest for using an illicit drug and she followed through with treatment and continued to be abstinent more than a year.

A profile of the typical cocaine user was compiled by M. S. Gold (1984) and his associates on the basis of 20- to 30-min structured telephone interviews with 500 randomly selected cocaine users who called a cocaine abuse hot line. At that time, according to the profile, the typical user was 30 years old, had been using the drug for 5 years, had completed a little more than 14 years of schooling, had an annual salary of $25,000–$50,000, had progressed from sniffing to injecting or freebasing, used about 6 g/week at a

cost of $637–$3,200, used compulsively, and was primarily motivated to stop use because of the cost of the drug. The population interviewed included college graduates, medical professionals, educators, and airline pilots.

Even though the drug had serious financial and personal ramifications for nearly all the users, they continued to use it to produce euphoria (82%) and energy and self-confidence (48%), to stimulate sexuality (21%), and to relieve boredom (57%).

A high percentage of the users had psychological and physical problems, including depression, anxiety, irritability (more than 80% of the sample), paranoia, loss of interest in activities not related to drug taking, and difficulty concentrating. The leading physical side effects were chronic insomnia, chronic fatigue, severe headaches, nasal problems, unsatisfactory sexual performance, loss of consciousness, seizures, nausea, vomiting, and suicidal ideations or attempts.

Of those interviewed, more than half (61%) thought they were addicted to cocaine, and most (83%) said they could not turn down the drug if it were offered to them. Most (80%) experienced withdrawal symptoms of depression and loss of energy and motivation when deprived of cocaine. About half rated cocaine as more important than sex (50%) and friends (64%), and a large percentage thought it was more important than food (71%) or family activities (72%).

About half reported stealing money from their family, employers, and friends to support the cocaine habit, 56% had spent at least half of their savings on the drug, half were deeply in debt, and 42% had spent all their assets on cocaine. More than one third had turned to crime, including drug dealing, to obtain the drug. Less than half (40%) reported career or job problems, but 17% had lost their jobs as a direct result of cocaine abuse. Twenty-six percent reported divorces or loss of relationships because of the drug, and another 28%

were being threatened with separation or divorce. Thus, most had risked all they had for the cocaine high (Gold, 1984).

ASSESSMENT

Medical examination of a person who abuses cocaine or amphetamine includes obtaining a medical, psychiatric, and psychosocial history, including family input if possible, and a physical examination. Laboratory tests include complete blood cell count, blood chemistry assays, urinalysis, urine and/or blood toxicological assays, electrocardiogram, and chest radiographs (Karan et al., 1991).

Indications for hospitalization include one or a combination of the following: current use of other drugs, serious coexisting or dependency-induced physical or psychiatric problems, compulsive intravenous or freebase use of the drug, severely impaired family or social functioning, strong resistance to treatment, and failure in other outpatient treatment programs (Karan et al., 1991).

If cocaine withdrawal is suspected in a neonate, a urine sample from the mother may help in the diagnosis (Sparks, 1993).

TREATMENT

Stimulant overdose can produce cardiorespiratory distress and seizures. Life support and the administration of thiamine, glucose, oxygen, and naloxone are indicated. Naloxone is an opioid antagonist that blocks the opioid receptor sites in the body. It is given because narcotics are often taken along with cocaine or amphetamines. Suggestions for treating specific signs and symptoms of severe overdose include the following:

- Coronary artery spasm: nitrates and calcium channel blockers.

- Arrhythmias: propranolol, lidocaine, or calcium channel blockers.

- Hypertension: sodium nitroprusside, phentolamine, and calcium channel blockers.

- Severe hyperthermia: physical cooling techniques and dantrolene sodium.

- Severe agitation or seizure activity: benzodiazepines such as diazepam or lorazepam.

- Hypotension: norepinephrine tartrate, dopamine, or both.

- Pneumothorax: oxygen, pneumocentesis.

Psychosis associated with use of cocaine or amphetamine can be treated with haloperidol (caution is needed because this drug may lower the threshold for seizures) or chlorpromazine. Depression continuing after 2 weeks may indicate an underlying major depression that should be evaluated more thoroughly by a psychiatrist (Karan et al., 1991).

Stimulant-intoxicated patients who have mild signs and symptoms of withdrawal need reassurance and a calm, nonthreatening environment. Agitation, paranoia, and violence are the most common management problems in amphetamine abusers undergoing withdrawal (Senay, 1983). Agitation may respond to such measures as frequent orientation and introduction of and visits by familiar persons such as friends and family members. Withdrawal from amphetamines may be helped by benzodiazepines and by good psychological care and support.

Protracted withdrawal is characterized by anhedonia, anergy, and dysphoria. It can be treated with monoamine oxidase inhibitors, amantadine, bromocriptine, and l-dopa. Continual evaluation for coexisting disorders is important so that the patient can receive appropriate treatment (Karan et al., 1991).

After withdrawal, the patient needs assistance to develop a relapse prevention plan involving education, individual therapy, group therapy, and community support groups (see chapter 2). Research on "anticraving" agents has had some promising results (Kleber, 1992).

Neonates in withdrawal from cocaine and amphetamines should be monitored closely for complications. They should also be comforted by being wrapped snugly, by the mother if possible, and kept in an area of reduced stimuli protected from loud noises, bright lights, and excessive handling (Sparks, 1993).

SUMMARY

The most potent of the CNS stimulants are cocaine, amphetamine, and amphetamine-like drugs. All of them can reverse fatigue, increase alertness, and temporarily promote a feeling of well-being. However, they also can produce profound dependence. The adverse effects of cocaine and stimulant abuse include sudden death, medical and psychiatric illnesses, reproductive disturbances, accidents, criminal activities, child neglect and abuse, and lost job productivity (Benowitz, 1992).

EXAM QUESTIONS

CHAPTER 5

Questions 41–48

41. Amphetamines are characterized as which of the following?

    a. Synthetically derived from ephedrine

    b. Schedule III substances

    c. Available in an oral form called "ice"

    d. Safer than cocaine

42. What is currently a medical use of amphetamines in the United States?

    a. Treatment of hypertension

    b. Long-term management of obesity

    c. Vasoconstriction during eye surgery

    d. Treatment of attention deficit hyperactivity disorder

43. What legislation passed by Congress in 1906 began the regulation of cocaine in the United States?

    a. Mariani Act

    b. Controlled Substance Act

    c. Harrison Act

    d. Pure Food and Drug Act

44. Which of the following statements about cocaine is correct?

    a. It is synthesized from ephedrine.

    b. It is a natural stimulant extracted from the leaves of the coca plant.

    c. It is a potent vasodilator.

    d. It is no longer used as an anesthetic.

45. Crack is an inexpensive smokable form of cocaine that is which of the following?

    a. Popular in inner-city lower socioeconomic groups

    b. Hard to manufacture

    c. Preferred by males

    d. Not as addictive as other forms of cocaine

46. Cocaine is least effective when taken by which route of administration?

    a. Sniffing

    b. Smoking

    c. Intravenous

    d. Oral

47. Which of the following statements about CNS stimulants is correct?

   a. They alter the function of norepinephrine, dopamine, and serotonin.

   b. They decrease the respiratory rate.

   c. They stimulate the appetite.

   d. They usually decrease existing circulatory problems.

48. CNS stimulant withdrawal is characterized by which of the following?

   a. A stable mood

   b. Numbness of the hands

   c. Cessation of cravings within 2 months of the last use of stimulants

   d. An initial "crash" followed in 1–4 hr by intense cravings

CHAPTER 6

THE OPIOIDS

CHAPTER OBJECTIVE

After studying this chapter, the reader will be able to describe the effects of opioids, the drugs' potential for addiction, and effective treatment.

LEARNING OBJECTIVES

After studying this chapter, the reader will be able to

1. Specify various types of abusers of opioids.

2. Recognize the role of methadone in opioid withdrawal.

3. Recognize therapeutic effects of opioids.

4. Indicate characteristics of tolerance to opioids.

5. Recognize signs and symptoms of opioid withdrawal.

6. Specify signs of opioid overdose.

7. Choose treatment for a neonate undergoing withdrawal from opioids.

8. Recognize characteristics of methadone.

INTRODUCTION

The term *opioid* is used in this book as it is used by several investigators (Arif & Westermeyer, 1988; Thomason & Dilts, 1991; Woolf, 1991c) to encompass naturally occur-ring drugs extracted from the opium poppy, semi-synthetic opioids produced by making minor chemical changes in the naturally occurring substances, and synthetic opioids that are chemically different from morphine but have similar pharmacological actions. The last group includes the agents often referred to as "narcotics" by addicts and professionals. These benevolent drugs with their soothing, pain-relieving qualities can, with inappropriate doses and long-term use, become highly addictive.

HISTORY

Opium has been used since at least 4000 B.C.E. and has been recognized and praised throughout history for its pain-relieving and sedating qualities. Hippocrates and Galen recommended and encouraged wide use of the drug. The resin from the ripe poppy was considered magical because it could be used to treat dysentery, decrease or eliminate pain, and suppress cough. In addition, it was considered a cure for anxiety and mental disorders, and the euphoria it produced gave much pleasure to the user.

However, as early as the 11th century physicians noticed and described its addictive potential. And during the 16th century, when the opium compound laudanum was the most popular medication in Europe, Arab scientists warned that long-term use of opium degenerates the mind. Nevertheless, by the 19th century opium was cheap, available and widely used by many nations, largely as a result of the legalization of opium in China (Zackon, 1986).

In 1805, the major ingredient in opium was isolated and was named *morphine* after Morpheus, the Greek god of sleep. Morphine is about 10 times stronger than opium and acts much more rapidly. It can be white, off-white, or light brown. It is dispensed in cubes, capsules, tablets, powder, and in solution.

In 1835, codeine, another natural constituent of opium, was synthesized from morphine and made available as phosphate or sulfate salts in syrups, tablets, and ampules for injection (Nahas, 1992).

During the Civil War, morphine and patent medicines containing opium and alcohol were used to treat dysentery and pain. Soldiers were given morphine freely as an analgesic. Also in the 1800s, recreational smoking of opium became popular in the United States when Chinese immigrants introduced the practice to Americans (Ray & Ksir, 1993). These immigrants began cultivating the opium poppy in Mexico, which eventually became the major source of illicit opium in North America (Arif & Westermeyer, 1988).

Growing the opium poppy is illegal in most countries, including the United States. In areas where it is legally grown for medicinal purposes, it is regulated by a network of international agreements. In India, the plant is grown legally as a cash crop. Interestingly enough, India has little illegal trade in opium. However, in other areas such as central Turkey, the opium poppy is an important illegal cash crop. In Pakistan, Afghanistan, and the "golden triangle" of Laos, Burma, and Thailand, growing the poppy is illegal.

Heroin was synthesized from morphine in 1874. In 1898, the Bayer Company promoted it as a cough suppressant until it was discovered to be 2.5 times stronger than morphine with twice the potential for addiction. Nevertheless, heroin became widely used, helped along by the invention of the hypodermic needle, and many physicians prescribed it, disclaiming its potential for addiction (Kaplan, 1983).

Heroin, a white, odorless, crystalline powder, is usually about 3% pure when bought illegally. The remaining filler substance may be lidocaine, procaine, quinine, or lactose (Schuckit, 1989). A dose of heroin is called a "bag" on the street and contains 1–5 mg of the drug (Woolf, 1991c).

The Harrison Narcotic Act of 1914 was an attempt to control opioid use by requiring a doctor's prescription for its sale. Opioid addicts turned to the black market, and in 1924, a federal law was passed making the use of heroin illegal. Individuals were prosecuted for the illegal possession of opioids, criminal organizations and city gangs flourished, the unemployed congregated in the cities, and crime increased (Zackon, 1986).

In the 1960s and 1970s, heroin use increased among young adults. In 1969, it was the No. 1 cause of teenage death in New York City (Woolf, 1991c). A 1978 survey of 24 urban areas showed an estimated 432,000–508,000 cases of heroin addiction in the United States, and another survey placed the figure closer to 1 million. (Kaplan, 1983).

Another upsurge of opioid abuse started in the late 1980s and is continuing. The number of methadone clinics is increasing, and the number of clients is on the upswing. Heroin is now being mixed with other drugs such as cocaine and marijuana, which increase the high that the user seeks. Heroin in some of the new forms can be taken orally, inhaled, and injected. Illegal drug use is never beneficial, but taking heroin orally or nasally has an advantage. Needles are not needed, so shared needle contact and transmission of HIV is reduced in addicts who use these routes.

CURRENT IMPACT

Use of the opioids is widespread, partly because the opium poppy is easy to grow but mostly because of the powerful effects induced by drugs in this group. Opioids are severely regulated in the United States. However, street demand continues to support a black market characterized by crime and poverty.

The drug most often associated with opioid abuse is heroin. It is difficult to estimate the extent of heroin addiction, because the statistics are usually fairly unreliable. However, according to recent estimates, 2 million persons in the United States have tried heroin, 1 million use it occasionally, and 500,000 are addicts (Horvath, 1996; Kreek, 1992).

Overall, there are three groups of opioid users: (1) "street" abusers, people who get their opioids illegally; (2) "medical" abusers, people who misuse opioids in a medical setting; and (3) "methadone" abusers, people whose opioid addiction is legally treated with the opioid methadone.

Street Abusers

The average street abuser is a young black or Hispanic male with a history of antisocial problems. Typically he was introduced to heroin by another heroin user, and he in turn has introduced the drug to others. Drug abuse usually starts in the midteens. The user starts with marijuana, and by the time he is 18 years old has proceeded to harder drugs, such as heroin. By age 20, he usually has been arrested for the first time (Schuckit, 1989).

A recent study (Hser & Booth, 1987) of patients admitted to six methadone programs in three cities showed that the patients shared some characteristics. For the 30 days before they were interviewed for maintenance therapy, heroin was the most commonly used drug. They also used cannabis, cocaine, and alcohol. More than 90% had been arrested, and most had been involved in some sort of criminal activity a mean of 6 of the 30 days

before the interview. Most of the subjects had never married, but few lived alone. The most common psychiatric problems reported were depression and anxiety. In general, the women in the study had been addicted for a shorter period than the men and had sought treatment earlier. Most of the women initially used narcotics because of the influence of a spouse or partner.

One half to two thirds or more of infants born to women addicted to opioids experience a withdrawal syndrome, with a mortality rate of 3–30% (Schuckit, 1989). Postnatal problems, including developmental delay, may need specialized treatment. Infants may have HIV infection at birth if their mothers use intravenous drugs or have sexual partners who are intravenous drug users (Allen, 1991; McKay & Scavicky-Mylant, 1991).

HIV is effectively spread by intravenous drug users, and in certain areas of the United States, intravenous drug use has superseded sex (male to male) as the leading risk behavior for AIDS. Reflecting trends of intravenous drug use in the United States, the incidence of AIDS is disproportionately high among blacks and Hispanics. Among males with AIDS, 25% are black and 15% are Hispanic. Among females, 52% are black and 21% Hispanic. Fifty percent of infants and children with AIDS are black, and 25% are Hispanic (Davis, 1991).

Medical Abusers

The medical abusers of prescription opioids are predominantly middle-class and include women, the elderly, health care professionals, and patients with pain syndrome. The histories of these abusers may be more like those of alcoholics than those of street abusers of opioids, although as they get older, street abusers also tend to rely on legal prescriptions from physicians (Schuckit, 1989).

In the 1960s and 1970s, propoxyphene (Darvon) was the most abused prescribed opioid in the United States; 500 deaths due to its use were reported in 1979 (Nahas, 1992). Many of those abusers obtained propoxyphene with prescriptions given them by physicians for pain relief and took the drug indiscriminately. Commonly abused opioids include meperidine (Demerol), morphine, and pentazocine (Talwin). Health care professionals are especially at risk for abuse of opioids because of their easy access to these drugs (Sullivan et al., 1988).

Methadone Abusers

Although given methadone at a clinic, methadone abusers may supplement their maintenance dose with black market methadone, alcohol, or other drugs. Or they may ask to go on methadone maintenance only because they temporarily cannot obtain opioids or because they want to decrease their tolerance to an amount they can afford (Schuckit, 1989; Thomason & Dilts, 1991).

SCHEDULE OF CONTROLLED SUBSTANCES

Heroin is a schedule I substance. Opium, morphine, codeine, hydromorphone, meperidine, and oxycodone are schedule II drugs. Nalorphine and paregoric are schedule III. Pentazocine is schedule IV. Medications that contain limited quantities of certain narcotic drugs for antitussive and antidiarrheal purposes and for which no prescription is required are classified as schedule V (Nahas, 1992).

Therapeutic Uses

All the opioids have analgesic, antitussive, antidiarrheal effects. Some are used as preoperative medications; others, as detoxification drugs. Particular opioids are used in the treatment of severe pain, severe-to-moderate pain, and mild-to-moderate pain (Nahas, 1992).

Nontherapeutic Uses

Opioids are used recreationally for euphoria and to relieve mental and physical pain. They are also used to decrease tolerance so the user can use smaller amounts of a drug and still get the same effects and in combination with other drugs to enhance the effects of the other drugs (Nahas, 1992).

Routes of Administration

Four factors determine heroin's effects on the user: (1) the amount of heroin administered; (2) the route of administration; (3) the amount of time between doses, which determines the concentration of the drug in the system; and (4) the degree of tolerance of the user.

Opioids can be taken orally, by inhalation (sniffing), by smoking, subcutaneously ("skin popping"), and by intravenous injection ("mainlining"). All opioids are less potent when taken orally than when taken by other routes. The intravenous route produces the most rapid and intense response and is the most efficient. The effects last up to 4 hr. Long-term sniffing of heroin can cause perforation of the nasal septum. Smoking heroin is popular in the Middle East and Far East, but the intravenous route is the most popular route in America (Arif & Westermeyer, 1988; Nahas, 1992; Schuckit, 1989; Woolf, 1991c).

In some parts of Asia, heroin is placed on a piece of aluminum foil and heated over a flame. The vapors are inhaled through a paper tube ("chasing the dragon"). It was common for American soldiers to smoke heroin in Vietnam, where the drug was widely available and inexpensive.

Street users can readily distinguish the two euphoric effects of heroin, the "rush" and the high. The rush comes quickly after the drug is injected intravenously and lasts only a minute or two. In medical treatment, morphine is almost always given orally or by intramuscular injection so that the rush does not occur.

The rush from heroin is caused by a sudden flood of the injected heroin bathing the brain before the drug can be diffused through the bloodstream and broken down into morphine. The high that follows the rush can last for 4 or 5 hr and is caused by the effects of the opiate diffusing from the bloodstream through the blood-brain barrier. It is not affected by the method of administration. Thus, the high can come from skin popping, smoking, or any other method that gets enough of the opioid into the bloodstream. The heroin reduces stimuli from both within the body and outside it in a way that is related to the medical use of opioids in "distancing the patient from his pain" (Schuckit, 1989; Woolf, 1991c).

BIOCHEMISTRY

Opioids can be separated in to three categories: substances that occur naturally, such as opium, morphine, and codeine; semisynthetic drugs produced by minor chemical changes in the natural substances, such as heroin, hydromorphone (Dilaudid), and oxycodone (Percodan); and synthetic analgesics such as propoxyphene (Darvon) and meperidine (Demerol). The prototype opioid with which all other opioids are contrasted and compared is morphine (Schuckit, 1989). Opioids can also be classified according to their action, as either agonist or antagonist at receptor sites. The opioids are similar in absorption, duration of effects, side effects, and signs and symptoms of withdrawal.

All members of the opioid group provide analgesia; act as an antitussive; depress respiration; and produce effects on the gastrointestinal system, smooth muscle, peripheral blood vessels, and endocrine system. They depress the CNS to produce changes in mood, drowsiness, mental cloud-

ing, and depression of the cardiac function at high doses.

Analgesic Effects

The primary reason for the use of opioids is for pain relief. These agents suppress the perception of pain without completely clouding the consciousness.

Each of the opioids relieves pain in dose-related increments, until a plateau is reached. This plateau differs for each opioid. Beyond the plateau, ever greater doses only produce greater side effects such as respiratory depression, sedation, seizures, and loss of motor control.

Among the most effective analgesics are parenterally administered heroin, morphine, and hydromorphone, because of their rapid absorption and high threshold for side effects. Codeine and methadone (Dolophine) have good oral absorption, but morphine and meperidine do not (Thomason & Dilts, 1991).

Antitussive Effects

Opioids (e.g., codeine or hydrocodone) suppress the cough reflex by decreasing the sensitivity of the central respiratory center to increases in the level of carbon dioxide. Death from respiratory arrest can result (Thomason & Dilts, 1991).

Respiratory Effects

Respiratory arrest is the major cause of death due to acute opioid overdose. The opiate antagonists (e.g., naltrexone) can dramatically reverse respiratory depression (Thomason & Dilts, 1991).

Gastrointestinal Effects

Nausea and emesis may be the initial reaction due to central stimulation, but as central depression occurs, emesis may not occur even with an emetic agent. Both the longitudinal and the circular muscular layers of the intestine contract simultaneously, sharply reducing peristaltic action. This effect can be helpful in patients with dysentery, minimizing loss of fluid and electrolytes. However, the effect can be unpleasant in patients being treated for pain because it leads to constipation (Thomason & Dilts, 1991; Woolf, 1991c).

Effects on Smooth Muscle

The smooth muscle of the urinary bladder is stimulated by opioids. This stimulation can produce a troublesome feeling of constant urgency. Most opioid abusers come to ignore this effect because of a reduced central perception of the stimulation. The uterine muscle is mildly affected by opioids, so that labor is often prolonged (Thomason & Dilts, 1991).

Peripheral Effects

Opioids induce a release of histamine that dilates peripheral blood vessels and may cause reddened skin and itching. Another mechanism causes reflex vasoconstriction inhibition resulting in orthostatic hypotension (Thomason & Dilts, 1991; Woolf, 1991c).

Endocrine Effects

Opioids act on thc pituitary gland to decrease thyroid activity and production of gonadotropins and ACTH. This effect leads to lessened sexual desire in both men and women (Thomason & Dilts, 1991).

CNS Effects

The CNS has receptor sites for endogenous, opioid-like substances called enkephalins, dynorphins, and endorphins. These substances, collectively called opiopeptins, attach to their receptor sites and act as neurotransmitters in the regulation of pain and other body functions. Apparently, opioid drugs mimic the natural endogenous opiopeptins, attach to the receptor sites for opiopeptins, and act in place of opiopeptins to regulate pain and certain other body functions (Woolf, 1991c).

Four receptor sites for opiopeptins have been identified. The mu receptors are thought to regulate

euphoria, physical dependence, withdrawal, respiratory depression, and supraspinal analgesia. The kappa receptors have prominent actions on diuresis, sedation, sleep, and spinal analgesia. Stimulation of the sigma receptors can produce emotional unease, dysphoria, hallucinations, and vasomotor stimulation. Delta receptors appear to affect cardiovascular function, contribute to analgesia, and cause changes in affective behavior (Schuckit, 1989; Woolf, 1991c).

When an opioid drug has the right shape to fit one of these receptors, it can attach and produce a response (agonist), produce a partial response (partial agonist) or prevent any response from occurring (antagonist) (Woolf, 1991c). For example, mu receptors are usually occupied by the morphinelike opioids (agonists), but these drugs can be displaced by other drugs such as naloxone (antagonist) so that the effects of the first type of drugs at the mu receptor cannot be felt (Nace & Isbell, 1991).All the opioids are addictive substances, but some are more rapidly addicting than others and more likely to be abused (Woolf, 1991c).

Tolerance

Tolerance occurs with long-term use of opioids. Therefore, over time the user must increase the dose to feel the euphoric effects, and other less desired effects, such as respiratory depression, nausea, emesis, and impairment of consciousness. Certain other effects, such as orthostasis, myosis, constipation, and urinary urgency continue to be felt with no increase in dose.

Tolerance to most opioids, especially the more potent analgesics, develops rapidly. However, a period of abstinence reverses tolerance, and the user can again experience the effects with a smaller dose (Thomason & Dilts, 1991). Intermittent use of small quantities of opioids does not appear to produce tolerance. It is estimated that about half of recreational opioid users, in certain settings, do not progress to long-term use (Arif & Westermeyer, 1988).

Cross-tolerance occurs among the opioids. Consequently, an addict who is experiencing withdrawal from one opioid can suppress the signs and symptoms of withdrawal by using another opioid. When the substituted opioid is stopped, he will experience the withdrawal syndrome characteristic for the second opioid. This procedure may be used in detoxification (Woolf, 1991c).

Effects on the Fetus

Opioids cross the placenta and affect the fetus. Newborns can have signs of intoxication or overdose and can experience a withdrawal syndrome similar to withdrawal in adults (Schuckit, 1989).

OPIOID-RELATED MEDICAL PROBLEMS

When pure opioids are taken in appropriate doses, their long-term use does not usually cause medical problems. The problems that do occur are usually due to contaminated needles, adulterants in opioid mixtures, and overdose.

Signs and symptoms of overdose include recent use, decreased respirations, pallor, blue mucous membranes, pinpoint pupils, pulmonary edema, cardiovascular dysfunction, convulsions, and coma (Thomason & Dilts, 1991).

Typical medical problems include AIDS; abscesses and infections of skin, muscle, bone, joint, and lung; tuberculosis; tetanus; malaria; and hepatitis. Patients may also have gastric ulcers, endocarditis and other cardiac problems, anemias, electrolyte disturbances, kidney failure, pneumonia, bronchospasm, depression, and sexual dysfunction (Schuckit, 1989).

TABLE 6-1
Opiod Withdrawal

Stage I—begins within hours of last dose and peaks at 36–72 hr

1. Craving for the drug
2. Tearing (lacrimation)
3. "Runny nose" (rhinorrhea)
4. Yawning
5. Sweating (diaphoresis)

Stage II—begins at 12 hr and peaks at 72 hr

6. Mild to moderate sleep disturbance
7. Dilated pupils (mydriasis)
8. Loss of appetite (anorexia)
9. "Goose flesh" or "cold turkey" (piloerection)
10. Irritability
11. Tremor

Stage III—begins at 24–36 hr and peaks at 72 hr

12. Severe insomnia
13. Violent yawning
14. Weakness
15. Nausea, vomiting, diarrhea
16. Chills, fever
17. Muscle spasms or "kicking the habit" (especially in the lower extremities)
18. Flushing
19. Spontaneous ejaculation
20. Abdominal pain

Source: Clinical Textbook of Addictive Disorders, R. Frances & S. Miller, Eds. New York: The Guilford Press, pp. 103–120.

WITHDRAWAL

The cessation of long-term moderate or heavy use of an opioid, a reduction in the amount used, or the administration of an opioid antagonist will produce signs and symptoms of acute withdrawal *(Table 6-1).*

The acute phase of opioid withdrawal lasts up to 2 weeks. This period is followed by a protracted withdrawal of up to 1 year, which is characterized by mild increases in blood pressure, body temperature, respirations, and pupillary diameter (O'Brien, 1992; Thomason & Dilts, 1991).

Signs of acute withdrawal in neonates include high pitched crying, fever, sleep disturbances, frantic fist sucking, yawning, sneezing, nasal stuffiness, increased respirations, tremors, convulsions, vomiting, diarrhea, and dehydration. These signs may not be apparent until several weeks after birth, because drugs are retained longer in neonates than in adults. A protracted withdrawal of up to 18 months is characterized by increased susceptibility to colds, flu, ear infections, viruses, and other conditions related to a deficient immune system (Beasley, 1990).

CASE STUDY

Some persons apparently can use heroin recreationally in a controlled fashion. Although studies have been done to differentiate this group of users from those who become addicted to the drug, so far no consistent differences have been found. The following is a case study of a man who uses heroin recreationally (Ray & Ksir, 1993).

A. D. is a 40-year-old man with a wife and three children. He works regularly as a union carpenter. He has no family history of alcoholism or drug dependency.

Drug use began with heavy consumption of alcohol and occasional use of marijuana when he was 16 and progressed to daily use by the time he was 18. By the time he was 19, he had stopped his heavy drinking, but he continued to use marijuana regularly and did some dealing in the drug. For about 18 months, from age 20 to 22, he experimented with psychedelics, and for 2 years, from age 21 to 23, he used amphetamines with some frequency.

A. D. first used heroin when he was 24. He used it sporadically for 2 years, but with growing frequency. At age 27, he recognized that he had a habit. When he was 32, he married a woman who disapproved of his use of narcotics. Although his drug use had sharply decreased, it never ceased. For the past 10 years, his use of heroin has been confined to weekends, with an occasional shot during the week. For the past 5 years, however, this occasional "extra" has virtually ceased. His wife does not use heroin at all but will smoke marijuana with him occasionally. Because of her disapproval of his drug use and the people with whom he uses drugs, on almost every weekend, he selects a time to go to a using friend's home and get high there.

ASSESSMENT

An opioid withdrawal syndrome should be suspected when a patient has areas of increased pigmentation over the veins; clotted veins; skin lesions or abscesses; clubbed fingers; constricted pupils (except when hydromorphone is being abused); swollen nasal mucosa, lymph glands, and liver; abnormal results on laboratory tests (indicative of AIDS, venereal disease, liver function problems, use of opiates); a history of visiting numerous physicians; or complaints of headaches, back pain, kidney pain, or abdominal pain. Opioid abuse should also be suspected when a health care professional requests analgesics for personal use.

Patients should be treated in a medical setting for life-threatening emergencies such as toxic reactions or overdoses. Patients should be assessed for physical signs and symptoms of opioid use, including depressed respirations, pallor, pinpoint pupils, hyperemia of the nasal mucosa, evidence of recent needle use, pulmonary edema, cardiac arrhythmias, lethargy, and coma (Schuckit, 1989).

Assessment of a neonate with possible opioid withdrawal is based on physical signs indicative of withdrawal, abnormal results on laboratory tests for the mother or the newborn, and history of the mother's drug use (Beasley, 1990; Schuckit, 1989).

TREATMENT

Emergency treatment of opioid withdrawal includes establishing an adequate airway and cardiac function, preventing aspiration, establishing intravenous access, treating blood loss and pulmonary edema, obtaining blood for laboratory tests, monitoring vital signs, possible dialysis, and administering a narcotic antagonist such as naloxone (Narcan) (Schuckit, 1989) or clonidine (Thomason & Dilts, 1991).

The patient should be given information about available treatment programs, support groups, the possibility of HIV infection if he used intravenous opioids, and a methadone program. After safe detoxification, the patient should be referred to a methadone program or to a trained addictions counselor for further evaluation and treatment (see chapter 2).

Treatment of opioid withdrawal in neonates includes swaddling, frequent small hypercaloric feedings, monitoring (sleep, body temperature, weight, electrolytes, other illness), intravenous fluids if needed, use of medications such as paregoric if needed until the baby is discharged from the hospital, and referral for follow-up care (Beasley, 1990). Local child protective services can be contacted for follow-up care of the neonate. Perinatal programs are available for both mother and infant that focus on issues related to substance abuse, life management skills, parenting, and child development (Sparks, 1993).

Methadone Maintenance

In the United States, the usual practice in opioid detoxification is to switch the addict to a longer acting opioid such as methadone. Methadone is a synthetic narcotic analgesic. It is nearly as potent as morphine, is well absorbed orally (thus avoiding use of the intravenous route), and has a 24-hr duration of action.

Because of these qualities methadone is offered to heroin addicts as a standard oral substitute for heroin. A daily dose of 30–50 mg can eliminate cravings for heroin. However, patients often take extra street methadone or other drugs such as alcohol or marijuana while on methadone maintenance, a dangerous practice that could result in overdose.

Methadone maintenance involves three phases. The first phase is a daily dose of 20–40 mg orally in fruit juice. This daily dose is gradually increased as tolerance develops until a stabilization (or maintenance) dose is reached. This dose can gradually be reduced in an effort to help the patient become drug-free without undergoing abrupt withdrawal.

In the second phase, the patient goes to the methadone clinic each day to receive the drug and leave a urine sample that will be tested for methadone levels and for the presence of other drugs, such as alcohol, other opioids, amphetamines, and barbiturates. During this time, the patient attends social rehabilitation programs and receives medical care.

The third phase begins after a year of stabilization. Some programs may allow the patient to take a supply of methadone home and return weekly for urine testing and a new supply. If he follows the program, he may be able to find a job and get back into the community. If there is any indication of abuse, the patient returns to phase 1.

Other long-acting opioids can be used in place of methadone. These include naltrexone (Trexan); buprenorphine (Buprenex); and L-∝-acetyl-methadol (LAAM), a longer acting methadone derivative (Johnson, Jaffe, & Fudala, 1992; Leavitt & Smith, 1993; Thomason & Dilts, 1991).

The effectiveness of methadone maintenance programs appears to vary with the way they are administered. For example, in some programs counseling is not available. Different programs provide different dosages of methadone; some monitor patients' dosages carefully, whereas others use too high a dosage. Successful methadone treatment depends on the motivation of the patient and the quality of ancillary services offered at the clinic (Kaplan, 1983; Nahas, 1992).

SUMMARY

Opium, the natural source of morphine and codeine, was used in its raw form for centuries both medically and recreationally. It became important in world politics in the late 1800s and 1900s, when its addictive potential led to federal regulations. A number of synthetic opioids are available, all of which can produce dependence and can result in overdose and death. The spectrum of opioid users ranges from middle-aged, middle-class women to inner-city lower-class youth. Some use to avoid painful signs and symptoms of withdrawal; others, for occasional pleasure.

EXAM QUESTIONS

CHAPTER 6
Questions 49–58

49. Which of the following is characteristic of street abusers of opioids?

    a. They often have a history of antisocial behavior.

    b. They are usually female.

    c. They typically use cocaine before turning to heroin.

    d. They are not responsible for spreading HIV via contaminated needles.

50. Heroin addicts on methadone maintenance are using the methadone program therapeutically when they do which of the following?

    a. Go on methadone maintenance to decrease their level of tolerance to an affordable amount

    b. Supplement the therapeutic methadone dose with black market methadone, alcohol, or other drugs

    c. Do not attend group support meetings or use other ancillary services offered at the clinics

    d. Take their methadone dose regularly at the clinic and abstain from using other drugs

51. All opioids have which of the following therapeutic effects?

    a. Laxative

    b. Emetic

    c. Anorectic

    d. Analgesic

52. Which of the following is a physiological effect of opioids?

    a. Suppression of histamine release

    b. Increased sensitivity of the respiratory center to carbon dioxide levels

    c. Suppression of pain perception

    d. Increased thyroid activity

53. Which of the following drugs would be the most effective analgesic?

    a. Any parenterally administered analgesic

    b. Cocaine administered by inhalation

    c. Orally administered meperidine

    d. Parenterally administered morphine

54. Which of the following statements about tolerance to opioids is correct?

    a. It is due to long-term use of the drugs.

    b. It always develops slowly.

    c. It cannot be reversed by a period of abstinence.

    d. It does not increase the danger of overdose.

55. Which of the following patients is least likely to have an opioid withdrawal syndrome?

    a. An adult whose pupils are pinpoint

    b. A newborn who emits a constant high-pitched cry

    c. A health care professional who requests analgesics for personal use

    d. A teenager who has areas of decreased pigmentation over the veins

56. Which of the following signs is commonly associated with opioid overdose?

    a. Decreased respirations

    b. Runny nose

    c. Fever and chills

    d. Contaminated needles

57. Treatment of a neonate undergoing withdrawal from opioids includes which of the following?

    a. Administration of large doses of methadone

    b. Avoidance of swaddling

    c. Frequent small hypercaloric feedings

    d. A bright and stimulating environment

58. Which of the following statements about methadone is correct?

    a. It is much less potent than morphine.

    b. Its effects last for 24 hr.

    c. It is a naturally occurring narcotic analgesic.

    d. It is typically given in daily doses of 100 mg.

CHAPTER 7

THE HALLUCINOGENS

CHAPTER OBJECTIVE

After studying this chapter, the reader will be able to indicate how the hallucinogens affect users and the best way to treat patients in crisis with these drugs.

LEARNING OBJECTIVES

After studying this chapter, the reader will be able to

1. Indicate the history of the discovery and uses of LSD.

2. Recognize the psychological effects of hallucinogens.

3. Specify the physiological effects of hallucinogens.

4. Indicate medical problems related to the use of hallucinogens.

5. Specify signs and symptoms of hallucinogen intoxication.

6. Choose treatment procedures for hallucinogen intoxication.

INTRODUCTION

The hallucinogens comprise a wide variety of substances of different chemical structures. This classification includes both natural products, such as morning glory seeds, and complex synthetic drugs, such as LSD, the most potent of the hallucinogens (Zackon, 1986). Hallucinogens, both natural and synthetic, alter perception of reality and produce hallucinations (Schuckit, 1989).

HISTORY

Hallucinogens have been used since ancient times. The Vedic writings in India (1600 B.C.E.) discuss a plant called *soma* that could alter consciousness. The plant was probably a mushroom, the fly agaric *(Aminita muscaria),* which is still used in parts of northeastern Siberia. The Greek writer Herodotus, who lived in the fifth century B.C.E., also described *soma.* Lysergic acid alkaloids, produced from ergot-infected grain, are mentioned in several other texts from ancient Greece.

Other drugs widely used in ancient Greece, Rome, Assyria, Persia, Egypt, and China are members of the Solanaceae, or potato family, which contains one or more of the hallucinogenic alkaloids scopolamine, atropine, and hyoscyamine. These drugs were used in religious rituals, sorcery, medicine, and as poison during the Middle Ages and the Renaissance. The odd behavior shown by persons who ingested these drugs was seen as proof that the persons had contact with Satan (Cox et al., 1983).

In the Western Hemisphere, at least 90 plants have hallucinogenic properties. Many of them contain atropine and scopolamine. These hallucinogenic substances were used by Indian tribes throughout North and South America in rituals and as medicines 3,000 years ago. The "magic mushroom" depicted as a god is carved on huge stones in Guatemala.

The Mayans and Aztecs cultivated and used hallucinogenic plants, including the morning glory *(Rivea corymbosa),* which has seeds that contain the alkaloid *d*-lysergic acid amide; mushrooms that contain psilocybin and psilocin; and varieties of the peyote cactus, which contains mescaline.

Attempts by the Spanish to suppress the cultivation and use of hallucinogenic plants were unsuccessful, and the use of peyote spread rapidly to bands of Mescalero Apaches (from whom the name mescaline is derived) and to tribes in northern Mexico, the Southwest, the West, and Canada (Zackon, 1986). In 1918, the Native American Church incorporated and, after lengthy court battles, won the right to use peyote (i.e., mescaline) in its rituals.

Except for use in specially approved research studies, these Indian rituals are currently the only legal use of hallucinogens in North America (Ray & Ksir, 1993).

In 1943, Albert Hofmann, a Swiss chemist, accidentally ingested some LSD (which he had synthesized in 1938) and experienced hallucinations, depersonalization, restlessness, vertigo, visual disturbances, and difficulty in concentrating (Holbrook, 1991b). LSD and some of the other hallucinogens, including psilocybin and mescaline, were evaluated for their therapeutic value in psychotherapy, but they were not shown to be helpful (Weiss & Millman, 1991).

Timothy Leary, an assistant professor of psychology at Harvard University, experimented with LSD on prisoners at Massachusetts prison and became convinced that it could "expand consciousness." He also held experimental sessions with his students in which they took LSD and related their experiences. After being fired from Harvard University, he remained active in the promotion of LSD and in the cultural revolution of the 1960s, which was characterized by psychedelic art and by language, music, and clothes reflective of the hallucinogenic experience (Ray & Ksir, 1993; Trulson, 1985).

In 1956, dimethyltryptamine (DMT) and diethyltryptamine (DET) became somewhat popular hallucinogens. DMT was known as a "businessman's trip," because the effects were short-lived and could be experienced during a lunch hour (Holbrook, 1991b).

During the 1960s and 1970s, it became fashionable to inhale nitrous oxide from plastic bags filled with the gas. Later amyl and butyl nitrite became popular among male homosexuals (Schuckit, 1989).

In the mid-1960s, PCP appeared in the illicit drug trade of San Francisco and New York. It was declared illegal in 1979 because of its wide abuse. PCP is easily made, is widely used as an adulterant in other street drugs, and may be one of the most commonly used drugs on the street (Schuckit, 1989).

Amphetamine-like hallucinogens, also called designer drugs, include methylenedioxyamphetamine (MDA), which was popular between 1960 and 1973, and methylenedioxymethamphetamine (MDMA), which was widely used from 1967 to 1985, when it was classified as a schedule I drug. Methoxymethylenedioxyamphetamine (MMDA), paramethoxyamphetamine (PMA), and methylenedioxyethylamphetamine (MDEA) were available up to the mid-1980s until they were given an emergency classification as schedule I drugs in 1985 (Holbrook, 1991b; Ray & Ksir, 1993; Weiss & Millman, 1991).

CURRENT IMPACT

Overall, the use of hallucinogens, both natural and synthetic, has increased tremendously in the past 30 years (Nace & Isbell, 1991). PCP is widely abused both deliberately as a drug of intoxication and unknowingly by people who think they are buying another drug. PCP and LSD are used primarily by young adults, adolescents, and even children at events such as parties and concerts, although some take the drugs regularly (Holbrook, 1991b).

Many health care officials have been particularly concerned about the upsurge in use of PCP among teenagers and have sought answers to why young people use this dangerous and unreliable drug. Schlaadt and Shannon (1986) found that most PCP users had been physically or emotionally battered, 60% of the girls had been part of an incestuous relationship, and chronic users were more likely to act out sexually. For others, the drug offered an escape from reality. Despite its poor reputation as a street drug, it is still widely used.

SCHEDULE OF CONTROLLED SUBSTANCES

LSD, peyote, mescaline, psilocybin and all the designer drugs are schedule I substances. PCP is a schedule II drug (Nahas, 1992).

Therapeutic Uses

Ketamine, a PCP analog, is used as an anesthetic in the United States. LSD has been tried unsuccessfully in the past as a psychotherapeutic agent, as part of the treatment for alcohol and opiate withdrawal, and as an agent to produce a calm state in terminally ill patients. The synthetic hallucinogens have no known therapeutic value.

Nitrous oxide is used as an anesthetic by dentists and obstetricians. Amyl and butyl nitrite were once used in the treatment of angina but now have limited medical use. MDMA was synthesized to be an appetite suppressant but was not put on the market (Holbrook, 1991b).

Nontherapeutic Uses

The hallucinogens are used recreationally and socially for their mind-altering effects (Schuckit, 1989). Amyl and butyl nitrite were once widely used by homosexual groups to delay orgasm and may also be used to counter the effects of CNS depressants such as alcohol and marijuana.

Routes of Administration

All the hallucinogens, except DMT, are well absorbed orally. They are almost never used intravenously (Beasley, 1990). PCP is usually smoked but can also be taken orally, sniffed, or used intravenously. The designer drugs (2,5-dimethoxy-4-methamphetamine [DOM or STP], MDA, MMDA, MDMA, PMA, and MDEA) are usually taken orally but may be inhaled or used IV. DMT and DET are orally inactive and therefore are inhaled or injected. LSD is usually taken orally in capsules or tablets, small chips of gelatin called "windowpanes," tiny pellets called "microdots," and "blotter" (Holbrook, 1991b).

Psilocybin mushrooms can be eaten fresh, dried, in tablets, or added to food. Mescaline and peyote are used orally. Nitrous oxide and amyl or butyl nitrite are inhaled. Nutmeg is ground up and inhaled or ingested, morning glory seeds are taken orally, and catnip used by humans is usually smoked (Schuckit, 1989).

BIOCHEMISTRY

The terms hallucinogen, psychedelic, mindbender, and psychotomimetic are used interchangeably to describe substances that produce alterations in thought, mood, and perception and usually hallucinations at some dosage (Holbrook, 1991b; Nahas, 1992; Weiss & Millman, 1991).

Alterations

The alterations vary according to the personality and mood of the user, the drug, the dose, the route of administration, and the setting in which the drug is taken. All the hallucinogens produce dizziness, weakness, drowsiness, nausea, paresthesia, tension, visual illusions, mood swings, hypervigilance and isolation, and wavelike recurrences of altered perceptions.

Other alterations may occur, including synesthesia (the strange and powerful feeling that the senses are all working together, e.g., "seeing" sounds and "hearing" colors), loss of somatosensory perception (disappearance of normal boundaries of identification between the self and the environment), distortion of body (the feeling that the body is heavy and being pulled downward or, in contrast, is weightless and floating), distorted perceptions of time and space, vivid and bizarre images, a sharpened sense of hearing, and a feeling of mental alertness and self-awareness.

The user believes these alterations of reality are an authentic emotional and psychological experience and does not recognize that they are symptoms of brain impairment. The hallucinogens are psychostimulants that affect the brain by altering the neurotransmission of central, cholinergic, adrenergic, and, especially, serotoninergic neurons (Holbrook, 1991b; Nahas, 1992).

Most of the hallucinogens produce adrenaline-like effects in addition to altered perception of reality. These include mydriasis (dilated pupils), increased salivation and lacrimation, flushed face, increased blood pressure, tachycardia, fine tremor, hyperglycemia, hyperthermia, piloerection, hyperactive reflexes, diaphoresis, and anorexia. High doses or sensitivity to the hallucinogens may produce anxiety, panic, depression, seizures, incoher-

ence, hemorrhaging, self-destructive behavior, visual disturbances, delirium, and coma (Beasley, 1990; Nahas, 1992; Schuckit, 1989; Weiss & Millman, 1991).

Tolerance

To experience both the behavioral and pharmacological effects, users must take increasingly larger doses of the hallucinogens after 3–4 days of use at even one dose per day. Tolerance is lost within 4–7 days after stopping use of the hallucinogen. Cross-tolerance occurs with most of the hallucinogens, but it does not appear to extend to marijuana. (Schuckit, 1989).

LSD

Biochemistry

Researchers think that LSD produces its hallucinogenic effect by stimulating the raphael nuclei. This section of the brain uses the neurotransmitter serotonin, which has a chemical structure similar to that of LSD. Serotonin regulates incoming sensory information and outgoing muscle impulses. It is theorized that LSD increases the sensitivity of this region of the brain, allowing more information to flow to higher brain regions, including those that control vision and emotion. Thus, persons who take the drug have heightened sensitivity to stimuli, which can then lead to distortions in depth, touch, texture, color, sound, and coordination (Holbrook, 1991b).

LSD also slows serotonin metabolism and causes the neurotransmitter to bind at nerve endings; at the same time, brain levels of norepinephrine are decreased. Drugs that deplete serotonin in the brain, either by blocking its synthesis or by impairing its storage, greatly enhance and prolong the effect of LSD. LSD is the most potent of the hallucinogens. It produces psychological and behavioral changes similar to those of psychosis (psychotomimetic symptoms) at doses as small as 50–100 µg.

Subjective effects. Symptoms occur within 30 min after ingestion and may last 4–6 hr (Nahas, 1992). They include vivid perceptual distortions, time distortion (minutes may seem to be hours), space distortions, body image distortions, loss of somatosensory perception, confusion, synesthesias, and heightened sensory experiences. In addition, parts of the body or trivial objects may suddenly become important and the subject of serious scrutiny, emotions may appear to exist simultaneously or rapidly follow each other, and the user may have a feeling of being powerful and capable of great insight.

Physiological signs and symptoms. Physiological signs and symptoms occur within 20 min after ingestion. They can include dizziness, hot and cold flashes, dry mouth or excessive salivation, dilated pupils, hyperthermia, hypertension, hyperactive reflexes, sweating, tremors, and nausea.

Related Medical Problems

Panic reactions. The most common LSD-related medical problems reported in the emergency department are a high level of anxiety and fear or panic reactions. Users who are in a panic state are highly stimulated, frightened, hallucinating, and usually fearful that they are losing their minds. Most often, the panic occurs after a bad experience in a person with relatively little experience with the drug. The emotional problems tend to ease as the effects of the drug wear off. The time required may be as long as 12 hr (Schuckit, 1989).

Toxic psychosis. The typical reaction in toxic psychosis is a rapid loss of contact with reality with very disturbed behavior, which closely resembles an acute psychotic break. Delusions can be dangerous; for example, patients may

try to destroy a part of their bodies or may attack another person. Patients in this condition need medically supervised detoxification. Toxic psychosis usually clears in a few hours or days. Improvement is uneven, but consistent improvement should be seen on a day-to-day basis. It is thought that this condition develops in patients who were prepsychotic in the drug-free state (Arif & Westermeyer, 1988; Holbrook, 1991b).

Flashbacks. The adverse effect most often connected with LSD use is flashbacks, sudden recurrences of specific experiences that occurred during an episode of taking LSD. Flashbacks may appear days to years after use, occur more often in regular users than in occasional users, can occur after a single dose, last only a few minutes, and diminish with time if the person stops using LSD. Flashbacks are unpredictable, although they seem to occur more often just before going to sleep, while driving, during periods of high stress, and when certain drugs such as marijuana are used.

Flashbacks can be pleasurable or distressing and have been divided into three types: perceptual (most common), somatic, and emotional. Perceptual flashbacks are often visual (colors of a nonspecific form), although any sensory modality can be affected. Somatic flashbacks are often a loss of a sense of reality or distortions of time, space, and body image. Emotional flashbacks may be distressing emotions originally associated with the acute LSD reaction.

Many users have had unpleasant reactions to LSD. Even experienced users may have anxiety, depression, and fearfulness after using the drug. A severely unpleasant drug reaction is called a "bad trip" and is one of the most common emergencies in patients who have taken

LSD (Holbrook, 1991b; Nahas, 1992; Weiss & Millman, 1991).

Amotivational syndrome. Another adverse effect from the long-term use of hallucinogens is a state called amotivational syndrome. It is characterized by a behavioral pattern of increased apathy and disinterest in the world or social contact, disregard for typical conventions such as appropriate dress and manner, anhedonia, and an inability to concentrate (Mirin & Weiss, 1991).

Chromosomal damage. One of the bigger controversies associated with use of LSD has been possible chromosomal damage due to the drug. Although some studies have shown white blood cell damage in LSD users, others have found no conclusive evidence of chromosomal changes (Holbrook, 1991b; Ray & Ksir, 1993).

Withdrawal

Signs and symptoms of withdrawal are not evident after the sudden cessation of LSD use (Nahas, 1992).

CASE STUDY

A 23-year-old man was admitted to the hospital after he stood uncertain whether to plunge a knife into his friend's back. His wife reported that he had been acting strangely since taking LSD approximately 3 weeks before admission. He was indecisive and often mute and shunned physical contact with her. On admission, the patient was catatonic, mute, and echopractic. He appeared to be preoccupied and hallucinating. On transfer to another hospital 1 month after admission, there was minimal improvement.

During his adolescence, the patient had alternated between acceptance of and rebellion against his mother's religiosity and warnings of the perils of sex and immorality. He had left college during his first year, after excessive use of amphetamines.

He attended, but did not complete, art school. In adulthood, he became increasingly puzzled about the meaning of life, his role in the universe, and other cosmic problems. This struggle apparently led to his ingestion of LSD. Shortly after ingestion, he was ecstatic and wrote to a friend, "We have found the peace, which is life's river which flows into the sea of Eternity." Soon afterward, in a brief essay, he showed some awareness of his developing psychosis: "I am misunderstood, I cried, and was handed a complete list of my personality traits, habits, goals, and ideals, etc. I know myself now, I said in relief and spent the rest of my life in happy cares asylum. AMEN." (Ray & Ksir, 1993)

Assessment

Information about the nature and amount of LSD used is difficult to obtain because most of these patients cannot give a lucid account. Because few illicit drugs are pure, urinalysis is needed for appropriate diagnosis. Assessment should include psychosocial history, medical history, and information on drug use. Data on any mental illness in the patient and his family should be obtained as soon as possible to rule out a psychiatric disorder.

Patients may laugh or cry or show panic, fear, euphoria, paranoia, hypervigilance, drowsiness, or withdrawal (Huggins, 1990). Other signs and symptoms include blindness (from contaminants such as quinine), dizziness, synesthesia, poor motor coordination, hyperventilation, aspiration, and nausea (Nahas, 1992).

Overdose, which rarely occurs with the hallucinogens, is a life-threatening emergency and requires hospitalization. Signs can include severe hyperthermia, hemorrhaging, delusions causing self-destructive behavior, and coma (Beasley, 1990).

Treatment

Patients should be reassured that the signs and symptoms will gradually subside. They should receive education about flashbacks. Hospitalization is not usually needed if a supportive nonthreatening environment can be provided. If possible, care should be given with family or friends present (Schuckit, 1989).

Treatment of overdose includes observation of vital signs, maintenance of a patent airway, cardiac monitoring, and medications if needed. Convulsions are treated with anticonvulsants and diazepam if needed and reduction in body temperature. If progress is inadequate after 24 hr, the drug ingested may be STP or PCP (Schuckit 1989; Holbrook, 1991b).

All medications other than diazepam or chlordiazepoxide should be avoided. Chlorpromazine (Thorazine) or any other antipsychotic drug is contraindicated for any patient with inadequate liver function. If a patient is given medication, both he and his family should be told that it must be continued until he is professionally reevaluated. Coexisting mental health problems should be ruled out or treated (Schuckit, 1989).

A follow-up visit should be arranged, and appropriate referrals for psychotherapy or a drug treatment program should be made to help the user and his family deal with his drug problems (Huggins, 1991).

PSILOCYBIN

Biochemistry

Psilocybin might be viewed as a minor hallucinogen. That is, although it produces the same types of hallucinations and side effects as LSD, it is about 150–200 times less potent. Its effects appear within 15 min after a dose of 4–8 mg, peak at 90 min, wane after 2–3 hr, and disappear after 5–6 hr (Schuckit, 1989).

Psilocybin comes from a natural source, a mushroom *(Psilocybe mexicana)*. It is thought to produce hallucinogens and perceptual distortions

by its effects on the serotoninergic fiber tracts (Arif & Westermeyer, 1988).

Subjective Effects

Psilocybin provides vivid visual hallucinations and distortions. Soon after eating the mushrooms, the user's face may feel numb, his pupils dilate, and his muscles twitch. He may feel intoxicated, laugh hilariously, experience emotional swings from extreme highs to deep depression or anxiety, lose the ability to concentrate, and experience hallucinations of pleasant but unfamiliar smells (Cox et al., 1983). Memory may be affected, so that past and perhaps repressed experiences suddenly become vivid and real; these then meld with the present so that all sense of the present and reality are lost. Users may feel they are undergoing a profound mystical, religious, or cosmic experience (Holbrook, 1991b; Ray & Ksir, 1993; Trulson, 1985).

Tolerance

Tolerance to psilocybin develops after the drug has been taken for several consecutive days. After tolerance has developed, the drug no longer produces any of the desired effects, and the user must abstain from it for several days before it will become effective again. Even trying other drugs such as LSD or mescaline during abstinence will not produce the desired effects. Each of these drugs produces cross-tolerance to the others in the group.

Related Medical Problems

Paranoia and accidental death. The real hazards of psilocybin and psilocin are acute paranoia and accidental or deliberate death during use. Even though psilocybin is much less potent than other hallucinogens, a bad trip can occur in some users, who become confused, disoriented, fearful, and unable to distinguish between reality and unreality. They may have true hallucinations, panic, terror, and severe agitation. The general lack of availability of the drug has made its potential for abuse very low.

Toxic psychosis. The signs and symptoms of toxic psychosis due to psilocybin are similar to those of LSD-induced toxic psychosis. They may include hyperthermia, flushing, euphoria, anxiety, panic, paranoia, and depersonalization.

Withdrawal

No signs or symptoms of withdrawal occur when use of psilocybin is stopped.

Assessment and Treatment

Assessment of patients with psilocybin toxic syndrome is essentially the same as that for patients with LSD intoxication. Treatment is essentially the same as that for users of LSD. The effects of psilocybin will be of shorter duration than those of LSD (Holbrook, 1991b).

MESCALINE

Biochemistry

Mescaline, the second most widely used hallucinogen, is derived from peyote cactus buttons. The usual oral dose is 300–500 mg (three to six peyote buttons). It produces approximately the same effect as 50–100 µg of LSD or 10 mg of psilocybin for about 1 or 2 hr (Schuckit, 1989).

Mescaline acts on both the peripheral and the central nervous systems to cause dilated pupils and increases in heart rate, blood pressure, and body temperature. Convulsion or death can occur because of respiratory depression (Holbrook, 1991b).

Subjective effects. The subjective effects of mescaline can include numbness, tension, anxiety, speeded-up responses, muscle twitching, dizziness, and attraction to a single object at which the user might stare for long periods. Mescaline particularly influences vision and hearing, producing vivid perceptual distortions and hallucinations such as brightly colored lights, geometric patterns, and visions of strange animals (Ray & Ksir, 1993; Trulson, 1985).

Related Medical Problems

Toxic psychosis due to mescaline is similar to that due to LSD. Characteristics include delusions, paranoia, and panic. Because mescaline is not very potent, toxic psychosis is rare (Arif & Westermeyer, 1988).

Withdrawal

No signs or symptoms of withdrawal occur when use of mescaline is stopped.

Assessment and Treatment

Assessment and treatment of patients with mescaline intoxication is the same as assessment and treatment of patients with LSD or psilocybin intoxication (Holbrook, 1991b).

AMPHETAMINE-RELATED HALLUCINOGENS

Biochemistry

The synthetic hallucinogens or designer drugs have potent hallucinogenic and stimulating properties. These drugs are chemically related to both amphetamine and mescaline. Most of them produce euphoria with lower doses and hallucinations with higher doses (Beebe & Walley, 1991).

At a dose of 35–79 mg, DMT produces effects similar to those of LSD. They develop quickly and last about 1 hr. Some think this drug is more likely than others to produce panic episodes because the rapid onset of effects does not allow the user to adjust quickly enough. He thus has a greater sense of losing control than with other agents.

Methylphenyltetrahydropyridine (MPTP), derived from heroin, was known for producing parkinsonian-like signs and symptoms. MDA, also called "love pill," produces euphoria and an increased sense of touch at low doses and effects like those of LSD at high doses. The effects begin about 30–60 min after ingestion and continue for about 8 hr. MDMA, also called "ecstasy" or the "yuppie psychedelic," has mainly stimulating effects, as does PMA.

At doses of 1–4 mg, STP or DOM, also called "serenity" and "peace pill," produces LSD-like effects that last 16–24 hr. Side effects include confusion, tremors, flushing, sweating, nausea, vomiting, and blurred vision. Bromodimethoxyamphetamine (DOB) is more potent than mescaline (Holbrook, 1991b; Nahas, 1992).

Related Medical Problems

Panic reactions due to the amphetamine-related hallucinogens are similar to those caused by LSD, psilocybin, and mescaline. Research is being done on possible neurotoxic effects of MDMA. A permanent form of parkinsonism can occur when MPTP is used. Death due to preexisting cardiovascular disease can occur when MDMA or MDEA is used.

Withdrawal

Signs and symptoms of withdrawal do not occur when use of amphetamine-related hallucinogens is stopped.

Assessment and Treatment

Assessment and treatment of patients with intoxication due to amphetamine-related hallucinogens is the same as assessment and treatment of patients with LSD, psilocybin, or mescaline intoxication (Holbrook, 1991b; Ray & Ksir, 1993; Weiss & Millman, 1991).

PCP

Biochemistry

PCP acts as an anticholinergic, a CNS depressant, an anesthetic, a tranquilizer, and a hallucinogen.

CNS effects. The main physiological effects of the phencyclidines are increases in blood pressure, heart rate, respiration, and reflexes. The increase in muscular reflexes produces muscle rigidity. Cholinergic effects include sweating, flushing, drooling, constriction of the pupils, dizziness, lack of coordination, slurred speech, and nystagmus.

The range and type of CNS effects caused by PCP vary with the dose. Doses of 2–5 mg typically lead to a mild depression and then stimulation. A dose of 10 mg produces the sensory alterations that most users want, such as intoxication, perceptual illusions, and numbness of the extremities. Doses of 20 mg or more can lead to catatonia, coma, and convulsions, and larger doses may induce seizures, respiratory depression, and cardiac irregularities (Schuckit, 1989).

PCP abuse syndrome. The PCP abuse syndrome can be divided into four successive phases of psychological change (Carroll, 1985; Holbrook, 1991b; Milhorn, 1991). In phase 1, acute toxic reaction to PCP, signs and symptoms are dose related, They include combativeness, catatonia, convulsions, and coma. Visual hallucinations and sometimes auditory hallucinations occur. High doses may cause death due to respiratory depression or cardiovascular failure. Within 72 hr, the sensorium clears, unless the patient progresses to the next phase.

Phase 2, PCP toxic psychosis, does not depend on blood levels of the drug and does not necessarily follow the first phase. However, it appears most often after long-term use. It lasts about 1 week and is characterized by paranoid delusions, agitation, hostility, impaired judgment, and visual and auditory hallucinations. The user may become a danger to himself and others.

Phase 3 consists of psychotic episodes. An episode can last a month or more after the drug was taken, can occur after a single use of PCP, and can strongly mimic schizophrenia. Users may have delusions of persecution, grandiosity, and global disasters, or they may feel that they have superhuman strength. They have a blunted affect and behave in an unpredictable manner. It is thought that most persons in whom PCP ingestion produces a schizophrenic-like state have psychotic or prepsychotic personalities.

Phase 4 is PCP-induced depression. The risk of suicide is high, and the user may take other psychoactive drugs to get relief from his symptoms. Like phase 2, phase 4 can follow any of the previous stages and may last a single day or several months.

Tolerance. Tolerance develops to the behavioral and toxic effects of PCP, but abrupt cessation of the drug usually results in only minor signs and symptoms of withdrawal. These include tremors, facial twitching, and fearfulness (Nahas, 1992; Schuckit, 1989).

Related Medical Problems

Overdose. Deaths due to acute PCP overdoses of usually 150–200 mg have been reported. Overdose is marked by extreme hypertension that lasts several days after ingestion of the drug. Muscular rigidity and horizontal and vertical nystagmus are always present. Other signs and symptoms include an inability to feel mild sensation, repetitive movements, flushing, hyperthermia, profuse sweating, increases in oral and bronchial secretions, and convulsions. A coma may occur. It can last as long as 10 days, and the patient may

than have an organic brain syndrome that may last a month or longer (Schuckit, 1989; Weiss & Millman, 1991).

Impaired thinking and loss of memory. Long-term users of PCP have cycles characterized by periods of heavy PCP use, anorexia, and insomnia that are followed by periods of abstinence and sleep. These cycles leave users depressed, disoriented, and unable to remember recent events for about 2 months (Carroll, 1985; Huggins, 1990; Schuckit, 1989).

Flashbacks. The flashbacks described by PCP users are similar to those experienced by LSD users (Arif & Westermeyer, 1988).

Speech problems. PCP users may have persistent speech problems such as stuttering, an inability to speak clearly, and an inability to speak at all (Arif & Westermeyer, 1988; Nahas, 1992; Weiss & Millman 1991).

Chronic and severe anxiety and depression. Some users of PCP are depressed enough to attempt suicide (McCardle & Fishbein, 1989).

Isolation. Long-term users of PCP may gradually withdraw from their family and non–PCP-using friends. Divorce, loss of jobs and career, and, among teenagers, dropping out of school are also common patterns. Abuse of other substances may contribute to the patient's downward spiral (Cox et al., 1983).

Accidental injury or death. Drowning is a major cause of death in teenagers who use PCP. Jumps from high places or automobile accidents can occur. Deaths from self-mutilation and homicide have been connected to PCP-induced bizarre behavior. Some evidence suggests that the behavioral response to PCP may be associated with certain personality traits and background features (Holbrook, 1991b; McCardle & Fishbein, 1989).

Effects on body systems. High doses of PCP can lead to kidney failure, brain hemorrhage, and repeated uninterrupted convulsions (Arif & Westermeyer, 1988).

Withdrawal

Because the chemical structure of PCP resembles that of the CNS depressants, a withdrawal syndrome after long-term use might be expected. However, only mild signs and symptoms occur when use of the drug is stopped. These include minor tremors, facial twitching, and fearfulness (Arif & Westermeyer, 1988; Holbrook, 1991b).

CASE STUDY

One PCP user reported the following (Ray & Ksir, 1993):

Immediately after smoking the "Dust," I started experiencing the effects. All my troubles seemed to go away. I felt a little drunk and had some trouble walking around the apartment. Objects appeared either very far away or very close and I couldn't really judge distance at all...I liked being apart from things, and felt outside my body for most of the trip. That was fun. Before I smoked I had been troubled about some exams coming up and felt I wasn't really prepared. All that anxiety vanished with the Dust...I felt at peace. It was a good feeling...I want to be there always.

Assessment

Because most PCP patients are in a hyperactive state with confusion, loss of control, and possibly amnesia, obtaining a complete history may not be possible initially (Nahas, 1992; Schuckit, 1989). A physical examination should be done. Urine and blood tests should be done, but the results may not be reliable because PCP remains in these fluids such a short time (Holbrook, 1991b). Signs and symptoms should be observed, and the patient should be assessed for the need for life support, potential harm to himself or others, coexisting conditions, and the degree of toxic effects (Carroll, 1985).

Treatment

The purpose of treatment is to protect the patient and others from harm, provide necessary life support, facilitate detoxification, and avoid the use of other medications unless they are necessary. The patient should be given a calm environment where he is not likely to hurt himself or others; physical restraints should be used only if necessary (Carroll, 1985; Holbrook, 1991b; Schuckit, 1989). The most important part of treating a PCP user who has a medical emergency is to support vital signs and body systems (Schuckit, 1989).

Recovery from PCP psychosis progresses from agitation to a mixed phase to resolution. In the resolution phase, all psychotic characteristics rapidly disappear and the patient's original personality reemerges.

The duration of recovery seems to depend on individual susceptibility to the drug, the relative dosage of antipsychotic medication used, and whether or not acidification of the urine has been used to speed the excretion of phencyclidine.The typical patient spends about 5 days in each phase of psychosis when he is receiving appropriate care in a secluded setting.indications that the patient is moving out of the agitated phase into the mixed phase include lack of hyperactivity. The patient also seems much less threatened by staff visits and is no longer openly hostile to visitors. He can follow simple concrete instructions or suggestions, and he accepts his medication without being suspicious and hostile. He may still have hallucinations and thought disorders, but he is relatively calm and reasonable and can accept some responsibility for controlling his behavior. He still has periods when he seems to regress to gross paranoia, terror, and hyperactivity; these alternate with quiet but paranoid watchfulness. In this phase, the goals are to keep the patient from harming himself, relieve the psychosis, reduce paranoia, and continue detoxification. Behavior must be monitored closely and continually, but a flexible isolation plan can be tried in which the patient can voluntarily seek seclusion at the first indication that he is losing control.

Usually, by about the 10th day of hospitalization, the patient begins to enter the resolution phase. His predrug personality begins to reappear, and he develops some insights into the chain of events that led him to the hospital. He may be able to switch over to voluntary hospitalization, and the groundwork for outpatient visits is developed. If he is taking an antipsychotic medication, it can be tapered off and eventually stopped.

However, the patient must have close follow-up, usually on a daily basis for several months, because the psychosis can recur within a few days, even in persons who seem to have made a complete recovery. Those who have not undergone formal, structured detoxification seem to need higher doses of an antipsychotic for a longer period to prevent recurrence of signs and symptoms (Schuckit, 1989; Weiss & Millman, 1991).

Despite the unpredictable and serious effects of PCP, more than half of users go back to the drug a short time after they have been treated (Carroll, 1985).

NITRITES

Three substances related to the hallucinogens are nitrous oxide and amyl and butyl nitrite. Nitrous oxide is a commonly used anesthetic gas and is a fairly weak agent that can be used with other products or alone (Schuckit, 1989). Health care workers are among the greatest abusers of this substance. When the drug is used each day for a number of months, a paranoid psychotic state accompanied by confusion may develop. The problem clears rapidly once the drug is stopped.

Amyl and butyl nitrite, or "poppers," were once widely used by homosexual groups to delay orgasm and are also used to counter the effects of depressants such as alcohol and marijuana. Amyl nitrite is sold illicitly under a variety of nicknames, such as "rush," "kick," and "belt." This potent vasodilator was once used for the treatment of angina but now has only limited medical use.

In one study (Schuckit, 1989), approximately 60% of a series of 150 homosexuals admitted using amyl nitrite. At least 20% said they used the substance once or twice a week. Heavier use of the vasodilator occurred in groups and accompanied high intake of alcohol. This pattern of use has also been loosely linked to AIDS: The drug appears to depress cell-mediated immunity and is associated with an increased incidence of pneumonia and Kaposi's sarcoma, a relatively rare form of cancer.

The most common clinical problems of amyl nitrite intoxication are a toxic reaction to the drug and a panic reaction. The panic reaction clears spontaneously with reassurance. The drug may also produce nausea, dizziness, and a feeling of faintness because of a drop in blood pressure. This feeling of dizziness or faintness may be the real cause of the euphoria that users report (Arif & Westermeyer, 1988; Schuckit, 1989).

SUMMARY

The hallucinogenic plants have offered medicinal, spiritual, and recreational assistance to humans for centuries. More recently, synthetic hallucinogens have become available. Of these, LSD, the prototype, is the most potent and popular. PCP, despite its serious psychological risks, continues to be abused, especially by younger people.

EXAM QUESTIONS

CHAPTER 7
Questions 59–71

59. In what situation in North America is it legal to use peyote?

    a. Detoxification of PCP users

    b. Treatment of depression

    c. Induction of cross-tolerance to other hallucinogens

    d. Rituals in the Native American Church

60. Timothy Leary is especially known for which of the following?

    a. Promoting medical uses of cocaine

    b. Experimenting with LSD

    c. Accidentally ingesting mescaline

    d. Discovering the anesthetic properties of PCP

61. Which of the following statements about PCP is correct?

    a. It is widely abused both deliberately and unknowingly.

    b. Most users are teenagers.

    c. It has an illegal analog called ketamine.

    d. The usual route of administration is oral.

62. Which of the following is a characteristic of LSD?

    a. It is usually smoked.

    b. It is available in small chips of gelatin called "windowpanes."

    c. It is poorly absorbed orally.

    d. It is the least potent of the hallucinogens.

63. The term hallucinogens is used interchangeably with which of the following terms?

    a. Marijuana

    b. Psychotropics

    c. Neuroleptics

    d. Psychedelics

64. Which of the following statements about hallucinogens is correct?

    a. They are currently the drug of choice in the treatment of asthma.

    b. They have only recently been discovered.

    c. They do not alter neurotransmitters.

    d. They produce alterations in thought, mood, and perception.

65. Ingestion of LSD can do which of the following?

    a. Produce signs and symptoms of psychosis only at high doses

    b. Produce panic attacks that may last up to 1 year

    c. Cause only minor physiological disturbances

    d. Cause flashbacks days or even years after use

66. Which of the following is characteristic of psilocybin?

    a. It is about 150 times more potent than LSD.

    b. It is derived from mushrooms.

    c. Its use is associated with severe signs and symptoms of withdrawal.

    d. It does not cause cross-tolerance to other hallucinogens.

67. Which of the following statements about mescaline is correct?

    a. It is the second most widely used hallucinogen.

    b. It acts on the CNS only.

    c. An average dose is 20 peyote buttons.

    d. It does not affect vision.

68. Which of the following statements about amphetamine-related hallucinogens is correct?

    a. They include MPTP derived from heroin.

    b. They cause severe withdrawal.

    c. They are chemically related to LSD.

    d. They are not as potent as other hallucinogens.

69. PCP actions include which of the following?

    a. Pain relief

    b. CNS excitation

    c. Hallucinations

    d. Appetite suppression

70. Which of the following is characteristic of PCP users?

    a. They experience severe withdrawal when they stop using the drug.

    b. They typically do not return to drug use after treatment.

    c. They have signs and symptoms that are readily differentiated from those of schizophrenia.

    d. They may have persistent speech problems.

71. Treatment for PCP abusers includes which of the following?

    a. Alkalinizing the urine

    b. Diuretics

    c. Avoiding oral suction

    d. A calm environment

CHAPTER 8

CANNABIS

CHAPTER OBJECTIVE

After studying this chapter, the reader will be able to indicate the short- and long-term effects of cannabis use.

LEARNING OBJECTIVES

After studying this chapter, the reader will be able to

1. Specify epidemiological characteristics of cannabis use.

2. Specify the metabolism of tetrahydrocannabinol (THC).

3. Recognize the subjective effects of marijuana.

4. Indicate therapeutic uses of marijuana.

5. Indicate medical problems related to use of cannabis.

6. Choose treatment for a patient in a marijuana-induced panic state.

INTRODUCTION

Few drugs have produced the controversy that surrounds the use of cannabis in all its forms, including marijuana, hashish, and hashish oil. On one side are the proponents who think that cannabis is harmless and perhaps even beneficial. On the other side are increasing numbers of physicians and researchers who are alarmed at the long half-life of THC, the major chemical found in cannabis, and who point to the serious short- and long-term physical and psychological effects of these drugs. Many of the opponents of cannabis urge much more stringent laws to reduce sales and use of this illicit drug (Ray & Ksir, 1993).

Marijuana is the common name for a herb known as hemp, or *Cannabis sativa*. It has been used for centuries and is a drug that has been tried by a significant part of the population. Currently, it is the most widely used illicit drug in Western society (Ray & Ksir, 1993).

HISTORY

Cannabis was used at least 6,000 years ago. The first detailed description of it appeared in the writings of the Chinese emperor Shen-Nung in 2700 B.C.E.

Marijuana was used for cult rituals and for relieving pain. Hashish, the concentrated resin of *C. sativa*, was eaten in the Middle East during the Middle Ages. The derivation of the word *hashish* may be from the Arabic word for dry grass or from "Hasan-ibn-al-Sabbah," a writer of the 11th century. Marco Polo reported use of hashish in his story about the old man of the mountain and the assassins (Hashishims), whose loyalty to their prince was due in part to the euphoria from a drug. Marco Polo mistakenly thought the drug was opium (White & Albana, 1974).

The Western world largely ignored cannabis until the late 1700s, when its medicinal qualities were praised by a British physician, W. B. O'Shaughnessy, then working in India. He reported the analgesic, anticonvulsant, and muscle-relaxant properties of the drug in 1841. Physicians in the Middle East and Far East had prescribed cannabis preparations for centuries. In 1840, marijuana was prescribed as a sedative, hypnotic, and analgesic and for treatment of uterine dysfunction, dysmenorrhea, and tetanus (Hofmann & Hofmann, 1975). Marijuana remained in the United States Pharmacopoeia until 1941.

By 1936, every state had laws regulating the use, possession, and sale of marijuana. In 1937, the federal government passed the Marijuana Tax Act, which made it extremely difficult to buy or sell marijuana but did not outlaw its use. Soon after, laws were enacted that made possession of the plant *C. sativa* illegal (Ray & Ksir, 1993).

In 1964, THC was first isolated by a team of Israeli scientists. THC is the most psychoactive cannabinoid, the chief intoxicant of hemp. Nine other cannabinoids are included in the THC class, but they have not been studied to any degree. In all, *C. sativa* contains 400 other compounds in addition to THC. These include 61 with psychoactive properties and more carcinogens than tobacco.

During the 1960s and 1970s, marijuana use increased among the middle-class, young, female, and rural populations. Use of marijuana among high school seniors peaked in 1979 (Weiss & Millman, 1991). In 1980, use began declining among young adults, but surveys showed that those who began using marijuana in high school tended to continue its use in adulthood (Hubbard et al., 1989).

CURRENT IMPACT

The National Household Survey on Drug Abuse reported that the number of marijuana users (use within the 30 days preceding the survey) declined 36% between 1985 and 1988, although visits to the emergency department related to marijuana intoxication more than doubled for unclear reasons (Sidney, 1990). Marijuana continues to be the most popular illicit drug in America. Up to 50 million to 60 million persons try it on at least one occasion, and 18 million smoke it on a regular basis (Lee & Bennett, 1991; Schuckit, 1989).

Cannabis users are reported from 120 countries, of which 25 fall into the high-use category. Users come from all age groups and social strata (Arif & Westermeyer, 1988). However, most users are young adults in urban or semiurban areas in almost all areas of the world (Weiss & Millman, 1991). The average marijuana user in the United States is 18–25 years old.

Marijuana is sometimes called the "gateway" drug to more drug use. Habits of drinking and using drugs are established during youth and often persist into adulthood. These habits lead to further experimentation and drug use. Use of drugs during the early years is associated with low educational achievement, dropping out of school, and increased incidence of mortality and morbidity (Yu & Williford, 1992).

SCHEDULE OF CONTROLLED SUBSTANCES

Marijuana and the tetrahydrocannabinols are schedule I drugs (Nahas, 1992).

Therapeutic Uses

Marijuana or THC has been evaluated for use as an analgesic, antiemetic, antidepressant, hypnotic, tranquilizer, and relaxant and as a treatment for withdrawal symptoms, and glaucoma. In general, the results are less than useful. However, THC has been used to decrease intraocular pressure in patients with glaucoma, as an antiemetic in terminal cancer, and as an agent to relieve signs and symptoms of asthma. It is also being studied for use in the treatment of multiple sclerosis (Nahas, 1992; Schuckit, 1989). Younger patients seem to do better with the drug. Older patients are more likely to complain about the unpleasant side effects, such as lack of coordination, dizziness, and ataxia (American Medical Association, 1986).

Recently, there has been a big push, especially in the western United States, to legalize cannabis for medical use. Legalization of marijuana is a matter of great controversy. AIDS patients think using marijuana would help relieve nausea and vomiting and decrease pain and anxiety. Some physicians and researchers think that the benefits do not outweigh the drawbacks. They also suspect this push is nothing more than an effort to legalize an illegal drug.

Nontherapeutic Uses

Marijuana is used recreationally at all levels of society. Small doses produce a feeling of euphoria, relaxation, and congeniality similar to those produced by small amounts of alcohol. The user may feel intoxicated, dizzy, sleepy, or dreamy. His vision seems sharper, and he seems more aware of his environment. Time seems to move very slowly, and he may have increased sexual interest. In this relaxed state, he laughs easily.

Routes of Administration

For illicit use, marijuana usually is rolled in paper (called a "joint") and smoked or is smoked through a water pipe or "bong." Marijuana can be boiled and served as a tea or eaten in food. The drug is rarely injected because of the unpleasant side effects of severe pain and inflammation at the injection site (Cox et al., 1983). Equipment used

for administering recreational drugs is called "drug paraphernalia."

For medical use, THC is prepared in gelatin capsules and given orally. The oral dose must be three to five times greater than the smoked dose to produce the same effects.

BIOCHEMISTRY

Cannabis sativa is a leafy plant that grows well in warm climates. As mentioned earlier, it contains more than 60 cannabinoids and more than 400 different chemicals. THC, derived from the resin secreted by *C. sativa,* has psychostimulating and psychodepressant properties as well as hallucinogenic properties (Weiss & Millman, 1991). THC can be categorized with the hallucinogens, but it differs from them in that it produces hallucinations only at very high doses.

Cannabis sativa is used primarily for hemp rope, chicken feed, bird seed, and an ingredient to speed drying of commercial paints. The THC content of hemp is about 0.2%.

Marijuana is made by drying a mixture of the plant's leaves, small stems, and flowering tops. Hashish oil is made by extracting the drug ingredients from the cannabis plant with solvents such as alcohol or petroleum products such as gasoline. The resulting dark syrup is the most potent form of cannabis.

The derivatives of *C. sativa* (marijuana, hash, and hashish oil) contain variable amounts of THC. For example, marijuana contains 1–10%, and hashish oil may contain up to 60%.

THC potency refers to the mind-altering potential of an individual sample of marijuana. For example, 1% THC potency is enough to produce a mild euphoria. Marijuana from Latin America has a THC potency of 3–4%, whereas sinsemilla (seedless) plants contain 8–10% THC or higher. The potency of the average marijuana cigarette is about

5–6% (Holbrook, 1991b). The potency of marijuana depends on which part of the plant it comes from. Stems are less potent than leaves, and leaves are less potent than flowering tops. THC is formed photochemically from other plant alkaloids, and its potency is increased by sunshine (Ray & Ksir, 1993).

When broken down by burning, the more than 400 chemicals in the natural form of marijuana produce more than 2,000 chemicals, many of which are irritating to the lungs. Marijuana smoke contains twice as many carcinogens as tobacco smoke does. Some of the nonpsychomimetic ingredients in marijuana, particularly cannabinol and cannabichromene, may be more damaging than THC to some body systems (Mann, 1985).

When THC is smoked, about half of it is absorbed, and the drug is metabolized primarily by the lungs. Effects develop in 20–30 min and last 2–3 hr, depending on the dose. With oral THC, more is absorbed, and the drug is metabolized primarily by the liver. Effects occur in 30–60 min and lasting about 8 hr.

THC moves rapidly from the bloodstream into the tissues, where it accumulates, especially in areas of high fat, including the, testes, spleen, adrenal glands, heart, and brain. THC is slowly released from the fat back into the systemic circulation.

THC has a half-life of about 7 days, and measurable amounts remain in the body as long as a month. If a person uses marijuana more than once a month, the residue levels of THC build up in the body.

Marijuana and individual cannabinoids such as THC may diminish the body's ability to manufacture DNA, RNA, and essential proteins. It is also thought that THC may have important effects on the dopamine system and that it may interact with benzodiazepine receptors (Schuckit, 1989).

Subjective Effects

The psychoactive effects of cannabis vary depending on the personality of the user, his expectations, the setting, and his degree of relaxation and feelings of well-being. The effects may include euphoria, relaxation, introspection, enhanced socialization, compulsive laughter, interest in performing tasks that usually seem boring and repetitive, altered perception of time and distance, floating sensations, depersonalization, and perceptual changes of hearing and vision.

The overall experience is generally perceived as pleasant. However, negative subjective effects may occur, including suspiciousness, aggressiveness, paranoid delusions, social withdrawal, hallucinations, confusion, and panic (Ray & Ksir, 1993).

Physiological Effects

Short-term physiological effects include an increased heart rate, tremors, slight hypothermia or hyperthermia, hypotension, loss of balance, decreased motor coordination, impaired short-term memory, decreased intraocular pressure, conjunctival irritation, increased hunger, nausea, vomiting, and restlessness. Long-term physiological effects include stuffy nose, bronchitis, decreased immune function, and abnormal sleeping and eating patterns (Beasley, 1990; Ray & Ksir, 1993).

Tolerance

Tolerance to most of the physiological and neuropsychological effects of THC occurs rapidly with long-term use even when the dose is low. Tolerance is quickly lost when the drug is no longer used or is used infrequently. Mild cross-tolerance of marijuana and alcohol occurs (Ray & Ksir, 1993).

MARIJUANA-RELATED MEDICAL PROBLEMS

Psychological Problems

Panic reactions. Cannabis-induced panic reactions usually last 5–8 hr. They may occur in any user but are more common in users with preexisting psychopathologic conditions. Most users do not have chronic cannabis-induced panic reactions. Others experience the reactions every time they use the drug, and some continue to experience panic reactions or agoraphobia or both even after they discontinue marijuana use (Schuckit, 1989; Weiss & Millman, 1991).

Flashbacks. Marijuana-induced flashbacks can occur in both frequent and infrequent users. The feelings and perceptions experienced in the intoxicated state recur at a lower intensity and last only a few minutes (Holbrook, 1991b; Schuckit, 1989).

Toxic reactions. At high doses, increased muscle rigidity, myoclonus, hallucinations and delusions, organic brain syndrome, and delirium can occur. The reaction is not generally life-threatening, even when induced by hashish (Holbrook, 1991b).

Temporary psychosis. A psychotic disorder characterized by paranoid delusions, visual hallucinations, bizarre behavior, violence, and panic can be precipitated by cannabis use. This state, which is indistinguishable from schizophrenia, clears up within a few weeks unless the patient has preexisting psychiatric problems (Schuckit, 1989; Weiss & Millman, 1991).

Organic brain syndrome. Organic brain syndrome is a temporary clouding of the mental processes characterized by impaired tracking ability, decreased short-term memory, decreased ability to concentrate, and impaired learning. It may be partly caused by adulterants, and it should clear up with abstinence (Schuckit, 1989).

Amotivational cannabis syndrome. Amotivational cannabis syndrome is characterized by apathy, decreased goal-directed activities, impaired concentration, abrupt mood swings, abnormal irritability and hostility, and neglect of personal appearance. Some patients also experience panic reactions, paranoia, depression, and suicidal ideations and attempts. Abstinence reverses these symptoms if the patient has no severe psychopathologic condition (Holbrook, 1991b; Weiss & Millman, 1991).

Physiological Problems

Lungs. The acute effect of marijuana is dilation of the bronchial tree, but long-term use may cause constriction and a form of asthma. Other problems include a decrease in vital capacity; pneumonitis; tracheobronchitis; tar deposits; and cancer, particularly of the tongue, jaw, and lung (Holbrook, 1991b; Schuckit, 1989).

The components of a marijuana cigarette and those of a tobacco cigarette, aside from the cannabinoids, contain many of the same ingredients. However, the two types of cigarettes are smoked differently. Generally, a tobacco smoker inhales and holds the smoke in his lungs for an average of 2 sec, whereas a marijuana smoker draws smoke more deeply into his lungs and holds it there more than 2 sec.

Hand-rolled marijuana cigarettes are not filtered as most commercially available tobacco cigarettes are. Also, most tobacco smokers put out their cigarettes without smoking the last half inch. Marijuana smokers, however, smoke the last half inch, where the cannabinoids and cancer-causing chemicals are found in the highest concentrations. About 80% of marijuana smokers also smoke regular cigarettes, doubling the smokers' exposure to tars, nicotine, and THC (DuPont, 1984).

Marijuana cigarettes also contain higher amounts of polynuclear aromatic hydrocarbons, a generic term used to describe a group of compounds isolated from coal tars and other products of combustion, many of which are carcinogenic (Mann, 1985). Marijuana smoke is almost always contaminated with spores of the common soil fungus *Aspergillus,* which can cause aspergillosis, a serious, resistant lung disease. In addition, marijuana smoke contains many more respiratory irritants than tobacco smoke does.

Marijuana is definitely more harmful than tobacco. Marijuana has more carcinogens, carbon monoxide, and hydrogen cyanide, and the smoke is much harsher. One joint can be equivalent to anywhere from three to five cigarettes to one pack of cigarettes. DuPont (1984) notes, "Whatever tobacco smoke does to human lungs, marijuana smoke does more and does it more quickly." Nose and throat. Marijuana use can cause laryngitis, sinusitis, and pharyngitis (Holbrook, 1991b).

Heart. Marijuana causes increases in blood pressure and heart rate and a decrease in the strength of cardiac contractions. Although the drug probably has little impact on a healthy heart, persons with cardiac dysfunction may be affected (Schuckit, 1989).

Immune system. Some evidence suggests that THC decreases the immune response of lymphocytes. Lingering colds, a flulike feeling, chest pain, chronic coughing, hoarseness, bronchitis, and irregular menstrual periods may be indications of a compromised immune system (Ray & Ksir, 1993).

Reproductive system. Heavy marijuana smoking can decrease testosterone levels in males. It

may also cause abnormalities in the structure of sperm (Ray & Ksir, 1993).

Endocrine system. Decreased levels of testosterone and possibly of growth hormone have been shown in heavy marijuana smokers (Schuckit, 1989).

Brain. Heavy marijuana users have abnormal findings on electroencephalograms (EEGs) for up to 3 months after their last use. THC also may act on the limbic system (emotions), and it impairs memory (Schuckit, 1989).

Injuries. Accidents can occur because of altered perceptions of time and distance, and decreased judgment (Schuckit, 1989).

Effects on the Fetus

Studies on the potential effects of THC on the unborn child are often inconclusive and contradictory. However, it seems likely that the drug can have an effect. Various studies have suggested that use of marijuana may cause low birth weight, fetal abnormalities, small head circumference, small size, and developmental delay. Others have not supported these findings. Nonlymphoblastic leukemia is 10 times more prevalent in newborns of mothers who smoke marijuana than in newborns of nonsmokers (Nahas, 1992).

WITHDRAWAL

Mild signs and symptoms of withdrawal can occur after cessation of high-dose, long-term use of marijuana. They include insomnia, rebound REM sleep, irritability, decreased appetite, nausea, weight loss, restlessness, and irritability of 4–5 days' duration (Holbrook, 1991b; Schuckit, 1989).

CASE STUDY

Dr. G., a specialist in adolescent psychiatry in Cleveland, described the case of a 17-year-old boy who came to the specialist after the teenager's grades dropped from A's to C's and D's (Mann, 1985). The teenager had dropped out of all extracurricular activities and had become progressively more irritable. He had given up his friends, schoolwork, and every activity except listening to high-volume rock music and had decided that he would become a keyboard player in a rock group—even though he had not played the piano since he took lessons in third grade.

Dr. G. noticed reversed letters in the teenager's handwriting and suggested obtaining an EEG to rule out a learning disability. The neurologist who examined the EEG results likened the 17-year-old's graphs to those of a 7- or 8-year-old with a pronounced learning disability.

The teenager said that his memory seemed to be going bad and that he felt stupid when he was in a group of other people. Further investigation revealed that the teenager regularly used marijuana. He was asked to stop smoking marijuana for 8 weeks, to see if the behavior would improve. He agreed, and another EEG was obtained at the end of the 8 weeks. The second EEG showed some improvement, but the most marked improvement was in the teenager's behavior. His attitude, mood, and humor had returned to presmoking levels, and his grades had improved. The teenager was so encouraged that he stopped smoking marijuana for 2 more months. The findings on an EEG obtained then were normal.

ASSESSMENT

Interview of a patient who uses marijuana might reveal an amotivational syndrome as described in the case study. However, the effects of THC vary with each person.

The history should include psychosocial and medical data and information on drug use and use of medications. A psychiatric history is particularly important for patients who appear to have a marijuana-related psychiatric problem. Laboratory tests may be necessary to rule out other drug use (Weiss & Millman, 1991).

TREATMENT

For most of those who use marijuana occasionally, the drug's effects are of short duration. A few have a drug-induced panic state that lasts 5–8 hr (Schuckit, 1989). In this state, all the effects of marijuana are exaggerated, and the user perceives the environment as threatening. He may fear he is losing control.

After other drug use and any preexisting psychopathological conditions are ruled out, reassurance is all that is needed. The patient can be placed in a quiet room and reassured that his signs and symptoms will clear within the next 4–8 hr. Friends can be allowed to visit to help calm the patient.

No drug treatment is usually needed. However, if the anxiety cannot be controlled, a benzodiazepine can be administered and repeated as needed. The patient should be advised that because of the lingering effects of THC, he may feel mildly drugged and intoxicated for the next few days.

If the anxiety or paranoia seems particularly severe, the patient should be referred to a center that specializes in treating chemical dependency. There he might be given drugs such as haloperidol (Haldol) or chlorpromazine.

Parents should be educated about the seriousness of marijuana use as a gateway to other drug use. They need encouragement to seek appropriate drug treatment for their adolescents or teenagers as early as possible. After the patient is discharged, he and his family should be referred to appropriate treatment programs and community support groups (Weiss & Millman, 1991).

SUMMARY

Cannabis contains many active chemicals, the most potent of which is THC. THC is absorbed through inhalation or ingestion and remains in the body for as long as a month. Marijuana use increases heart rate, alters perception of reality, acts as a sedative, and, at high doses, can produce hallucinations.

Tolerance can occur, and signs and symptoms of withdrawal have been observed. Other current medical concerns are possible adverse effects to the fetus, and increased risk of lung cancer. Use of marijuana impairs driving ability, and marijuana may be a gateway to other drug use.

EXAM QUESTIONS

CHAPTER 8

Questions 72–79

72. Which of the following statements about marijuana (THC) is correct?

    a. It is used most often by older adults.

    b. It is the most popular illicit drug in America.

    c. It is usually injected.

    d. It is used predominately by those in lower income levels.

73. Which of the following statements about the metabolism of THC is correct?

    a. It has a half-life of 7 days.

    b. It accumulates in areas of low fat.

    c. Measurable amounts remain in the body for up to 6 months.

    d. Oral doses are metabolized primarily by the lungs.

74. Which of the following statements about the psychoactive effects of marijuana is correct?

    a. The overall experience is always pleasant.

    b. Panic reactions are common.

    c. Adverse effects include a temporary psychosis easily distinguishable from schizophrenia.

    d. The effects vary according to the personality of the user.

75. Which of the following is characteristic of marijuana-induced organic brain syndrome?

    a. It usually lasts 5–8 hr.

    b. It causes a decrease in long-term memory.

    c. It is unlikely to clear up with abstinence.

    d. It may be due in part to adulterants.

76. Which of the following is a pulmonary effect of long-term use of marijuana?

    a. Dilation of the bronchial tree

    b. Ventilation-perfusion mismatch

    c. Increase in vital capacity

    d. Constriction of the bronchial tree

77. THC has been used therapeutically to do which of the following?

    a. Cause emesis

    b. Decrease intraocular pressure

    c. Suppress the appetite

    d. Increase motivation level

113

78. Medical problems related to use of THC include which of the following?

    a. Increased testosterone levels in males

    b. Agoraphobia

    c. Increased immune response by lymphocytes

    d. Initial amotivational syndrome that resolves with continued use

79. Treatment of a patient in a marijuana-induced panic state includes which of the following?

    a. Starting methadone treatment

    b. Reassuring the patient that the symptoms will clear in 3–4 days

    c. Not allowing friends to help calm the patient

    d. Evaluating the patient for other drug use

CHAPTER 9

SOLVENTS, GLUES, AND AEROSOLS

CHAPTER OBJECTIVE

After studying this chapter, the reader will be able to identify solvents, glues, and aerosols that are abused and recognize their physiological and psychological effects.

LEARNING OBJECTIVES

After studying this chapter, the reader will be able to

1. Indicate the epidemiological characteristics of abuse of inhalants.

2. Specify a therapeutic use of inhalants.

3. Recognize signs and symptoms of solvent inhalation.

4. Specify common routes of administration used by solvent abusers.

5. Indicate the metabolism of inhalants.

6. Recognize medical problems related to abuse of inhalants.

INTRODUCTION

Inhalants, which include solvents, glues, and aerosols, are volatile chemicals at ordinary temperatures. When inhaled, they can alter mood, thinking, and feeling.

The inhalants are favorite drugs of abuse for young persons and, like marijuana, may be the first step on the road to more dangerous drugs. As teenagers mature, most abandon use of these substances and move on to other drugs. However, a small percentage continue to use inhalants as a drug of choice (Ray & Ksir, 1993).

HISTORY

The use of inhalants for their effects goes back to ancient times when ointments and perfumes were used to enhance religious ceremonies in Egypt, Babylon, and Biblical Palestine. In the 16th century, alcohol fumes were inhaled as an anesthetic, and in 1847, chloroform was discovered and used as an anesthetic for surgery and childbirth. Nitrous oxide was first synthesized and used socially in 1776. In the mid-1800s, along with ether, it was used as an anesthetic. These substances were widely abused during the mid-1800s to mid-1900s, generally by patients who had been treated for a legitimate medical problem.

The first cases of abuse of a volatile substance appeared in 1951, when a physician reported two cases of young boys who sniffed glue. During the 1950s and early 1960s, the number of cases involving youths and some adults grew rapidly. Most abused model airplane cements and lighter and cleaning fluids. Various aerosols, gases, propellants, and refrigerants also became popular with inhalant abusers (Schuckit, 1989; Weiss & Millman, 1991).

In the early 1960s, in response to the number of deaths due to benzene and carbon tetrachloride, the Hobby Industry Association of America and toy manufacturers took these products off the market. In a further effort to stop young persons from sniffing glue, the Testor Corporation, the largest manufacturer of plastic cement of the type most often abused in the United States, began adding oil of mustard to the basic formula. When sniffed, this ingredient leads to severe nasal irritation similar to that caused by eating a chunk of horseradish. Cements that include this oil do not affect persons who use the products appropriately.

The federal government banned the use of carbon tetrachloride in any product sold directly to the public, and by the mid-1960s, 26 cities and six states had passed statutes to gain control of the inhalation of solvents. Nevertheless, abuse of the inhalants increased significantly in the late 1960s and 1970s along with multiple-drug use. *Table 9-1* lists some commonly abused products and their solvents (Glowa, 1986; Nahas, 1992; Schuckit, 1989).

CURRENT IMPACT

According to the National Annual High School Senior and Young Adult Survey, inhalant use has fluctuated but has remained within a stable range since 1979. In the 1988 survey, 17.5% of high school seniors reported that they had tried inhalants (Weiss & Millman, 1991).

The percentage of users appears to decrease from junior high school through college. Rates are higher in some minority groups, including Native Americans and Mexican-Americans (Schuckit, 1989).

The average solvent user is 14–17 years old. About four times as many males as females use regularly, and most are multi-drug abusers. School performance is generally poor, emotional disturbance and tension are common, and most users fit the profile of antisocial personality disorder. Users have a less stable home environment than their peers who do not abuse solvents, and most are in the lower socioeconomic classes (Glowa, 1986). In one study of 130 solvent users (Dinwiddie, Reich, & Cloninger, 1991), solvent use did not clearly precede the use of other substances. Typically, alcohol and cannabis were used first and then the solvents. In addition, solvent users were 5 to 10 times more likely than nonusers to abuse opioids, stimulants, depressants, and hallucinogens.

As in other types of abuse, solvent sniffing usually occurs as experimentation in a group setting. Most children sample an inhalant a few times and then never do so again, either because the experience was unpleasant or because it did not provide enough reinforcement for continued use. Others occasionally or "socially" abuse inhalants, perhaps using once a month or so. Sniffing the solvent is often only a way to be one of the group, and does not become a habit. Others use inhalants daily and are at the greatest risk of physical and psychological damage from these agents. Solvent sniffing, especially of the halogenated hydrocarbons (often found in cleaning fluid) is associated with a significant risk of death (Schuckit, 1989).

Although solvent abuse is primarily a problem among the young and the poor, these substances are also abused by high-functioning, affluent, educated, middle-class persons. In a study of attitudes of Native American youth, eighth-grade reservation youth had low belief that drugs are harmful and thought that marijuana and the inhalants were easy to obtain (Beauvais, 1992).

TABLE 9-1
Household Products Containing Psychoactive Solvents Product

Product	*Solvent*
Adhesives	Toluene
Aerosol propellant	Fluorocarbons, trichloroethylene, toluene
Antifreeze	Isopropanol
Bottled fuel gas	Isobutane, propane, butane
Cleaning fluid	Trichloroethane, naphtha, perchloroethylene, trichloroethylene, carbon tetrachloride, toluene, methylene chloride
Fingernail polish remover	Acetone, aliphatic acetates
Fire extinguisher	Bromochlorodiflouromethane
Gasoline	Hydrocarbons, lead, tricresyl phosphate
Industrial solvents	Chlorinated hydrocarbons, hexane, toluene, benzene, aliphatic acetates
Ink	Toluene, chlorinated hydrocarbons
Lacquer thinner	Toulene
Lighter fluid	Naphtha
Liquid shoe polish	Toluene, chlorinated hydrocarbons
Plastic (styrene) cement	Toluene, acetone, hexane, trichloroethylene, benzene
Room deodorizers	Butyl nitrite
Rubber cement	Benezene, hexane, trichloroethylene
Toy model cements	Toluene, acetone, naphtha, hexane, alcohols, aliphatic acetates, tricresyl phosphate, hexane

Source: A Manual on Drug Dependence by G. Nahas. Essential Medical Information Systems, Inc. 1992. Reprinted with permission.

SCHEDULE OF CONTROLLED SUBSTANCES

The inhalants are not controlled substances.

Therapeutic Uses

Alcohol, chloroform, ether, and trichloroethylene were once used as analgesics and anesthetics. They have been superseded by less inflammatory and more predictable gaseous agents. Nitrous oxide is currently used as an anesthetic in dentistry. Amyl and butyl nitrite have been used in the treatment of angina (Arif & Westermeyer, 1988).

Nontherapeutic Uses

The inhalants are used recreationally mostly by adolescents and teenagers for the euphoric effects. Nitrous oxide and amyl and butyl nitrite are often abused by a particular group of adults (Nahas, 1992).

Routes of Administration

Legitimate and therapeutic administration of an anesthetic by a dentist or doctor is guided by current medical regulations. Solvents are usually inhaled through the nose and mouth, but they can be taken orally in liquid form.

Nontherapeutic methods of inhalation include inhaling from an open container, filling a bag or balloon with the inhalant and holding it over the head, and pouring the solvent on a cloth and holding the cloth to the mouth and nose (Nahas, 1992; Schuckit, 1989). The concentration of the solvent can be increased by warming the bottle or can. Warming can produce vapor concentrations 50 times the maximum allowable industrial concentration (Arif & Westermeyer, 1988).

Euphoria occurs in a few minutes. Continuous inhalation of the vapors eventually causes loss of consciousness. If the bag falls from the hand and mouth, deep respiratory depression and death can be avoided. This sequence does not occur when a plastic bag is used. The plastic is nonporous, and a tight seal is established between the mouth and the bag. The bag does not automatically fall away when consciousness is lost. When it does not, suffocation is eminent. Plastic bag suffocation is one of the leading causes of death among young persons who sniff solvents. Suffocation may also occur when a user inhales freon gas, because the gas can freeze the airway, cutting off all air flow (Glowa, 1986).

BIOCHEMISTRY

Solvents, glues, and aerosols produce rapid intoxication because they are quickly absorbed over the large surface of the lungs, enter the bloodstream, and are carried directly to the brain and other body tissues.

Solvents are fat soluble and concentrate in fat-rich tissues such as the brain, lungs, heart, and kidneys. The liver and intestines have fewer blood vessels, so the solvent concentration in these areas increases more slowly.

Solvents are metabolized in both the kidneys and the liver and are eliminated from the body primarily through the lungs. They also can be metabolized into a water-soluble form and eliminated through the urine or skin. Some of the water-soluble forms are more harmful than the original solvent (e.g., acetaldehyde, which is a metabolite of alcohol).

Solvents are thought to alter the neurotransmitter systems in the brain and produce a depressive effect (Glowa, 1986; Miller, 1991; Weiss & Millman, 1991).

Psychological Effects

Inhalation produces an immediate effect, ranging from mild dizziness to delusions (extraordinary strength, or the ability to fly), or auditory hallucinations similar to those experienced with other psychomimetic drugs. Almost all abusers feel giddy, carefree, drunk, and euphoric and have a sense of increased power and reckless abandon. Some feel numb or as if they are floating on air.

These feelings last for the duration of the inhalation, usually 15–45 min. This period is followed by 1 or 2 hr of drowsiness and stupor and then a return to normalcy. Several unpleasant side effects can occur during the sniffing episodes; most of the effects are transient (Beasley, 1990; Schuckit, 1989; Weiss & Millman, 1991).

The most dangerous time, with the exception of unconsciousness, is in the midst of the feeling of power and weightlessness. During this period, a user may injure himself by jumping from a high place.

Physiological Effects

Signs and symptoms of inhalant use include ataxia, slurred speech, photophobia, conjunctivitis, double vision, tinnitus, nasal inflammation, chest pain, heart beat irregularities or arrhythmias, faintness, loss of consciousness, peripheral neuropathy, organic brain syndrome, wheezing, coughing, rhinitis, aplastic anemia, leukopenia, weakness, nausea, vomiting, anorexia, diarrhea, hepatitis, pancreatitis, and renal failure (Beasley, 1990; Schuckit, 1989; Weiss & Millman, 1991).

Although many organic solvents, in large doses, can induce an acute, reversible narcotic state, few induce long-term, long-lasting, or irreversible changes in the structure or function of the nervous system (Spencer & Schaumby, 1985). However, at high doses, inhalants can lead to rapid loss of control and loss of consciousness, putting the abuser at risk for potential overdose and for death due to respiratory arrest, cardiac arrhythmias, or irreversible damage to the brain and other body tissues.

Tolerance

Many users become psychologically dependent on the effects they get from sniffing solvents. Some even have a favorite brand of solvent, glue, or aerosol. However, there is little evidence that any solvents are physically addicting. Large doses induce tolerance within a week, and sudden deaths have occurred because of collapsed lungs and suffocation. Smaller amounts induce tolerance after a longer period of exposure. Signs and symptoms of withdrawal do not occur, even after long-term use (Schuckit, 1989; Weiss & Millman, 1991).

INHALANT-RELATED MEDICAL PROBLEMS

Most fatalities are caused by the inhalation of butane (28%), adhesive solvents (23%), cleaning-fluid solvents (26%), aerosols (5%), and material in fire extinguishers (5%) (Nahas, 1992).

Psychological Effects

Panic attacks are quickly over, because the period of intoxication is only 15 min to 1 hr (Schuckit, 1989). Flashbacks do not occur with use of inhalants (Schuckit, 1989). Organic brain syndrome is common in long-term abusers of inhalants. Characteristics of the syndrome include confusion, decreased intellectual functioning, impairment of recent memory, and an inability to think through problems (Schuckit, 1989).

Benzene Toxic Effects

Benzene, which is classified as an aromatic hydrocarbon, is extremely toxic. It can produce bone marrow aplastic anemia and necrosis or fatty degeneration of the heart, liver, and adrenal glands. It can also cause dyspepsia, anorexia, and chronic gastritis. Its CNS effects include headache, drowsiness, and irritability. Benzene is often implicated in toxic effects that involve the bone marrow and in cases of leukemia (Senay, 1983). It is a common ingredient in many dry-cleaning fluids (Arif & Westermeyer, 1988).

Toluene Toxic Effects

Toluene is much less toxic than benzene. Until the 1970s, commercial toluene was combined with as much as 20% benzene, a practice that led to marked toxic effects among workers who handled these compounds. More recently, toluene has been highly purified and now contains only a small amount of benzene. Long-term exposure of laboratory animals to toluene causes scattered abnormalities in the brain and spinal cord, patchy loss of myelin, and decreased Purkinje fibers in the CNS.

Long-term effects of toluene include nausea, vomiting, discomfort, anorexia, jaundice, and hepatomegaly. The urinary tract is also affected, and patients may have pyuria, hematuria, proteinuria, and renal tubular necrosis. Hematopoietic abnormalities, such as reversible anemia, have been reported. Mental dullness, tremors, emotional liability, nystagmus, cerebellar ataxia, and permanent encephalopathies also can occur (Arif & Westermeyer, 1988; Weiss & Millman, 1991).

Trichloroethylene Toxic Effects

Trichloroethylene is halogenated hydrocarbon that can produce cardiac arrhythmias, a well-known problem when it is used to induce anesthesia during surgery and a cause of death in industrial settings. Carbona, a cleaning fluid that contains trichloroethylene, has been linked to hepatotoxic effects (Arif & Westermeyer, 1988).

Carbon Tetrachloride Toxic Effects

Carbon tetrachloride, a highly toxic solvent, can produce renal and hepatic failure, which are accompanied by convulsions. Because of its violent effects, it has been almost eliminated from commercial products (Nahas, 1992; Weiss & Millman, 1991).

CASE STUDY

Although it is difficult to predict who will use inhalants, researchers have created a profile of the typical abuser. The following case study describes a woman who closely fits the picture (Glowa, 1986).

The patient was a 23-year-old woman with a high school education and a 10-year history of drug abuse. She was physically dependent on aerosol spray paints. For 2 years, she sniffed paints, plastic enamels, and paint thinners daily for up to 5 hr/day. She would place a paint-saturated cloth in her mouth and inhale the vapors, a practice that kept her continuously intoxicated. Typically, the paint contained toluene.

The woman's parents, both alcoholics, were separated. Her social life was limited, and her own marriage had ended in separation. She had been arrested at least 30 times, once for assaulting a policeman. Twice, she had become so depressed that she had taken drugs in an attempt to commit suicide.

When she was admitted to the hospital, she complained of chronic muscular pain and a loss of sensation in her hands and feet. However, a routine physical examination revealed no sensory or neuromuscular problems. Although toxicological tests did not detect the presence of any drugs, the results of further tests suggested the possibility of a developing muscular abnormality. Previously, she had been hospitalized for acute organic brain syndrome, or brain damage, a common diagnosis given to solvent abusers. After 16 days of treatment, she was discharged.

ASSESSMENT

During the initial interview, patients with suspected solvent intoxication should be assessed for indications of impaired judgment, slurred speech, ataxia, impulsiveness, inappropriate affect, and delusions. The level of care needed should be determined at this time.

The initial history should include psychosocial, medical, and psychiatric information and data on drug use (Schuckit, 1989). Laboratory tests can detect toluene and many other inhalants or their metabolites in the blood for 4–6 hr after use of the substance and in the urine for 4 hr after use (Weiss & Millman, 1991).

TREATMENT

Some young abusers of inhalants have life-threatening conditions, including respiratory depression and cardiac arrhythmias, which can cause rapid loss of consciousness and sudden death. Sudden death sometimes occurs after the user has engaged in some form of physical activity just before or while sniffing the solvent. Most persons who seek medical help are anxious and have some degree of mental impairment.

Inhalant abusers need treatment in structured treatment programs that include participation by the abuser's family (see chapter 2). Ideally, adolescents should be treated in adolescent treatment programs. Hospitalization is needed for severe signs and symptoms, most of which are quickly reversible (Arif & Westermeyer, 1988; Schuckit, 1989; Weiss & Millman, 1991).

SUMMARY

Inhalants are breathable chemicals that produce mind-altering effects. Most of them produce effects similar to those of anesthetics. That is, low doses cause a slight stimulation, larger doses cause a decrease in inhibition and control, and high doses can produce loss of consciousness. Inhalants are especially popular among children and teenagers, probably because the products containing the solvents are easily obtained and inexpensive.

EXAM QUESTIONS

CHAPTER 9
Questions 80–87

80. Which of the following statements about solvents, glues, and aerosols is correct?

   a. They are dangerous only if they result in a loss of consciousness.

   b. They are especially popular among adolescents and teenagers.

   c. Moderate signs and symptoms of withdrawal occur when use is discontinued.

   d. Products containing them are difficult to obtain.

81. Which of the following is characteristic of abuse of inhalants?

   a. Abuse appears to increase from junior high school through college.

   b. Four times as many females as males are abusers.

   c. Persons who abuse inhalants usually do not use other drugs.

   d. Abuse usually occurs as an experimentation in a group setting.

82. Which of the following is a current use of nitrous oxide?

   a. Treatment of depression

   b. Treatment of angina

   c. Recreational use by scuba divers

   d. Anesthesia in dentistry

83. Which of the following is a common route of administration used by solvent abusers?

   a. Swallowing a tablet soaked with the solvent

   b. Filling a bag with the solvent and holding the bag over the head

   c. Inhaling the smoke produced by burning a paper soaked with the solvent

   d. Cooling an aerosol can that contains the solvent and spraying the cooled solvent into the mouth

84. Which of the following statements about the metabolism of solvents is correct?

   a. They concentrate in tissues that are high in fat.

   b. Their water-soluble metabolites are less harmful than the fat-soluble ones.

   c. They are metabolized solely in the liver.

   d. They are eliminated primarily through the urine.

85. How long after the last use can many of the inhalants or their metabolites be detected in the blood?

   a. No more than 30 min

   b. 4–6 hr

   c. 1–2 days

   d. 3–4 weeks

86. Under what circumstances can inhalant abuse cause sudden death?

    a. If the user has pancreatitis

    b. If the user exercises after inhaling the solvent

    c. If use of the solvent is suddenly stopped

    d. If respiratory depression and cardiac arrhythmias develop

87. Which of the following statements about the effects of inhalants is correct?

    a. Low doses produce intense stimulation.

    b. Intoxication occurs rapidly.

    c. Decreasing the dose causes decreased inhibition.

    d. High doses always cause loss of consciousness.

CHAPTER 10

OVER-THE-COUNTER DRUGS

CHAPTER OBJECTIVE

After studying this chapter, the reader will be able to recognize how OTC drugs are abused and the population most likely to abuse them.

LEARNING OBJECTIVES

After studying this chapter, the reader will be able to

1. Indicate characteristics of various OTC products.

2. Select characteristics of abusers of OTC products.

3. Recognize the effects of OTC products that are most commonly abused.

4. Specify medical problems that can result from abuse of various OTC products.

INTRODUCTION

A large variety of OTC substances are available on the market, including diet pills, antihistamines, antianxiety agents, sleeping aids, and laxatives. These products are legal, inexpensive, and often misused (Schuckit, 1989; Woolf & Moore, 1991).

HISTORY

Use of OTC products dates back to the earliest times when pharmacists prepared compounds to improve sleep and boost energy. In many parts of the world, this practice continues, and natural herbs and ingredients are freely dispensed. As noted in earlier chapters, even hazardous products such as opium, cocaine, and hashish were once thought to be beneficial medications and were available either locally or through mail-order catalogs (Schuckit, 1989).

CURRENT IMPACT

More than 500,000 different OTC drugs are on the market in the United States (Schuckit, 1989). These drugs are often addictive and are often abused by persons who self-medicate. The abuse may occur because the user cannot afford medical care, does not have a regular physician, or lacks knowledge about the products. General information offered on television or as advertisements in magazines and newspapers is not sufficient to inform the public of potential dangers.

The most frequent users of OTC drugs are white, middle-class women. The elderly, particularly elderly women, are far more likely to self-medicate with OTC products than are any other age group. This group accounts for the purchase of two of every five OTC products (Schuckit, 1989).

Seven groups of potentially addictive OTC products are stimulants, antihistamines (sedative-hypnotics), cold and allergy products, analgesics, laxatives, weight control aids, and bromides. Each of these is discussed later in the chapter.

SCHEDULE OF CONTROLLED SUBSTANCES

Most of the OTC drugs are classified as schedule V drugs (Nahas, 1992).

Therapeutic Uses

OTC drugs are nonprescription substances that have a variety of uses. Examples are analgesics, hypnotics, antianxiety drugs, antihistamines (for colds and allergies), laxatives, stimulants, diet pills, and diuretics (Schuckit, 1989; Woolf & Moore, 1991).

Nontherapeutic Uses

OTC drugs can be used for their effects, as part of socialization (caffeine in coffee), or as adulterants for street drugs (Woolf & Moore, 1991). Usually the OTC drugs are not indicated by patients as their primary drugs of choice. These medications have a low abuse potential in persons who do not have preexisting psychopathologic conditions (Woolf & Moore, 1991).

Routes of Administration

OTC medications are taken orally in the form of liquids, powders, and pills. As adulterants in street drugs, OTC drugs may unknowingly be sniffed, smoked, or injected (Woolf & Moore, 1991).

STIMULANTS

Of the approximately 16 million Americans who use OTC stimulants, two thirds are men, and use by employed men and students is increasing (Schuckit, 1989). Stimulants found in OTC products include caffeine, ephedrine, and phenylpropanolamine (see section on weight control aids).

Biochemistry

Caffeine is a bitter alkaloid found in teas, coffee, and kola nuts. It is the most powerful ingredient found in most OTC stimulants. A cup of coffee contains about 75–125 mg of caffeine. The OTC stimulant No-Doz contains 100 mg, and Vivarin contains 200 mg. A mild stimulating effect that restores mental alertness makes caffeine the most popular psychotropic drug in North America. Adults consume 200 mg per capita daily, 90% in the form of coffee. The average coffee drinker consumes 500–600 mg of caffeine each day (Ray & Ksir, 1993; Schuckit, 1989). Low doses of caffeine have mild and often beneficial effects, but high doses can cause adverse effects.

When taken orally, caffeine appears in body tissues within 5 min and is entirely absorbed from the gastrointestinal tract within 45–120 min. It is metabolized in the liver into xanthine metabolites, which are excreted through the kidneys. Its half-life is 2.5–7.0 hr (Beasley, 1990).

Physiological Effects

At higher doses caffeine has significant physiological effects, including the following.

Cardiovascular effects. Caffeine increases heart rate, contractility, and output. It can cause arrhythmias and possible heart attacks from the increase in fatty acids. It also increases blood pressure, cerebral vascular constriction, and systemic vascular dilation.

Respiratory effects. Respiratory effects of caffeine include an increase in breathing rate. It may also relax smooth muscle (bronchi).

CNS effects. Caffeine increases motor activity by directly stimulating all levels of the CNS. The effects include an increased capacity for skeletal muscle work and increased muscle tension.

Renal and gastrointestinal effects. Initially, caffeine has a direct diuretic action. It also increases gastric secretion and acidity, contraction of gut muscle, and esophageal sphincter pressure.

Endocrine effects. Caffeine causes reactive hypoglycemia.

Psychological Effects

At recommended doses, caffeine causes productive flow of thought and increased efficiency and a decrease in drowsiness and fatigue (Arif & Westermeyer, 1988; Holbrook, 1991c; Ray & Ksir, 1993).

Tolerance

High doses of caffeine, 600 mg/day, produce tolerance, especially to cardiovascular effects. Small daily amounts of caffeine can cause mild tolerance (Arif & Westermeyer, 1988; Holbrook, 1991c). Toxic effects can occur in patients who drink coffee after taking therapeutic doses of theophylline (Beasley, 1990).

Related Medical Problems

Fibrocystic breast disease. Fibrocystic breast disease is characterized by the development of benign lumps in the breast and is thought to be due to the production of a growth-promoting substance in the breast tissues. In some studies, women with fibrocystic breast disease had levels of the growth-promoting substance at least 50% higher than the levels in women without the disease (Schuckit, 1989; Ray & Ksir, 1993).

Insomnia. Forty percent of regular heavy users of caffeine report sleeplessness (Schuckit, 1989).

Headache. Caffeine's vasoconstrictive effects can reduce headaches both in users and in persons who do not use the stimulant regularly (Ray & Ksir, 1993).

Neuromuscular problems. Neuromuscular problems associated with use of caffeine include "restless" legs and arms and persistent tremors.

Cancer. Cancer of the bladder and lower urinary tract, kidney, and pancreas are more likely in users than in persons who do not use caffeine (Beasley, 1990; Schuckit, 1989).

Drug interactions and effects. Caffeine in high doses can interact with other drugs to increase urinary levels of catecholamines. Excessive caffeine may cause a hypertensive crisis when used in conjunction with monoamine oxidase inhibitors. Oral contraceptives can reduce the excretion of caffeine, and caffeine given to patients taking large doses of propoxyphene (Darvon) can cause convulsions.

Some nasal sprays and antiasthmatic products, for example, contain ephedrine. Ingestion of large amounts of these products can cause amphetamine-type psychosis. Ephedrine and phenylpropanolamine have also been found in street samples of cocaine and amphetamines (Holbrook, 1991c).

Coexisting psychiatric disorders. Schizophrenia-type disorders can be exacerbated when caffeine is ingested. The caffeine acts as an antagonist of antipsychotic medications (Schuckit, 1989).

Effects on the fetus. The half-life of caffeine is prolonged in pregnancy and in the newborn. The drug is excreted in breast milk (Nahas, 1992). If a mother continues to breast-feed while using caffeine, the baby may respond by being restless. For a while after birth, all babies, whether full-term or premature, lack the enzyme required to metabolize caffeine. If, in addition to using caffeine, the mother smokes tobacco, the baby has an increased risk of having a lower birth weight (McKay & Scavnicky-Mylant, 1991).

Withdrawal

Signs and symptoms of withdrawal from caffeine include headache, increased sleep, depression, lethargy, excessive yawning, restlessness, constipation, dull mental state, cravings, and irritability. People who drink high doses of coffee during the week at work find that they need to consume caffeine on the weekends to avoid withdrawal (Holbrook, 1991c; Ray & Ksir, 1993; Schuckit, 1989).

Assessment

Assessment of patients who overuse caffeine includes a history and a physical examination. They should be evaluated for emergency medical needs and for detoxification.

Treatment

Detoxification of a person who overuses caffeine consists of a gradual reduction in intake. The number of cups of coffee drunk daily is reduced by one cup each day until the person is caffeine-free. If necessary, decaffeinated coffee, tea, or juice can be substituted for regular coffee. Constipation may be a problem and can be treated with a mild laxative or high-fiber diet and water (Beasley, 1990).

The person should be educated about the health implications of caffeine use and should be referred for further medical or psychiatric treatment as needed, particularly if the person has a coexisting psychiatric disorder or is pregnant (Holbrook, 1991c; Ray & Ksir, 1993; Schuckit, 1989).

Psychiatric patients who are taking antipsychotic medications should be informed that restricting the use of coffee results in improvement in caffeine-related problems within a few days, even within hours for some patients (Schuckit, 1989).

ANTIHISTAMINES

Women tend to use antihistamines much more often than men do. Two thirds of the women are more than 35 years old, and half are more than 50 years old. The average user of OTC tranquilizers tends to be younger, usually less than 35 years old (Schuckit, 1989).

Biochemistry

All the OTC sleep-inducing products, including Unisom, Sominex, Sleep-eze, Miles Nervine, and Nytol, contain 25–50 mg of diphenhydramine. Some also contain aspirin or acetaminophen. These preparations no longer contain scopolamine.

Antihistamines are quickly absorbed. They acting as antagonists to the histamine released by the body during allergic reactions (Schuckit, 1989).

Related Medical Problems

Overdose with antihistamines may be due to an attempt to achieve hallucinations, to multiple-drug interactions (e.g., antihistamines in combination with an antipsychotic or a tricyclic antidepressant may cause anticholinergic toxic effects), or to combining an antihistamine with a drug of abuse (antihistamines are usually abused in combination with alcohol, an opioid, or a sedative) (Arif & Westermeyer, 1988). Toxic reactions, including a toxic-induced psychosis, usually resolve in 2–48 hr (Schuckit, 1989).

Withdrawal

The antihistamines are not physically addicting, although they are occasionally abused by addicts for purposes of sedation (Woolf, 1991d)

Assessment

Assessment of a patient with toxic reactions to antihistamines includes a history and a physical examination. During the initial interview, the patients should be assessed for emergency medical problems and other drug use, because some persons use antihistamines in combination with other drugs.

Treatment

Provisions should be made for safe detoxification. Treatment of patients who are having a toxic reaction includes providing reassurance and support. Patients should receive appropriate referrals for follow-up care (Schuckit, 1989; see also chapter 2). Patients and their families should be educated about reactions caused by combining antihistamines with drugs of abuse such as pentazocine (Schuckit, 1989).

COLD AND ALLERGY PRODUCTS

Cough syrups containing codeine were once widely used and abused by young persons and by heroin addicts who could not get a supply of heroin (Wilford, 1982). For example, a 4-oz (120 ml) bottle of codeine cough syrup contains 240 mg of codeine and is the equivalent of 20–25 mg of oral morphine. Better controls have made codeine a prescription drug and have dramatically changed abuse of OTC codeine.

Biochemistry

Cold and allergy products contain antihistamines, analgesics, decongestants, expectorants, and cough suppressants. Some inhalers contain adrenaline-like substances (Schuckit, 1989).

Nasal and pulmonary decongestants can worsen the very problems they were designed to relieve. For example, nasal stuffiness, caused by airborne chemical or allergenic substances, may at first be relieved by nasal decongestants. However, with repeated frequent use, a rebound phenomenon occurs in which chronic swelling of the nasal mucosa results in redness and swelling. After the decongestants are withdrawn for a few days, signs and symptoms usually subside. Some patients may

need an oral decongestant or systemic steroid to provide relief while the topical decongestant is being discontinued (Arif & Westermeyer, 1988).

Related Medical Problems

Depression and other psychiatric signs and symptoms can occur when decongestant and anti-asthma inhalers containing adrenalin-like substances are abused (Schuckit, 1989). Overdose of cough suppressants that contain codeinelike substances can cause respiratory impairment (Schuckit, 1989).

Withdrawal

Rebound phenomenon occurs with frequent use of cold and allergy products. This effect subsides after a few days if use of the products is discontinued (Arif & Westermeyer, 1988).

Assessment

Assessment of patients with problems related to use of cold and allergy products includes a history and a physical examination. They should be assessed for any medical emergencies and for appropriate detoxification.

Treatment

Medical emergencies are treated as needed. Provisions should be made for safe detoxification. Treatment is generally symptomatic. Patients should be educated about use of nasal and pulmonary decongestants (Arif & Westermeyer, 1988). Referrals for further evaluation and counseling as needed should be provided.

ANALGESICS

Analgesics, particularly salicylates, are the most commonly used OTC products. Currently, more than 300 aspirin-containing products are available. According to estimates, these products are used regularly by 33 million Americans (Schuckit, 1989).

Biochemistry

Analgesic drugs (an analgesic and an antiin-flammatory) contain aspirin and similar substances such as acetaminophen and caffeine (Schuckit, 1989) and are very effective for relieving pain and stiffness. Aspirin is an excellent drug for treatment of active rheumatoid arthritis, juvenile rheumatoid arthritis, osteoarthritis, headache, arthralgias, and myalgia. It is rapidly absorbed, primarily in the small intestine and secondarily from the stomach, and has a half-life that lengthens as the dosage is increased. Some analgesics (e.g., Bromo Selzer and Vanquish) also contain antacids such as sodium bicarbonate.

Related Medical Problems

Gastric distress, heartburn, and nausea are the most common adverse effects of overdoses of analgesics. Other effects include profound acid-base imbalances, tinnitus, asthmatic attacks, skin reactions, and electrolyte problems (Schuckit, 1989). Long-term use of analgesics can cause peptic ulcers, anemia, renal disease, and neuropathy (Ray & Ksir, 1993; Schuckit, 1989).

Withdrawal

No withdrawal associated with use of analgesics has been observed (Schuckit, 1989).

Assessment

Assessment includes a history and a physical examination. Patients should be assessed for medical emergencies, detoxification, and other drug use.

Treatment

Medical emergencies are treated as needed. Provisions should be made for safe detoxification. Patients and their families should be educated about use of OTC drugs (Ray & Ksir, 1993; Schuckit, 1989). Referrals should be provided for further evaluation and counseling as needed.

LAXATIVES

Abuse of laxatives is widely known and documented, especially in the elderly. According to estimates, more than 30% of persons 60 years and older take a laxative at least once a week (Schuckit, 1989).

Biochemistry

Laxatives include dietary fiber, saline, osmotic, and colonic mixtures (Schuckit, 1989). Products that are most likely to cause systemic problems generally contain phenolphthalein, which when absorbed can cause cardiac and respiratory distress in susceptible persons.

Related Medical Problems

Long-term use of laxatives can cause toxic effects due to digitalis, fecal impaction from a flaccid colon, osteomalacia, melanosis coli, gastric irritation, and protein loss. Hypovitaminosis syndrome occurs as a result of mineral-oil laxatives preventing the absorption of minerals and fat-soluble vitamins. Excessive use of saline laxatives can cause dehydration and electrolyte imbalance. Some stimulant laxatives containing anthraquinone can be transferred from mother to infant in breast milk. The laxative can cause nephritis and gastrointestinal pain in the infant (Schuckit, 1989).

Withdrawal

No signs or symptoms of withdrawal are associated with use of laxatives. The problems that occur are medical and psychological (Schuckit, 1989).

Assessment

Assessment of patients who overuse laxatives includes a history and a physical examination. Patients should be assessed for medical emergencies and eating disorders.

Treatment

Medical emergencies are treated as needed. Patients should be given information about the short- and long-term physiological and psychological effects of laxatives and the concept of addiction and assisted in exploring appropriate ways to deal with health problems (Schuckit, 1989). Referrals should be provided for further evaluation to rule out eating disorders and other medical problems and for counseling as needed.

WEIGHT CONTROL AIDS

Many persons, especially adolescent girls, use diet pills and diuretics to improve appearance (Litt, 1991).

Biochemistry

Phenylpropanolamine, which is usually combined with caffeine, is a weak stimulant of the sympathetic nervous system with actions similar to those of ephedrine. Although most often used as a decongestant in combination with an antihistamine in OTC cold preparations, phenylpropanolamine is also often used in weight control products, because in high doses it stimulates the CNS to produce anorexia. High doses also elevate mood and confidence, although headaches, irritability, and even psychosis develop in some users (Woolf & Moore, 1991).

Methylcellulose is a bulk producer that gives a feeling of fullness. However, it is no more effective for weight control than a low-calorie, high-fiber diet is (Schuckit, 1989).

Related Medical Problems

Side effects of phenylpropanolamine can occur at any dosage level, particularly if the daily dose exceeds 75 mg. Typical signs and symptoms of overdose are tinnitus, nervousness, restlessness, insomnia, headache, malaise, and excessively high blood pressure. Because it has adrenergic proper-

ties, phenylpropanolamine can also cause cardiac stimulation and elevate blood glucose levels. Phenylpropanolamine can interact with monoamine oxidase inhibitors and indomethacin or other agents that inhibit prostaglandin synthesis, such as aspirin and other antiinflammatory products (Woolf & Moore, 1991).

If the doses are high enough, phenylpropanolamine can induce psychoses almost identical to those caused by CNS stimulants (Woolf & Moore, 1991). Long-term misuse can cause depression and mania-like states or mania (Woolf & Moore, 1991).

Methylcellulose can produce esophageal obstruction, particularly in persons who have esophageal or gastric disease (Schuckit, 1989).

Withdrawal

If the doses of phenylpropanolamine are high enough, discontinuance of use can cause signs and symptoms of withdrawal. The signs and symptoms are similar to those outlined for CNS stimulants.

Assessment

Assessment of patients who abuse weight control aids includes a history and a physical examination. Patients should be assessed for emergency medical needs, detoxification, eating disorders, and psychiatric problems.

Treatment

Medical emergencies are treated as needed. Provisions should be made for safe detoxification. Patients and their families should be educated about alternatives for weight loss (Schuckit, 1989; Woolf & Moore, 1991). Referrals should be provided for further evaluation to rule out an eating disorder and for nutritional counseling.

BROMIDES

Products that contain bromides, usually in the form of bromide salts, have been used since the Civil War. Problems with abuse were first reported in the 1920s and continued in the 1940s and 1950s. At that time, abuse was thought to be a major reason for psychiatric hospitalization. Bromides were once a common ingredient in OTC sleep aids but are no longer on the market in this form (Schuckit, 1989).

Related Medical Problems

Because bromide has a long half-life of about 12 days, patients with bromide intoxication have gradual onset of signs and symptoms over months. Physical effects include a fine tremor, a maculopapular rash, slurred speed, lack of coordination, and dizziness. Psychological side effects range from irritability to confusion, depression, and maniclike behavior. Patients often complain about being too nervous to stand still and about being unable to organize their thoughts (Ray & Ksir, 1993; Schuckit, 1989).

Withdrawal

No signs and symptoms of withdrawal are associated with use of bromides (Schuckit, 1989).

Assessment

Assessment of a patient with bromide intoxication includes a history and a physical examination. Patients should be assessed for medical emergencies. Hospitalization is required for detoxification (Ray & Ksir, 1993; Schuckit, 1989).

Treatment

A bromide level greater than 10–20 mEq/L indicates the patient is intoxicated. Intravenous solutions containing sodium or ammonium chloride can be given, or normal saline can be alternated with 5% dextrose in saline (Schuckit, 1989). The patient should be reassured and placed in a calm environment. Patients and their families should be educated about the appropriate use of OTC and other medications (Ray & Ksir, 1993; Schuckit, 1989). Referrals should be provided for further counseling and evaluation.

EXAM QUESTIONS

CHAPTER 10
Questions 88–96

88. Which of the following statements about OTC drugs in the United States is correct?

    a. Most of them are classified as schedule II drugs.

    b. Their use is limited to the treatment of colds and allergies.

    c. More than 500,000 different preparations are available.

    d. They are most often used by white, middle-class men and the elderly.

89. Which of the following is characteristic of abusers of OTC drugs?

    a. They are typically persons who self-medicate.

    b. They usually identify an OTC drug as their primary drug of choice.

    c. They typically avoid using other drugs or alcohol as long as the OTC drugs are available to them.

    d. They usually do not abuse laxatives.

90. OTC drugs may be used for which of the following?

    a. Their narcotic effects

    b. Adulteration of street drugs

    c. Hallucinogenic effects

    d. Slow withdrawal from other drugs

91. Which of the following statements about caffeine is correct?

    a. It is rarely the major ingredient in OTC stimulants.

    b. It usually does not produce even mild tolerance unless the dose exceeds 600 mg/day.

    c. It has a half-life of 8–10 hours.

    d. It can exacerbate schizophrenia-type disorders.

92. At high doses, caffeine does which of the following?

    a. Decreases gastric acidity

    b. Can cause a hypertensive crisis when used in conjunction with monoamine oxidase inhibitors

    c. Does not cause toxic effects when combined with therapeutic doses of theophylline

    d. Can cause reactive hyperglycemia

93. Which of the following is a caffeine-related medical problem?

    a. Decease in night vision

    b. Pancreatitis

    c. Anxiety attacks

    d. Fibrocystic disease

94. Which of the following is a medical problem related to overdose with OTC analgesics?

    a. Gastric distress

    b. Depression

    c. Osteoporosis

    d. Increased glucose levels

95. Which of the following statements about laxatives is correct?

    a. Laxatives containing phenolphthalein are less likely than others to cause cardiac and respiratory distress.

    b. Laxatives containing anthraquinone are safer than others for nursing infants.

    c. Laxatives can cause in fecal impaction if used repeatedly.

    d. Laxatives containing saline are the only ones that do not upset electrolyte balance.

96. Which of the following is a side effect of phenylpropanolamine?

    a. Hypotension

    b. Elevated blood glucose levels

    c. Increased prostaglandin synthesis

    d. Somnolence

CHAPTER 11

IMPAIRED HEALTH PROFESSIONALS

CHAPTER OBJECTIVE

After studying this chapter, the reader will be able to recognize the scope, indications, and resolutions to substance abuse among health care professionals.

LEARNING OBJECTIVES

After studying this chapter, the reader will be able to

1. Recognize historical aspects of substance abuse among health care professionals.

2. Indicate the primary purpose of state boards of nursing in regard to substance abuse.

3. Recognize signs that might indicate substance abuse in a health care professional.

4. Specify appropriate interventions for impaired health care professionals.

INTRODUCTION

According to estimates, drug and alcohol use costs American businesses $50 billion to $100 billion annually as a result of problems ranging from decreased productivity to outright theft. Productivity losses may be subtle, such as tardiness or increased absenteeism, or may be as obvious as accidents on the job.Some workplace settings, and some jobs in particular, seem to contribute to increased drug use; for example, stimulant drugs are often used by truck drivers and some prescription medicines by health care workers (Crouch, Webb, Buller, & Rollins, 1989; Gerstein & Grossman, 1989).

HISTORY

Alcohol and drug use among nurses has a long history. Before the reformation of nurse's training programs by Florence Nightingale (1820–1910), nursing care was generally provided by convicts, prostitutes, and alcoholics.

The establishment of training schools and the restructuring of nursing into a quasi-religious vocation of care for the sick inaugurated the modern era of nursing on which books on nursing ethics are based. These reforms promoted professionalism in nursing. They also contributed to the bias perceived by the public toward the nursing profession (Haack, 1989).

In 1975, the AMA held the first biennial national conference focusing on disabled doctors. Subsequently, it began publishing a newsletter called *Impaired Physician* and providing backup services for state committees.

In 1982, the ANA adopted a policy stating that treatment should be offered to impaired nurses before disciplinary action is taken. In 1984, the association published a position paper, *Addictions and Psychological Dysfunctions in Nursing: The Profession's Response to the Problem,* that defined impairment due to drug and alcohol dependency. The definition is as follows: "When alcohol or drug use is causing continuing problems in one or more areas of an individual's life, such as problems at home, on the job, physically, or legally, an individual is said to be dependent on that drug." A task force was formed to set up assistance programs for chemically dependent nurses, and in 1985 the ANA held its first national biennial conference on impaired nurses.

In 1987, the AMA declared chemical dependency a disease and defined dependency to all psychoactive drugs, from cocaine to alcohol, as a bona fide medical entity termed chemical dependency (McElmurry, Church, & Haack, 1989).

CURRENT IMPACT

Substance abuse costs both the abuser and society. It causes decreased productivity, absenteeism, tardiness, poor interaction with patients, poor decisions, decreased staff morale, and mistakes and accidents that might lead to legal problems (Sullivan et al., 1988).

Because of the secretive nature of abuse and the many opportunities to abuse chemical substances in a medical setting, determining how widespread substance abuse is among health care professionals is difficult. A survey of 300 medical students in 1987 (Schwartz, Lewis, Hoffmann, & Kyriazi, 1991) showed that drug use included use of alcohol, marijuana, cocaine, and tobacco. A smaller survey of 68 medical students (Grafton & Bairnsfather, 1991) reported the use of these drugs as well as use of amphetamines and unprescribed sedatives.

A 1989 survey of 260 former anesthesiology residents (Lutsky, Abram, Jacobson, Hopwood, & Kampine, 1991) showed that 77.2% had used alcohol while in residency, 20.0% had used marijuana, 15.7% had used cocaine, and 24.2% had used unprescribed psychoactive drugs. In addition, 15.8% admitted they had been problem users while in residency.

Dentists have been linked with drug abuse of volatile gases such as nitrous oxide. Health care professionals, especially physicians and nurses, are thought to be the most frequent abusers of analgesic medications of any middle-class population (Schuckit, 1989). Other studies (Sullivan et al., 1988) have shown drug use among pharmacists and nurses. The ANA reported in 1984 that 68% of all state board actions over a 12-month period resulted from impaired functioning related to drug or alcohol use (Haack, 1989). In the 1990s, the percentage has increased to approximately 80% of all board actions. Psychologists and social workers are less likely to be reported to their professional regulatory boards for substance abuse than are nurses, pharmacists, and physicians. When reported, nurses, pharmacists, and physicians are more likely to be disciplined for stealing drugs from work than for using alcohol or illicit drugs.

Currently, each state has a nursing board consisting of political appointees whose primary purpose is to ensure the public safety. The boards set standards and grant approval to nursing schools, determine eligibility for licensure and relicensure, and take disciplinary action against persons who violate the nurse practice acts.

Specialty organizations also exist to assist nurses with addiction problems. In addition, almost every state medical association has assistance programs for physicians who are impaired because of substance abuse. However, only about 15 states have an organized assistance program for impaired nurses.

RECOGNITION OF IMPAIRMENT

Recognizing which health care professionals are impaired because of substance abuse is difficult. Denial is strong both in the abuser and in his colleagues and significant others.

If an addicted nurse is discovered, employers often find a different reason for termination to avoid the inconvenience of assisting the nurse with recovery or reporting the addiction to the board of nursing as required by law. Often the nurse goes on to find employment elsewhere, allowing the addiction to progress (Sullivan et al., 1988).

Addicted persons may admit to their drug use and see that their drug-related behavior is causing problems yet truly not believe that they are addicted. Denial may be strengthened by the belief that their education as health professionals will protect them from becoming addicted. In addition, their strong ethical principles as members of the helping professions make it painful to admit that they are compromising patients' care. Denial is further strengthened when the legal implications are not considered. The stigma from peers must be avoided at all costs. To avoid attention, impaired health care professionals must maintain a normal appearance and job performance. Ways of concealing drug use vary with the particular drug and workplace of the professional.

Vaillant (1983) found that physicians who become substance abusers commonly had had unstable childhoods and difficulty adjusting during their teens. They often had serious long-standing marital problems and in some cases serious psychopathological problems as well. Physicians who abused substances were likely to be psychologically isolated; many had numerous social contacts but most of the contacts were superficial. As physicians, the professionals had access to drugs in pure form, and were thus able to have much higher levels of intake than are possible with drugs obtained from illicit street vendors. The physicians were more likely to abuse substances on their own, rather than as members of a group, because of the need to protect their career investments.

Signs and Symptoms of Addiction

The signs and symptoms of addiction in nurses and other health care providers form a pattern. Those who recognize the pattern can help nurses and others seek evaluation from a professional.

History. Indicators of increased risk for substance abuse include a family history of substance abuse; a history of physical, emotional, or sexual abuse as a child; and a chronic medical condition that requires pain medications.

Physical indicators. Physical indicators of addiction include an odor of alcohol; red, bleary, bloodshot eyes; spider veins, especially around the nose; Band-Aids on hands and arms; watery eyes; and runny nose, with clear mucous drainage. The abuser is unkempt, avoids eye contact, and sometimes shows evidence of premature aging.

Mental and emotional indicators. Mental indicators include loss of memory, confusion, and blackouts. Emotional signs include rapid mood swings, from depression to euphoria; irritability in a person with a formerly stable temperament; and suicide threats or attempts.

Behavioral changes. Behavioral changes include marital and family problems, illnesses and accidents or other emergencies, complaints from others about work performance or substance use, excuses for tardiness or absence, and difficulty meeting schedules. The abuser eats alone and is increasingly isolated from staff members. Abusers may request to work night shifts or assignments that facilitate access to drugs. They may have a strong interest in pain control medications, disappear into a bathroom right after assessing the narcotics cabinet, and have unexplained absences and trips to the bathroom. Nurses who are impaired may become illogical or sloppy in charting, wear long-sleeved clothing continuously, and appear on their unit during their days off.

Narcotics discrepancies. Drug diversion should be suspected if there are frequent incorrect narcotic counts; apparent alteration of narcotic vials; an increase in the number of patient reports of ineffective pain medication; discrepancy between patients' reports and hospital records of pain medications being given; discrepancies in physicians' orders, progress notes, and narcotics records; unusual amounts of narcotics wasted; frequent corrections and erratic patterns of corrections on narcotics records; and unusual variation in the quantity of drugs needed on a unit (Sullivan et al., 1988).

Prescribed medications. Addicted nurses have reported getting prescribed drugs from a number of doctors simultaneously by complaining of fictitious symptoms or by stopping a doctor in the hallway and asking for a prescription. Some nurses have reported that they were given presigned prescription blanks for their use.

Hospital drugs. Addicted nurses may falsify patients' records or the narcotics records by charting that a dosage was given when it was instead diverted partly or entirely for the nurse's use. Or the nurse may sign out medications and report spillage or medication errors or make substitutions (e.g., a tube of saline in place of a tubex of meperidine). Some nurses have siphoned out a drug and replaced it partly or entirely with water. Nurses have also stolen drugs from the patient's bedside after drug supplies were accounted for at change of shifts. Some nurses have taken an entire delivery of drugs along with the sign-out sheet so that the loss looks like an accounting error.

Alcohol. Because alcohol is a legal drug, most hospitals do not have a written policy about drinking off the premises unless work performance is affected.

INTERVENTION

Early in the course of addiction, a pattern of the signs and symptoms just described may not be easily discerned. However, objective documentation by the nursing supervisor of unsatisfactory or deteriorating job performance will eventually make such a pattern obvious. The supervisor can then set a conference time to present the data to the nurse who is suspected of substance abuse (Benjamin & Curtis, 1986).

After the data are presented, the nurse is given an opportunity to explain his or her behavior. An agreement is made detailing a plan for correcting the situation within a specific time. A clear set of procedures for approving and monitoring the plan or taking further administrative action is established. If referrals are made for treatment, the nurse has the responsibility to comply.

Intervention can take a number of other approaches. However, all of them should have the element of surprise to prevent the nurse from finding an excuse to avoid participating or to manipulate the confrontation so that it is ineffective.

Johnsonian Intervention

In Johnsonian intervention, a professional counselor prepares a group of people significant in the nurse's life (spouse, children, friends, parents, colleagues, employers) to confront the nurse with their observations of the nurse's drug-related behavior that concern them. The group meets in advance, rehearses the material to be presented, decides on goals, sets the time and place for the intervention, and decides where the nurse will receive treatment and what each member of the group will do if the intervention is rejected. Persons who are too upset are eliminated from the group to keep a therapeutic atmosphere. The counselor facilitates the group in the intervention (Sullivan et al., 1988).

Peer Intervention

Peer intervention is a colleague-to-colleague approach. Usually two volunteer members of a peer assistance committee (in some states) from the state nurses' association tell the nurse, without revealing their source, information that has been given them about the nurse's unprofessional and possibly illegal drug-related behavior. The volunteers, one of whom is usually a recovering nurse, give the nurse information about the disease and treatment available and may threaten to report to the nurse's employer or the state board if their recommendations of treatment are not followed through. Vindictive use of the procedure is avoided by requiring two verifications of the problem before intervention is planned (Sullivan et al., 1988).

Employment-Related Intervention

With employment-related intervention, the employee assistance person and a group of recovering employees confront the nurse about drug-related problems they have observed in the areas of job performance, relations with patients and coworkers, theft, and others. Documentation before this intervention is important. The goal is to express concerns about the person and the job performance and to arrange for an evaluation with a professional counselor (Sullivan et al., 1988).

Combined Approaches

In some states, a hospital representative contacts the peer assistance committee of the state nurses' association and arranges for two of the committee members to work with the hospital to plan an intervention once just cause is shown. This committee does not have the authority to investigate, but it does threaten further reporting if the nurse refuses to be evaluated and follow treatment recommendations. The nurse is offered the support of the committee and the opportunity to become involved in the peer assistance program (Sullivan et al., 1988).

Guidelines for Intervention

The intervention should occur shortly after the precipitating event, and the persons intervening should have written documentation of the event. They should state the goal of the intervention and the consequences if it is rejected, confront the nurse in a kind and caring manner, and follow through after the intervention by going with the nurse to the treatment center immediately for evaluation. Nurses who are intoxicated should not be allowed to drive. The intervention should be documented (McElmurry et al., 1989).

Acute Intoxication

When a nurse is intoxicated on the job, the nurse supervisor documents the following: the nurse's behavior before, during, and after the interview; the time; the extent of impairment (e.g., slurred speech, errors in judgment, uncontrolled anger, poor coordination, errors in handling patients); and the action taken. If possible, a urine or blood specimen is collected for analysis as part of the documentation (Sullivan et al., 1988).

The nurse is confronted in private and is placed on personal leave. A relative, friend, or coworker can provide transportation home or directly to a treatment center for evaluation if the nurse is willing.

TREATMENT

Nurses have been successfully treated in both inpatient and outpatient programs with a multidisciplinary team approach, in which trained therapists have an understanding of the dynamics of nursing and are familiar with the professional and regulatory environment to which recovering nurses return. The curriculum usually includes education in disease concepts of substance abuse, individual and group therapy, development of support systems with both self-help groups such as AA (or Narcotics Anonymous or Cocaine Anonymous) and groups for the impaired nurse, and a minimum of 1 year of continuing care. Documentation of the nurse's progress may be provided to the state board of nursing on its request and with the nurse's written permission as well as other needed verification of abstinence (Sullivan et al., 1988).

REENTRY

Most employers might not wish to hire a recovering nurse. However, federal law specifies that drug-dependent persons are handicapped and cannot be discriminated against. Consequently, employers must hire solely on the potential for job performance.

Although federal law also protects the confidentiality of treatment records, licensing agencies may place sanctions on a nurse's license that reveal chemical dependency. Because these records are open to the public, an employer can obtain information of past disciplinary action as well as the nurse's responses to questions on dependency.

Some employers allow a recovering nurse to work in the nurse's former unit but stipulate that if the nurse's patients require mood-altering medications, the medications must be administered by a designated nurse other than the recovering nurse.

The nurse is monitored for continued abstinence to protect the patients and the employer and to provide the nurse with documentation of continuing abstinence. On return to work, the recovering nurse signs a contract agreeing to (1) consistently attend self-help groups, including a nurses' support group if available, and provide documentation of attendance; (2) provide documentation of continu-

ing care as recommended by the nurse's therapist; (3) attend sessions with a counselor from the employee assistance program or with an administrator on a regular basis; and (4) continue to report to the former employer after resignation or until a new employer is found and is notified of the contract and its provisions. If the contract is not honored, or relapse occurs, the recovering nurse can be terminated and the state board of nursing informed.

Other monitoring devices include frequent random drug screens done over a long period and paid for by the nurse or employer and occasionally the use of naltrexone (Trexan) or disulfiram (Antabuse). Monitoring is done by the designated monitor only. If staff personnel on the unit become aware that the nurse is recovering from drug dependency, they should be reassured that the disease is treatable though chronic and that management is responsible for the supervision. Confidentiality is important in monitoring. The impaired nurse should be scheduled to work the same hours as the monitor, thereby diminishing the number of persons who need to know that the nurse is recovering from drug dependency (Robbins, 1987).

Recovering nurses may face a variety of legal, career, and ethical problems. These problems can be more easily addressed and resolved with the support and encouragement of the state nurses' association peer assistance program, the hospital employee assistance program, or both (Sullivan et al., 1988).

DISCIPLINARY ACTION

Steps for disciplinary action may differ somewhat from state to state but basically follow the following format: The employer files a complaint with the state board of nursing that the nurse is in violation of the nurse practice act (which varies from state to state and includes legally binding definitions of the practice of professional nurses).

This complaint is thoroughly investigated for probable cause, sometimes by a committee called a "probable cause panel" composed of nurses as well as attorneys. If probable cause is found, an official administrative complaint is filed, and the nurse is notified of impending prosecution. If the nurse chooses to dispute the charges, he or she is given an opportunity to be heard by an administrative hearing officer (formal hearing).

Nurses who do not dispute the charges are given an opportunity to be heard by the board of nursing at one of its regular meetings (informal hearing). The administrative hearing office makes recommendations to the board of nursing that the board may accept, reject, or modify. The nurse may testify, be represented by an attorney, and provide witnesses whether the hearing is formal or informal.

The state board of nursing decides on a disciplinary action on the basis of violation of the nurse practice act. Discipline may involve a fine, a reprimand, probation, suspension or revocation of the nursing license, or a combination of any of these, and it becomes a permanent part of the nurse's record (Penny, Catanzarite, & Ritter, 1989; Sullivan et al., 1988).

State nursing boards generally consist of political appointees who may be uneducated about the disease concept of drug dependency and whose primary purpose is protecting the health and welfare of the public rather than rehabilitating impaired nurses. To address issues of rehabilitation, many state boards have established peer assistance programs (Penny et al., 1989).

CASE STUDY

T. S., a 31-year-old R.N., was referred to the Intervention Project for Nurses by the director of nursing at a major hospital. The employer expressed concern that Ms. S.'s nursing practice had been affected by the use of drugs. The director of nurses reported that for 2 years, Ms. S. was a "casual" employee who floated to different units in the hospital. T. S. had excellent nursing skills and was working on a graduate degree in hospital administration.

Documentation related to practice issues included behavioral changes and a pattern of discrepancies in the charting of narcotics. This pattern was observed on all units to which T. S. floated. Also noted were mood swings, flushed appearance, constricted pupils, and frequent absences from the unit.

With the specific documentation, an intervention was carried out by the director of nurses. Ms. S. agreed to treatment and participation in the Intervention Project for Nurses. She completed the initial (28 day) phase of treatment and, on recommendation of the treatment staff, continued in extended residential treatment for 6 weeks. After completing the residential program, Ms. S. began the continuing care program at the treatment center and accepted the restriction of remaining out of nursing practice for 3 months. Ms. S. was permitted to return to nursing after the 3-month period. She was evaluated as stable in recovery and committed to her ongoing recovery program. She returned to her employer (who had referred her) and resumed working in the medical-surgical area. Her practice was restricted only in the area of controlled drugs: She could not administer controlled drugs or assume responsibility for the narcotic cabinet keys.

T. S. has continued to progress in her recovery. She established a relationship with the Intervention Project for Nurses and continues to adhere to the requirements of the project. Reports have been received every 2 months to monitor her progress and her continued safe practice.

During the second year of recovery, Ms. S. resumed graduate work toward her master's degree in nursing. Her licensure record at the board of nursing reveals no evidence of disciplinary action (Penny et al., 1989).

SUMMARY

No conclusive evidence indicates that substance abuse is more likely to develop in health care workers because of their stressful work and lifestyles. Those who do become abusers often have a family history of substance abuse and are more likely to use alcohol than other drugs.

Nurses with substance abuse problems can enlist the help of their state peer assistance program. More education in the area of substance abuse is currently needed by the health care professionals.

The curricula for both nurses and doctors should be updated to provide adequate education on drug addiction, including addiction to prescription medications. A survey of 298 nurses (Long & Gelfand, 1992) showed a lack of knowledge about alcoholism. Sixty-six of the respondents could not answer correctly questions about social aspects of alcohol, and 93% could not define and identify the pharmacological characteristics of alcohol. Physicians must increase their awareness of prescription drugs of abuse and avoid prescribing the drugs for persons who are addicted (Elder, 1991).

EXAM QUESTIONS

CHAPTER 11
Questions 97–100

97. During the time of Florence Nightingale, which group of people usually provided nursing care?

    a. Volunteers

    b. Trained nurses and doctors

    c. Religious groups

    d. Convicts, prostitutes, and alcoholics

98. What is the primary purpose of state nursing boards?

    a. Ensure the public safety

    b. Assist nurses with addiction problems

    c. Provide health education for nurses

    d. Protect the reputation of recovering nurses

99. Which of the following is an indication of possible drug diversion in a health care setting?

    a. Occasionally incorrect narcotic counts

    b. A decrease in the number of patients' reports of ineffective pain medication

    c. Minor errors in the charting of narcotics

    d. Unusual variation in the quantity of drugs needed on the unit

100. Intervention for drug-dependent health care professionals includes which of the following?

    a. Confronting an intoxicated professional in public

    b. Presenting the data on a nurse's drug dependency to the entire nursing staff

    c. Prohibiting active involvement by the involved health care worker

    d. Objectively documenting deterioration of or unsatisfactory job performance

GLOSSARY

Abuse: The use of a mood-altering substance in a manner that is generally different from the manner in which social and cultural guidelines permit or for which the substance is medically prescribed. All chemically dependent persons abuse chemicals, but not all persons who use chemicals abusively become chemically dependent.

Addiction: Loss of control when using a mood-altering substance characterized by the inability to quit despite harmful life consequences. Consequences include physical health problems, legal difficulties, financial difficulties, relationship problems, and employment problems. The addict uses the mood-altering substance either continually or has periodic loss of control over use, is preoccupied with use of the mood-altering substance, and goes to any length to protect or hide his ability to use. Addiction involves a physical or a psychological dependency or both.

Alcoholism: A primary disease related to addiction to alcohol. Without treatment, alcoholism is often progressive and fatal. The frequency of drinking and the amount consumed are less important than the effect of the drinking on the person's life.

Antabuse: A medication (disulfiram) that inhibits the metabolism of alcohol. If a person ingests alcohol while taking this drug, he can become severely ill.

CAGE Inventory: An assessment questionnaire used during an interview with a client to determine if the client is an alcoholic. The results provide an indication of the appropriate level of treatment.

Chemical dependency: *See* Addiction.

Codependency: A pattern of painful dependency on compulsive behaviors and on approval from others in an attempt to find safety, self-worth, and identity. It is frequently the result of efforts by family members to cope with the behaviors of the person who is chemically dependent.

Controlled Substances Act: Legislation enacted in 1970 that made an increased number of drugs subject to stricter requirements for obtaining and using. The Drug Enforcement Administration is the federal agency responsible for enforcing this act. This legislation divides drugs subject to this act into five schedules related to the risk, if any, the drug poses to public health.

Schedule I: Drugs with no accepted medical use in the United States. The potential for abuse of these drugs is high.

Schedule II: Drugs approved for medical use in the United States. The potential for abuse of these drugs is high.

Schedule III: Drugs approved for medical use in the United States. The potential for abuse of these drugs is less than that of drugs in schedules I and II. Schedule III drugs contain limited amounts of narcotic drugs and nonnarcotic drugs.

Schedule IV: Drugs approved for medical use in the United States. The potential for abuse of these drugs is less than that of drugs in schedule III.

Schedule V: Drugs approved for medical use in the United States that can be distributed without a doctor's prescription. The potential for abuse of these drugs is less than that of drugs in schedule IV.

Cross-dependence: A person who is dependent on one drug in a class will be dependent on all other drugs in that class.

Delusion: A false belief held despite evidence to the contrary and despite the fact that others do not share the belief. Substance abusers use delusion as a defense mechanism to avoid admitting their drug dependency. The person typically distorts reality to avoid acknowledging the destructive nature of the chemical use.

Denial: A defense mechanism in which the existence of unpleasant realities is kept out of conscious awareness. Among substance abusers, denial involves self-deception that prevents the person from admitting the self-destructive nature of his chemical use to himself or others. The abuser may minimize his problems, blaming them on others, while considering that his substance use is under control.

Detoxification: Cleansing the body of accumulated toxins or poisons that are the result of prolonged use of a drug. Depending on the substance(s) involved and severity of the signs and symptoms experienced by the person during the process, detoxification can be accomplished on an inpatient or an outpatient basis and with or without direct medical supervision.

Drug half-life: The time it takes for half the concentration of a drug in a person's body to clear from the body. The longer the half-life is, the longer the effects of the drug linger.

Drug dependency: *See* Addiction.

Federal Privacy Act (CRF-42): Federal law that clearly spells out the rights of the individual to confidentiality in chemical dependency treatment.

Fetal alcohol syndrome (FAS): A syndrome caused by exposure to alcohol in utero; the leading preventable cause of mental retardation. No safe limits for use of alcohol in pregnancy have been established.

Impaired health professional: A health professional whose ability to practice his or her chosen profession in a safe manner is impaired because of the use of a mood-altering chemical. The most frequent cause of disciplinary action by professional boards.

Intervention: A carefully planned meeting of family, friends, and other concerned persons, often with the assistance of a professional, to confront an alcoholic or a drug addict about the destructive nature of the alcohol or drug use. The goal is to break through the substance abuser's denial and delusions and start him on the road to recovery.

Loss of control: The inability to consistently predict the amount a person will consume and the time, place, or duration of a drinking or a drug-taking episode.

MAST (Michigan Alcoholism Screening Test): An assessment tool used to provide information about the severity of alcoholism and to assist in determining the most appropriate level of treatment.

Physical dependency: A physiological craving by the body, the result of tissue tolerance; caused by prolonged use of a substance in greater amounts than normally ingested. To quit using the substance will result in signs and symptoms of withdrawal.

Psychological dependency: A strong, persistent desire to use a mood-altering substance that is not related to any physiological need.

Recovery: The process of healing from an addiction. It includes stopping all use of mood-altering substances and making changes in attitudes, beliefs, lifestyle, and behaviors.

Relapse: Return to the use of alcohol or drugs after a period of abstinence.

Risk factors: Factors thought to increase a person's susceptibility to substance use.

Self-help group: Any group that meets without professional leadership or direction to help the members of the group deal with a common problem. The best known self-help group is Alcoholics Anonymous.

Sobriety: A state achieved by abstaining from use of all mood-altering substances.

Substance abuse: *See* Addiction

Support group: *See* Self-help groups.

Tolerance: A reduced response to a drug over time; the substance abuser must take a larger amount of the substance to receive the same effect obtained previously. Tolerance is related to adaptations by the liver and the brain.

Treatment: A planned, systematic program designed to help a substance abuser become abstinent and remain so while improving the quality of his life through recovery. The three most common forms of treatment are outpatient, inpatient, and residential.

Withdrawal: Signs and symptoms that develop when a person with tissue tolerance to a mood-altering substance abstains (whether voluntarily or involuntarily) from using the substance, and levels of the drug in the body begin to diminish.

COMMON DRUG TERMS

Many drug terms have become standards in everyday conversation in the movies, in books, and on television. However, the following terms are heard mostly in the underground drug culture.

A: LSD.

ab: Abscess, an abscess that forms at the site of injection.

ace: One of anything, a 1-year prison term, a person of high repute in the drug culture.

acid: LSD.

airplane: A marijuana cigarette butt, or a "roach."

amped, to be amped: To be under the influence of or addicted to methamphetamine.

angel dust: Specially treated marijuana, often laced with PCP.

artillery: Equipment used by addicts to inject drugs. It usually includes a hypodermic syringe or a disposable syringe without the plunger to which is attached a baby bottle or pacifier nipple at the open end. Attached at the lower end is a hypodermic, sewing machine, or other type of needle. Other necessary equipment includes a piece of cotton or fragment of paper or cloth to use as a seal or "gasket" to keep air from entering the injection site, a spoon or bottle cap, and a match or matchbook for dissolving and preparing the solution for injection. Also known as q.v., dingus, dropper, gasket, gimmick, gun, hype, kit, layout, machine, outfit, point, and spike.

baby: Any girl, a man, marijuana.

backtrack: To withdraw the plunger within the syringe after the needle is inserted into the vein. If the action draws blood into the syringe when the needle is properly inserted, no air is present.

bag: A packet of drugs, often a small, clear cellophane or glassine square folded to hold an ounce or less of a drug. Bags usually sell for $5–8, depending on the supply.

bagman: A narcotics peddler.

bake a cake, bake the cake: To heat a substance in water to prepare it for injection as a narcotic and discover that it becomes sticky or pasty, to discover a prepared preparation contains no drugs.

bale: One pound (454 g) of marijuana.

ball, to ball: To engage in sexual intercourse, to absorb stimulants such as cocaine through the genitals.

bamboo: An opium pipe.

bang, to get a bang: The euphoric effect of a narcotic injection.

barbs, barbies: Barbiturates.

beat, to be beat: To buy a substance as a drug and discover it is an inert material (e.g., sugar, crushed aspirin, or the like), to be cheated when buying drugs.

Beast: LSD.

bent, to be bent out of shape: Under the influence of a drug or severely depressed.

Bernice, bernies: Cocaine in crystalline form.

big D: LSD.

big Joe, big John: The police.

big man, the big man: The brains or executive of a drug ring, often a person with political connections.

big O: Opium.

bit: A jail term.

biz: The drug artillery (*See* artillery).

black beauty: Benzedrine, amphetamine sulfate.

black bomber: Benzedrine, amphetamine sulfate.

black columbus: Marijuana.

black mote: Marijuana cured with sugar.

blank: Very low grade, highly diluted drugs, inert material sold as drugs.

block: A cube of morphine, an ounce of hashish.

blue angels: Amytal (amobarbital).

blue birds: Amobarbital.

blue bullets: Amobarbital.

blues: Amobarbital.

blue velvet: Paregoric, camphorated tincture of opium plus Pyribenzamine (tripelennamine), mixed for injection.

boot: Prolonging the injection of a drug by depressing the plunger slowly.

brick: A compressed brick of marijuana or morphine weighing 2.2 lb (1 kg).

bundle: A packet or quantity of dugs, usually containing 25 bags.

c: Cocaine.

caca: Spanish slang for "shit," heroin.

candy: Cocaine, barbiturates

candy man: A drug pusher, a cocaine peddler.

carga: Spanish slang for heroin.

Carrie Nation: Cocaine.

cartwheels: Double-scored, cross-scored amphetamine tablets, benzedrine.

cecil: Cocaine.

chalk: Cocaine.

Christmas cake, Christmas tree: Spansules containing amphetamines and barbiturates.

coast to coast, coasting: To subjectively enjoy the sensation of a drug, a term often used by heroin addicts to describe their introverted satisfaction after an injection of the drug.

cocktail: A marijuana cigarette attached to the butt of a standard tobacco cigarette.

copilots: Benzedrine, amphetamine sulfate.

courage pills: Barbiturates.

croaker: A street term for a physician, particularly a physician who sells drugs.

crooker: A physician who sells narcotics illegally.

crutch: A holder for marijuana cigarettes.

dabble: To take small amounts of narcotics on occasion.

dillies: An opium derivative.

dirty: In possession of narcotics or liable for arrest for possession.

double blue, double trouble: An amphetamine and a barbiturate taken together, such as amobarbital sodium and secobarbital (Tuinal).

down habit: Extreme addiction.

dreamer: Morphine.

dropper, dripper: The medicine dropper used in place of a hypodermic syringe.

dummy: A purchase that was thought to be narcotics but was only inert material.

eye openers: The first injection of narcotics taken in the morning, amphetamines.

finger wave: To be searched rectally or vaginally for narcotics hidden in a condom.

gage: Marijuana.

garbage: Very weak, severely diluted, heroin.

gee: A collar or gasket used to keep air from entering the vein during injection.

gee, geeze: A injection of narcotics.

gee head: A paregoric addict.

greenies: Dextroamphetamine sulfate with amobarbital, oval-shaped amphetamines.

ground control, controller: The person who watches an LSD taker while the taker is under the influence of the drug.

hag: An addict with a severe craving for any type of narcotic, in any quantity, or an addict with a craving for enormous doses; PCP.

heeled: Possessing narcotics.

hog: PCP.

hot shot: Fatal overdose of narcotics.

ice cream man: Opium or narcotics dealer.

J: A marijuana cigarette.

jack off, jack off the needle: To depress and withdraw the plunger of a hypodermic needle in a vein so as to inject a small part of the narcotic into the vein and then to draw blood into the syringe. The aim is to see that no air bubbles are in the syringe and to prolong the injection of the narcotic; in effect, the needle is washed out with blood.

jolly beans: pep pills, stimulants, amphetamines.

LA: A long-lasting amphetamine.

lame, lame duck: A person who does not use narcotics.

lemonade: Poor quality or very dilute heroin.

load: A stock of illegal drugs, 30_40 $3- to $8-bags of heroin.

machine: The kit used to inject narcotics.

magic pumpkin, magic mushroom: Mescaline.

manicure: To remove the dirt, stems, and seeds from marijuana.

mojo: Hard drugs such as heroin or cocaine.

nimbies, nembies: Yellow-coated barbiturates.

nod, be on the nod: A state of drowsiness while under the influence of narcotics.

orange wedge: Acid.

panic: A shortage of drugs on the market.

peaches: Amphetamines.

peanuts: Barbiturates.

P.G.: Paregoric.

pinks: Secobarbital sodium.

purple haze: LSD.

purple hearts: Dexamyl, a combination of Dexedrine (dextroamphetamine) and Amytal.

quill: A matchbook cover used as a holder through which methedrine, cocaine, or heroin is sniffed.

rainbows: Tuinal, a barbiturate combination of Amytal and Seconal (secobarbital) in a red and blue capsule.

reds and blues: Secobarbital and amobarbital combined in one dosage form, usually a red and blue capsule.

red birds: Secobarbital sodium.

red devils: Seconal barbiturates.

roses: Amphetamines.

salt shot: An injection of normal saline under the skin, given to persons who have overdosed on heroin.

scoff: To eat or ingest a drug by mouth.

script: A drug prescription.

sleepers: Sleeping pills.

speedball: An injection of a stimulant and a depressant mixed, usually heroin and cocaine.

splash: A sensation usually described in sexual terms and accompanied by excitation of the sex organs experienced at the initiation of an injection of methamphetamine or other narcotics.

take off: Injection.

teahead: A marijuana user.

tie: A tourniquet used to raise a vein for injection of narcotics.

turkey: A capsule containing nonnarcotic ingredients.

turps, turpie: Elixir of terpin hydrate with codeine.

uncle: A Federal agent.

valley, in the valley: The elbow flexure, the favored site for narcotic injection.

whites, white cross, whities: Double-scored, cross-scored amphetamine tablets, benzedrine.

wild Geronimo: An alcoholic beverage laced with barbiturates.

yellow bullets, yellows: Pentobarbital sodium in capsules.

yellow jacket: Pentobarbital sodium in capsules.

yan shee: The residue of opium in a pipe.

zig zag: The paper used to roll marijuana cigarettes.

Source: North American Symposium on Drugs and Drug Abuse.

BIBLIOGRAPHY

Abuse of benzodiazepines: The problems and the solutions. A report of a committee of the Institute for Behavior and Health, Inc. (1988). *American Journal of Drug and Alcohol Abuse, 14*(Suppl. 1), 1–69.

Alcoholics Anonymous (3rd ed.). (1976). New York: Alcoholics Anonymous World Services.

Alexander, B. (1988). The disease and adaptive models of addiction: A framework evaluation. In S. Peele (Ed.), *Visions of addiction* (pp. 45–66). Lexington, MA: D. C. Heath.

Allen, J. (1991). AIDS and human immunodeficiency virus infections in drug abusers. In G. Bennett & D. Woolf (Eds.), *Substance abuse* (pp. 317–331). Albany, NY: Delmar.

American Medical Association. (1983). *AMA drug evaluations* (5th ed.). Chicago: Author.

American Medical Association. (1986). *AMA manual of alcoholism.* Chicago: Author.

American Psychiatric Association. (1994). *Diagnostic and statistical manual of mental disorders: DSM-IV* (4th ed.). Washington, DC: Author.

Arif, A., & Westermeyer, J. (Eds.). (1988). *Manual of drug and alcohol abuse.* New York: Plenum.

Barr, M. (1990). Patient records and policy issues. In W. Lerner & M. Barr (Eds.), *Hospital-based substance abuse treatment* (pp. 202–209). New York: Pergamon.

Beasley, J. D. (1990). *Diagnosing and managing chemical dependency.* Amityville, NY: Essential Medical Information Systems.

Beattie, M. (1987). *Codependent no more* (pp. 169-183). New York: Harper & Row.

Beauvais, F. (1992). Attitudes about drugs and the drug use of Indian youth. *American Indian and Alaska Native Mental Health Research, 5*(1), 38–42.

Beebe, D. K., & Walley, E. (1991). Substance abuse: The designer drugs. *American Family Physician, 43*(5), 1689.

Benjamin, M., & Curtis, J. (1986). *Ethics in nursing* (2nd ed.). New York: Oxford University Press.

Bennett, G. (1991a). Substance abuse among the youth. In G. Bennett & D. Woolf (Eds.), *Substance abuse* (pp. 142–156). Albany, NY: Delmar.

Bennett, G. (1991b). Substance abuse in adulthood. In G. Bennett & D. Woolf (Eds.), *Substance abuse* (pp. 157–170). Albany, NY: Delmar.

Bennett, G., & Woolf, D. (Eds.). (1991). *Substance abuse.* Albany, NY: Delmar.

Benowitz, N. L. (1992). How toxic is cocaine? *Ciba Foundation Symposium, 166,* 125–148.

Blum, K., & Payne, J. E. (1991, November/December). Addiction: Maybe it's in the genes. The somatopsychic syndrome: A blueprint for behavior. *Addiction and Recovery.*

Borders, C. R. (1986). Identifying and motivating the alcoholic. *Patient Care, 15,* 59.

Boyd, M. (1991). Substance abuse in the aging. In G. Bennett & D. Woolf (Eds.), *Substance abuse* (pp. 171–186). Albany, NY: Delmar.

Burton, B. T. (1991). Heavy metal and organic contaminants associated with illicit methamphetamine production. In M. Miller & N. Kozel (Eds.), *Methamphetamine abuse: Epidemiologic issues and implications* (Research Issues No. 115, pp. 47–59). Rockville, MD: National Institute on Drug Abuse.

Cahalan, D. (1991). *An ounce of prevention.* San Francisco, CA: Jossey-Bass.

Carroll, M. (1985). PCP. In S. Snyder, B. Jacobs, & J. Jaffe (Eds.), *The encyclopedia of psychoactive drugs.* New York: Chelsea.

Chatlos, C. C. (1987). *Crack: What you should know about the cocaine epidemic.* New York: Perigree.

Cook, C. (1991). Pyrolytic characteristics, pharmacokinetics, and bioavailability of smoked heroin, cocaine, phencyclidine, and methamphetamine. In M. Miller & N. Kozel (Eds.), *Methamphetamine abuse: Epidemiologic issues and implications* (Research Issues No. 115, pp. 6–23). Rockville, MD. National Institute on Drug Abuse.

Cox, T. C., Jacobs, M. R., LeBlanc, A. E., & Marshman, J. A. (1983). *Drugs and drug abuse: A reference text.* Toronto: Addiction Research Foundation.

Crist, D., & Milby, J. (1990). Psychometric and neuropsychological assessment. In W. Lerner & M. Barr (Eds.), *Hospital-based substance abuse treatment* (pp. 18–33). New York: Pergamon.

Crouch, D., Webb, D., Buller, P., & Rollins, D. (1989). A critical evaluation of the Utah Power and Light Company's substance abuse management program: Absenteeism, accidents and costs. In D. Gerstein & E. Grossman (Eds.), *Drugs in the workplace* (Research Issues No. 91, pp. 169–193). Rockville, MD: National Institute on Drug Abuse.

Czyrko, C., Del Pin, C. A., O'Neill, J. A., Jr., Peckham, G. J., & Ross, A. J. (1991). Maternal cocaine abuse and necrotizing enterocolitis: Outcome and survival. *Journal of Pediatric Surgery, 40,* 414–416, 419–421.

Davis, I. (1991). What drug treatment professionals need to know about medical aspects of HIV illness. In M. Shernoff (Ed.), *Counseling chemically dependent people with HIV illness* (pp. 17–29). New York: Haworth.

Diamond, I. (1992). Alcoholism and alcohol abuse. In J. Wyngaarden, L. Smith, Jr., & J. Bennett (Eds.), *Cecil textbook of medicine* (pp. 14–47). Philadelphia: Saunders.

Dinwiddie, S. H., Reich, T., & Cloninger, C. R. (1991). The relationship of solvent use to other substance use. *American Journal of Drug and Alcohol Abuse, 17*(2), 173–186.

Dodes, L., & Khantzian, E. (1991). Individual psychodynamic psychotherapy. In R. Frances and S. Miller (Eds.), *Clinical textbook of addictive disorders* (pp. 391–405). New York: Guilford.

Dhopesh, V., Maany, I., & Herring, C. (1991). The relationship of cocaine to headache in polysubstance abusers. *Headache, 10,* 17–19.

DuPont, R. L. J. (1984). *Getting tough on gateway drugs: A guide for the family.* Washington, DC: American Psychiatric Press.

DuPont, R. L., & Saylor, K. E. (1991). Sedatives/hypnotics and benzodiazepines. In R. Frances & S. Miller (Eds.), *Clinical textbook of addictive disorders* (pp. 69–102). New York: Guilford.

Dyer, J. (1991). Stopping the spread of crack-related syphilis (Screening people at locations where crack cocaine is sold or used). *American Journal of Nursing, 91*(6), 16.

Editorial Experts, Inc. (1990). *Senate special report to the U.S. Congress on alcohol and health.* Alexandria, VA: U.S. Department of Health and Human Services.

Elder, N. C. (1991). Abuse of skeletal muscle relaxants. *American Family Physician, 44*(4), 1223.

Epstein, G. M. (1990). Evaluation and short-term treatment techniques. In. W. Lerner and M. Barr (Eds.), *Hospital-based substance abuse treatment* (pp. 142–144). New York: Pergamon.

Finney, J. W., & Moos, R. H. (1992). The long-term course of treated alcoholism: Predictors and correlates of 10-year functioning and mortality. *Journal of Studies on Alcohol, 53*(2), 142.

Frances, R., & Miller, S. (Eds.). (1991). *Clinical textbook of addictive disorders.* New York: Guilford.

Galanter, M., Egelko, S., De Leon, G., Rohrs, C., & Franco, H. (1992). Crack/cocaine abusers in the general hospital: Assessment and initiation of care. *American Journal of Psychiatry, 149*(6), 810–815.

Gerstein, D., & Grossman, E. (1989). Building a cumulative knowledge base about drugs and the workplace. In S. Gust & J. Walsh (Eds.), *Drugs in the workplace* (Research Issues No. 91, pp. 319–333). Rockville, MD: National Institute on Drug Abuse.

Giuliani, D., & Schnoll, S. H. (1985). Clinical decision making in chemical dependence treatment: A programmatic model. *Journal of Substance Abuse Treatment, 2,* 203–208.

Glowa, J. R. (1986). Inhalants. In S. Snyder, B. Jacobs, & J. Jaffe (Eds.), *The encyclopedia of psychoactive drugs.* New York: Chelsea.

Gold, M. S. (1984). *800-COCAINE.* New York: Bantam.

Goodwin, D. W. (1988). *Is alcoholism hereditary?* New York: Ballantine.

Goodwin, D., & Warnock, J. (1991). Alcoholism: A family disease. In R. Frances & S. Miller (Eds.), *Clinical textbook of addictive disorders* (pp. 485–500). New York: Guilford.

Gordis, E. (1993). Alcohol and the liver. In *Alcohol alert* (Research Issues No. 19, pp. 1–30). Rockville, MD: National Institute on Alcohol Abuse and Alcoholism.

Grafton, W. D., & Bairnsfather, L. E. (1991). Use of psychoactive substances by medical students: A survey. *Journal of the Louisiana State Medical Society, 143,* 27–29.

Haack, M. R. (1989). Future directions in research and prevention. In M. Haack & T. Hughes (Eds.), *Addiction in the nursing profession* (pp. 218–237). New York: Springer.

Helschober, B., & Miller, M. A. (1991). Methamphetamine abuse in California. In M. Miller & N. Kozel (Eds.), *Methamphetamine abuse: Epidemiologic issues and implications* (Research Issues No. 115, pp. 60–71). Rockville, MD: National Institute on Drug Abuse.

Hendrickson, E., & Schmal, M. (1993). Dual disorder. *The Lines, 10*(1).

Hofman, F., & Hofman, A. (1975). *A handbook on drug and alcohol abuse: The biomedical aspects.* New York: Oxford University Press.

Holbrook, J. (1991a). The autonomic and central nervous systems. In G. Bennett & D. Woolf (Eds.), *Substance abuse* (pp. 2–12). Albany, NY: Delmar.

Holbrook, J. (1991b). Hallucinogens. In G. Bennett & D. Woolf (Eds.), *Substance abuse* (pp. 68–80). Albany, NY: Delmar.

Holbrook, J. (1991c). CNS stimulants. In G. Bennett & D. Woolf (Eds.), *Substance abuse* (pp. 44–54). Albany, NY: Delmar.

Horst, E., Bennett, R. L., & Barrett, O., Jr. (1991). Recurrent rhabdomyolysis in association with cocaine use. *Southern Medical Journal, 84*(2), 269–270.

Horvath, B. (1996, September). CD Nursing in the new millennium. *Chemical Dependency.*

Hser, Y. I., & Booth, M. B. (1987). Sexual differences in addict careers. *American Journal for Drug and Alcohol Abuse, 3,* 231–251.

Hubbard, R. L., Marsden, M. E., Rachal, J. V., Harwood, H. J., Cavanaugh, E. R., & Ginzburg, H. M. (1989). *Drug abuse treatment.* Chapel Hill, NC: University of North Carolina Press.

Huggins, N. (1990). Psychiatric and psychological consequences of substance abuse. In W. Lerner & M. Barr (Eds.), *Hospital-based substance abuse treatment* (pp. 66–80). New York: Pergamon.

Irvine, G. D., & Chin, L. (1991). The environmental impact and adverse health effects of the clandestine manufacture of methamphetamine. In M. Miller & N. Kozel (Eds.), *Methamphetamine abuse: Epidemiologic issues and implications* (Research Issues No. 115, pp. 33–46). Rockville, MD: National Institute on Drug Abuse.

Johnson, R. E., Jaffe, J. F., & Fudala, F. (1992). A controlled trial of buprenorphine treatment for opioid dependence. *Journal of the American Medical Association, 267,* 2750–2755.

Kandall, S. R., & Gaines, J. (1991). Maternal substance use and subsequent sudden infant death syndrome (SIDS) in offspring. *Neurotoxicology and Teratology, 13*(2), 235–240.

Kaplan, J. (1983). *The hardest drug: Heroin and public policy.* Chicago: University of Chicago Press.

Karan, L., Haller, D., & Schnoll, S. (1991). Cocaine. In R. Frances & S. Miller (Eds.), *Clinical textbook of addictive disorders* (pp. 121–145). New York: Guilford.

Kato, I., Nomura, A. M., Stemmermann, G. N., & Chyou, P. H. (1992). Prospective study of the association of alcohol with cancer of the upper aerodigestive tract and other sites. *Cancer Causes and Control, 3*(2), 145–151.

Kaufman, E. (1985). Family systems and family therapy of substance abuse: An overview of two decades of research and clinical experience. *International Journal of Addictions, 20,* 897–916.

Kelley, D., & Lynch, J. B. (1992). Burns in alcohol and drug users result in longer treatment times with more complications. *Journal of Burn Care and Rehabilitation, 13*(2, Pt. 1), 218–220.

Ketcham, K., & Gustafson, G. (1989). *Living on the edge.* New York: Bantam.

Kharasch, S. J., Glotzer, D., Vinci, R., Weitzman, M., & Sargent, J. (1991). Unsuspected cocaine exposure in young children. *American Journal of Diseases of Children, 145*(2), 204–206.

Kinney, J., & Leaton, G. (1987). *Loosening the grip* (3rd ed.). St. Louis: Times-Mirror Mosby.

Kirvin, J. L., & Phillips, M. F. (1990). *Resources and informational care manual for drug, alcohol, and AIDS-exposed infants.* San Diego: Janice Kirvin.

Kleber, H. D. (1992). Treatment of cocaine abuse: Pharmacotherapy. *Ciba Foundation Symposium, 166,* 195–206.

Kolata, G. (1988, May). Alcoholic genes or misbehavior? *Psychology Today,* p. 34.

Kreek, M. J. (1992). Effects of drugs of abuse and treatment agents in women. In L. Harris (Ed.), *Problems of drug dependence 1991* (Research Issues No. 119, pp. 106–109). Rockville, MD: National Institute on Drug Abuse.

Leavitt, S., & Smith, S. (Eds.). (1993). NDA due for LAAM in March 1993. *Forum 6*(1).

Lee, J., & Bennett, G. (1991). Substance abuse in adulthood. In G. Bennett & D. Woolf (Eds.), *Substance abuse* (pp. 157–170). Albany, NY: Delmar.

Lewin, L., Caetano, R., Courtwright, D., Deitch, D., Fraser, D., Haughton, J., Hubbard, R., Isbister, J., Kleber, H., Lave, J., Mactas, D., McConnell, D., Moxley, J. III, O'Donnell, P., Richman, H., Stitzer, M., Gerstein, D., Harwood, H., Kearney, L., McGarraugh, E., Mazade, L., & Yordy, K. (1990). A study of the evolution, effectiveness, and financing of public and private drug treatment systems. In D. Gerstein & H. Henrick (Eds.), *Treating drug problems* (Vol. 1). Washington, DC: National Academy Press.

Lewis, J. A., Dana, R. Q., & Blevins, G. A. (1988). *Substance abuse counseling.* Pacific Grove, CA: Brooks/Cole.

Lewis, R., Piercy, F., Sprenkle, D., & Trepper, T. (1990). The Purdue Brief Family Therapy Model for adolescent substance abusers. In T. Todd & E. M. Selkelman (Eds.), *Family approaches with adolescent substance abusers* (pp. 29–48). Boston: Allyn and Bacon.

Lisse, J. R., Thurmond-Anderle, M., & Davis, C. P. (1991). Deep venous thrombosis in intravenous cocaine abuse mimicking septic arthritis of the shoulder. *Southern Medical Journal, 84*(20), 278–289.

Litt, I. F. (1991). Adolescent medicine. *Journal of the American Medical Association, 265*(23), 310.

Long, J. W. (1990). *The essential guide to prescription drugs.* New York: Harper & Row.

Long, P., & Gelfand, G. (1992). Alcohol education as primary prevention in health care. *Journal of Studies on Alcohol, 53*(2), 101.

Lukas, S. E. (1985). Amphetamines. In S. Snyder, B. Jacobs, & J. Jaffe (Eds.), *The encyclopedia of psychoactive drugs.* New York: Chelsea.

Lutsky, I., Abram, S. E., Jacobson, G. R., Hopwood, M., & Kampine, J. P. (1991). Substance abuse by anesthesiology residents. *Academic Medicine, 66*(3), 164–166.

Mackay, P., Donovan, D., & Marlatt, G. (1991). Cognitive and behavioral approaches to alcohol abuse. In R. Frances & S. Miller (Eds.), *Clinical textbook of addictive disorders* (pp. 452–481). New York: Guilford.

Magarian, G. J., Lucas, L. M., & Kumnar, K. L. (1992). Clinical significance in alcoholic patients of commonly encountered laboratory test results. *Western Journal of Medicine, 156*(3), 287–294.

Mann, P. (1985). *Marijuana alert.* New York: McGraw-Hill.

Mayfield, D., McLeod, G., & Hall, P. (1974). More detailed interview screening. *American Journal of Psychiatry, 131,* 1121.

McCardle, L., & Fishbein, D. H. (1989). The self-reported effects of PCP on human aggression. *Addictive Behaviors, 14*(4), 465–472.

McElmurry, B., Church, O., & Haack, M. (1989). Intervention with nurses in academia and administration. In M. Haack & T. Hughes (Eds.), *Addiction in the nursing profession* (pp. 97–112). New York: Springer.

McKay, S., & Scavnicky-Mylant, M. (1991). Substance abuse during the childbearing year. In G. Bennett & D. Woolf (Eds.), *Substance abuse* (pp. 102–126). Albany, NY: Delmar.

McNichol, R. W., Sowell, J. M., Logsdon, S. A., Delgado, M. H., & McNichol, J. (1991). Disulfiram: A guide to clinical use in alcoholism treatment. *American Family Physician, 44*(2), 481–484.

Merlin, S. (1990). Treatment of the alcohol withdrawal syndrome. In W. Lerner & M. Barr (Eds.), *Hospital-based substance abuse treatment* (pp. 81–100). New York: Pergamon.

Milhorn, H., & Thomas, J. (1991). Diagnosis and management of phencyclidine intoxication. *American Family Physician, 43*(4), 1293.

Miller, N. (1991). Special problems of the alcohol and multiple-drug dependent: Clinical interactions and detoxification. In R. Frances & S. Miller (Eds.), *Clinical textbook of addictive disorders* (pp. 194–218). New York: Guilford.

Miller, N. S., & Giannini, A. J. (1991). Drug misuse in alcoholics. *International Journal of the Addictions, 26*(8), 851–857.

Miller, N. S., & Gold, M. S. (1991a). Dual diagnoses: Psychiatric syndromes in alcoholism and drug addiction. *American Family Physician, 43*(6), 201.

Miller, N. S., & Gold, M. S. (1991b). Organic solvent and aerosol abuse. *American Family Physician, 44*(1), 183.

Mirin, S., & Weiss, R. (1991). Substance abuse and mental illness. In R. Frances & S. Miller (Eds.), *Clinical textbook of addictive disorders* (pp. 271–293). New York: Guilford.

Musto, D. F. (1992). Cocaine's history, especially the American experience. *Ciba Foundation Symposium, 166*, 7–19.

Nace, E., & Isbell, P. (1991). Alcohol. In R. Frances & S. Miller (Eds.), *Clinical textbook of addictive disorders* (pp. 43–68). New York: Guilford.

Naegle, M. (1989). Professional issues, ethical constraints, and legal considerations. In M. Haack & T. Hughes (Eds.), *Addiction in the nursing profession* (pp. 1–19). New York: Springer.

Nahas, G. G. (1992). *A manual on drug dependence.* New York: Essential Medical Information Systems.

Newcomb, M. D., Maddahian, E., Skager, R., & Bentler, P. M. (1987). Substance abuse and psychosocial risk factors among teenagers: Associations with sex, age, ethnicity, and type of school, *American Journal of Drug and Alcohol Abuse, 13*, 413–433.

Nowinski, J. (1990). *Substance abuse in adolescents and young adults.* New York: W. W. Norton.

O'Brien, C. (1992). Drug abuse and dependence. In J. Wyngaarden, L. Smith, Jr., & J. Bennett (Eds.), *Cecil textbook of medicine* (pp. 47–55). Philadelphia: Saunders.

Oetting, E., & Beauvais, F. (1988). Common elements in youth drug abuse: Peer clusters and other psychosocial factors. In S. Peele (Ed.), *Visions of addiction* (pp. 141–161). Lexington, MA: D. C. Heath.

O'Malley, S., & Gawin, F. (1990). Abstinence symptomatology and neuropsychological impairment in chronic cocaine abusers. In J. Spencer & J. Boren (Eds.), *Residual effects of abused drugs on behavior* (Research Issues No. 101, pp. 179–188). Rockville, MD: National Institute on Drug Abuse.

Parker, S., Zuckerman, B., Bauchner, H., Frank, D., Vinci, R., & Cabral, H. (1990). Jitteriness in full-term neonates: Prevalence and correlates. *Pediatrics, 85*(1), 17–23.

Peele, S. (1988). A moral vision of addiction: How people's values determine whether they become and remain addicts. In S. Peele (Ed.), *Visions of addiction* (pp. 201–233). Lexington, MA: D. C. Heath.

Penny, J., Catanzarite, A., & Ritter, J. (1989). Florida's alternative to disciplinary action. In M. Haack & T. Hughes (Eds.), *Addiction in the nursing profession* (pp. 50–63). New York: Springer.

Pol, S., Durand, F., Bernuau, J., Colin, J. F., Dubois, F., Hautekeete, M., Rouzioux, C., Degott, C., Rueff, B., & Benhamou, J. P. (1992). Herpesvirus infection of the respiratory tract in patients with alcoholic hepatitis. *Alcoholism, Clinical and Experimental Research, 16*(5), 979–981.

Randall, T. (1992). Cocaine, alcohol mix in body to form even longer lasting, more lethal drug. *Journal of the American Medical Association, 267*(8), 1043.

Rawson, R. A., Obert, J. L., McCann, M. J., Castro, F. G., & Ling, W. (1991). Cocaine abuse treatment: A review of current strategies. *Journal of Substance Abuse, 3*(4), 457–491.

Ray, O., & Ksir, C. (1993). *Drugs, society and human behavior* (5th ed.). St. Louis: Mosby.

Rerucha, M. (1986, October/November). Alcohol dependence syndrome in women: Perspectives on disability and rehabilitation. *Journal of Rehabilitation,* pp. 67–70.

Rex, D. K., & Kumar, S. (1992). Recognizing acetaminophen hepatotoxicity in chronic alcoholics. *Postgraduate Medicine, 91*(4), 241–245.

Reulbach, W. (1991). Counseling chemically dependent HIV positive adolescents. In M. Shernoff (Ed.), *Counseling chemically dependent people with HIV illness* (pp. 31–43). New York: Haworth.

Roberts, L. J., Shaner, A., Eckman, T. A., Tucker, D. E., & Vaccaro, J. V. (1992). Effectively treating stimulant-abusing schizophrenics: Mission impossible? *New Directions for Mental Health Services, 53,* 55–65.

Robbins, C. E. (1987). A monitored treatment program for the impaired health care professional. *Journal of the Operating Nurses Association, 17,* 17–21.

Rogers, R. L., & McMillin, C. S. (1989). *The healing bond.* New York: W. W. Norton.

Ropers, R. H., & Boyer, R. (1987). Perceived health status among the new urban homeless. *Social Science Medicine, 32,* 669–678.

Runeson, B. (1990). Psychoactive substance use disorder in youth suicide. *Alcohol and Alcoholism, 25*(5), 561–568.

Salzman, C. (1990). *Benzodiazepine dependence, toxicity, and abuse* (A task force report of the American Psychiatric Association). Washington, DC: American Psychiatric Association.

Schlaadt, R. G., & Shannon, P. T. (1986). *Drugs of choice: Current perspectives on drug use* (2nd ed.). Englewood Cliffs, NJ: Prentice-Hall.

Schleifer, S., Delaney, B., Tross, S., & Keller, S. (1991). AIDS and addictions. In R. Frances & S. Miller (Eds.), *Clinical textbook of addictive disorders* (pp. 313–316). New York: Guilford.

Schuckit, M. A. (1989). *Drug and alcohol abuse.* New York: Plenum.

Schwartz, R. H., Lewis, D. C., Hoffmann, N. G., & Kyriazi, N. (1991). Cocaine and marijuana use my medical students before and during medical school. Published erratum appears in *Archives of Internal Medicine, 151*(1), 196.

Scott, J. (1990). Laboratory evaluation. In W. Lerner & M. Barr (Eds.), *Hospital-based substance abuse treatment* (pp. 34–43). New York: Pergamon.

Selekman, M., & Todd, T. (1991). Crucial issues in the treatment of adolescent substance abusers and their families. In T. Todd & M. Selekman (Eds.), *Family therapy approaches with adolescent substance abusers* (pp. 3–28). Boston: Allyn and Bacon.

Senay, E. C. (1983). *Substance abuse disorders in clinical practice.* Boston: John Wright/PSG.

Sercarz, J. A., Strasnick, B., Newman, A., & Dodd, L. G. (1991). Midline nasal destruction in cocaine abusers. *Otolaryngology and Head and Neck Surgery, 105*(5), 694–701.

Shernoff, M. (Ed.). (1991). *Counseling chemically dependent people with HIV illness.* New York: Haworth.

Sidney, S. (1990). Evidence of discrepant data regarding trends in marijuana use and supply, 1985–1988. *Journal of Psychoactive Drugs, 22*(3), 319–324.

Solari-Twadell, A. (1991). Detoxification. In G. Bennett & D. Woolf (Eds.), *Substance abuse* (pp. 214–227). Albany, NY: Delmar.

Sparks, S. N. (1993). *Children of prenatal substance abuse.* San Diego: Singular.

Spencer, P. S., & Schaumby, H. H. (1985). Organic solvent neurotoxicity: Facts and research needs. *Scandinavian Journal for Work and Environmental Health, 11*(S), 53–60.

Stainback, R., & Walker, C. (1990). Discharge planning and selection of aftercare. In W. Lerner and M. Barr (Eds.), *Hospital-based substance abuse treatment* (pp. 184–198). New York: Pergamon.

Streissguth, A. (1992). Fetal alcohol syndrome: Early and long-term consequences. In L. Harris (Ed.), *Problems of drug dependence 1991* (Research Issues No. 119, pp. 126–130). Rockville, MD: National Institute on Drug Abuse.

Sullivan, E., Bissell, L., & Williams, E. (1988). *Chemical dependency in nursing.* Menlo Park, CA: Addison-Wesley.

Sumners, A. (1991). Women in recovery. In G. Bennett & D. Woolf (Eds.), *Substance abuse* (pp. 280–292). Albany, NY: Delmar.

Svikis, D., & Pickens, R. (1988). Methodological issues in family adoption and twin research. In R. Pickens & D. Svikis (Eds.), *Biological vulnerability to drug abuse* (Research Issues No. 89, pp. 120–133). Rockville, MD: National Institute on Drug Abuse.

Tabakoff, P., & Hoffman, P. (1991). Neurochemical effects of alcohol. In R. Frances & S. Miller (Eds.), *Clinical textbook of addictive disorders* (pp. 509–513. New York: Guilford.

Tarter, R., & Edwards, K. (1988). Vulnerability to alcohol and drug abuse: A behavior-genetic view. In S. Peele (Ed.), *Visions of addiction* (pp. 67–83). Lexington, MA: D. C. Heath.

Thomason, H., Jr., & Dilts, S. (1991). Opioids. In R. Frances & S. Miller (Eds.), *Clinical textbook of addictive disorders* (pp. 103–120). New York: Guilford.

Toufexis, A. (1991, May 13). Innocent victims. *Time Magazine,* pp. 56–60.

Trulson, M. E. (1985). LSD. In S. Snyder, B. Jacobs, & J. Jaffe (Eds.), *The encyclopedia of psychoactive drugs.* New York: Chelsea.

Vaillant, G. E. (1983). *The natural history of alcoholism.* Cambridge, MA: Harvard University Press.

Vannicelli, M. (1992). *Removing the roadblocks.* New York: Guilford.

Weiss, C., & Millman, R. (1991). Hallucinogens, phencyclidine, marijuana, inhalants. In R. Frances & S. Miller (Eds.), *Clinical textbook of addictive disorders* (pp. 146–170). New York: Guilford.

West, L. J., Maxwell, D. S., & Noble, E. P. (1984). *Alcoholism. Annals of Internal Medicine, 100,* 405–416.

Westermeyer, J. (1991). Historical and social context of psychoactive substance disorders. In R. Frances & S. Miller (Eds.), *Clinical textbook of addictive disorders* (pp. 23–39). New York: Guilford.

White, W., & Albana, R. (Eds.). (1974). *North American Symposium on Drugs and Drug Abuse.* Philadelphia: North American Publishing.

Wilford, B. (1982). *Drug abuse: A guide for the primary care physician.* Chicago: American Medical Association.

Wise, R. A., & Bozrath, M. A. (1985). Brain mechanisms of drug reward and euphoria. *Psychiatric Medicine, 3,* 445–460.

Woolf, D. (1991a). CNS depressants: Alcohol. In G. Bennett & D. Woolf (Eds.), *Substance abuse* (pp. 13–27). Albany, NY: Delmar.

Woolf, D. (1991b). CNS depressants: Other sedative-hypnotics. In G. Bennett & D. Woolf (Eds.), *Substance abuse* (pp. 30–43). Albany, NY: Delmar.

Woolf, D. (1991c). Opioids. In G. Bennett & D. Woolf (Eds.), *Substance abuse* (pp. 44–54). Albany, NY: Delmar.

Woolf, D. (1991d). Polypharmacy and the addict. In G. Bennett & D. Woolf (Eds.), *Substance abuse* (pp. 87–92). Albany, NY: Delmar.

Woolf, D., & Moore, D. (1991). Over-the-counter-drugs. In G. Bennett & D. Woolf (Eds.), *Substance abuse* (pp. 81–86). Albany, NY: Delmar.

Yang, R. D., Han, M. W., & McCarthy, J. H. (1991). Ischemic colitis in a crack abuser. *Digestive Diseases and Sciences, 36*(20), 238–240.

Yu, J., & Williford, W. R. (1992). The age of alcohol onset and alcohol, cigarette, and marijuana use patterns: An analysis of drug use progression of young adults in New York State. *International Journal of the Addictions, 27*(11), 1313–1323.

Zackon, F. (1986). Heroin. In S. Snyder, B. Jacobs, & J. Jaffe (Eds.), *The encyclopedia of psychoactive drugs.* New York: Chelsea.

Zimmerman, E. F. (1991). Substance abuse in pregnancy: Teratogenesis. *Pediatric Annals, 20*(10), 541–547.

INDEX

PRETEST KEY

1.   b   Chapter 1
2.   d   Chapter 1
3.   d   Chapter 1
4.   b   Chapter 2
5.   a   Chapter 2
6.   d   Chapter 2
7.   a   Chapter 3
8.   d   Chapter 3
9.   b   Chapter 3
10.   b   Chapter 4
11.   b   Chapter 4
12.   d   Chapter 5
13.   d   Chapter 5
14.   d   Chapter 6
15.   d   Chapter 6
16.   c   Chapter 7
17.   b   Chapter 7
18.   d   Chapter 7
19.   c   Chapter 8
20.   d   Chapter 8
21.   c   Chapter 9
22.   c   Chapter 10
23.   d   Chapter 10
24.   c   Chapter 11
25.   d   Chapter 11